The Body Populace

Transformations: Studies in the History of Science and Technology

Jed Z. Buchwald, general editor

The Body Populace

Military Statistics and Demography in Europe before the First World War

Heinrich Hartmann
translated by Ellen Yutzy Glebe

The MIT Press
Cambridge, Massachusetts
London, England

© Wallstein Verlag, Göttingen 2011

This is a slightly revised and expanded translation of *Der Volkskörper bei der Musterung: Militärstatistik und Demographie in Europa vor dem Ersten Weltkrieg.*

This translation was financed in part by the *Freiwillige Akademische Gesellschaft Basel* and the *Christine Bonjour-Stiftung.*

This book was set in ITC Stone Sans Std and ITC Stone Serif Std by Toppan Best-set Premedia Limited. Printed and bound in the United States of America.

Library of Congress Cataloging-in-Publication Data

Names: Hartmann, Heinrich, 1977- author.
Title: The body populace : military statistics and demography in Europe before
    the First World War / Heinrich Hartmann ; translated by Ellen Yutzy Glebe.
Other titles: Volkskörper bei der Musterung. English
Description: Cambridge, MA : MIT Press, [2018] | Series: Transformations:
    Studies in the history of science and technology | Includes bibliographical
    references and index.
Identifiers: LCCN 2018013620 | ISBN 9780262536325 (pbk. : alk. paper)
Subjects: LCSH: Europe--Population--History--19th century. | Europe--History,
    Military. | Europe--Population--Statistics. | Europe--Statistics, Medical.
Classification: LCC HB3581.A3 H3713 2018 | DDC 355.0094/021--dc23 LC record
    available at https://lccn.loc.gov/2018013620

10 9 8 7 6 5 4 3 2 1

Contents

Introduction: A History of Knowledge—Military Statistics

Gruber begins to climb, first violently, recklessly, hoisting his legs under him and directing his gaze upward, gauging with a certain anxiety the immeasurable length of pole still ahead. Then his movement slows, and as if he were relishing each grip as something new and pleasurable, he hoists himself higher than the exercise normally requires.[1]

Contrary to all his earlier tendencies, the cadet Karl Gruber, normally the weakest and most unathletic in his class, suddenly overcomes his fear of the gymnastics apparatus and his own body in a euphoric episode. Fellow cadets, as well as the noncommissioned officer responsible for his education, are surprised to the point of incapacitation by his sudden ecstasy. The story takes a tragic turn, however: the sudden burst of power is too much for the pupil's young body. When he reaches the ceiling, he suffers a heart attack and slides—or rather crashes—down the pole, standing still for a time in one spot, and then sinking lifelessly to the floor. A short time later, without having regained consciousness, Gruber dies. His teacher and the other officers forbid his fellow students from expressing any emotion about these events.

The twenty-three-year-old Rainer Maria Rilke recorded this story of his experience at an Austrian military school in Sankt Severin in his diary in 1899 and published it three years later under the title "Die Turnstunde"[2] (translated later into English as "The Gym Class"), and these events seem to have occupied the author for a long time. But what is this story really about? Certainly, it is a story rooted in a militaristic and chauvinist milieu devoid of emotional warmth, of society before the First World War, the story of an adolescent generation often strained to the breaking point by social pressure. It is also, however, a story built around Karl Gruber's physical and mental frailty. It is a story in which emotion becomes a conveyor of corporal strength. It is a story about the nationalization of the body: the noncommissioned officer Jastersky, who is characterized as Polish; the muscular "Tirolean classmate" who shows off his muscles; the good friend with the French name Jérôme, who always has an "English bandage" (i.e., "court plaster"[3]) at hand and who allows himself to be overwhelmed by his emotions after Gruber's death.

The Military Strength of the "Collective Body"[4]

The body of the pupil who fell victim here is what scholars who study the history of science and knowledge might call "overdetermined." In his strengths and weaknesses and his premature death, overlapping levels of interpretation and meaning are necessary in illuminating the individual in the context of a "larger whole." In the years leading up to World War I, concepts of corporal strength and weakness emerged from a ceaseless interplay between individuality and modern society, person and nation, and positivist Cartesian analogies between physical and mental strength in medicine. New scientific methods of statistical analysis connected the individual with "national populations" and contributed to the emerging field of demographic studies.[5] These factors converged in a significant way for the institutionalized military examinations and the statistical interpretation of the collective results. The test of fitness for service combined individual bodies into the large number of the total population and the abstract concept of their "military strength." Many contemporaries, in fact, viewed "fitness" as a concept that could bridge the gap between the individual and the broader collective society.

There were then and still are no absolute criteria for what makes a good soldier. Physical structure, age, constitution, and mental capabilities: all of these were factors that could be considered in the appraisal of military strength around 1900, but they were not mandatory. The definition of military strength as characteristically masculine should not be considered a matter of fact. This book does not seek to fill the void which results from this lack of universal criteria, but to historicize it. The aim here is not to contribute to any quest to establish a definition of the fit, male solider, nor is it my intention to base the analysis on the demographic data that resulted from the physical screenings performed during recruitment. Instead, the aim is to take a closer look at the circumstances that helped to shape the collective understanding of fitness—a process that was often spurred on by wars and conflicts. Defining the individual criteria and their relative importance to each other was a process of negotiation between the military and the political, economic, and social realms of society—or better, of societies.

We will analyze such a new anthropometric knowledge as circular, or as circulating between European nation states and their colonial territories.

This book examines to what extent these entwined discourses and practices between the mid-nineteenth century and World War I were dependent upon parallel and in fact interdependent dynamics of society and scholarship. This was an era that seethed with nationalism and the militarism that fed on the same in a kind of symbiosis. As a new form of scholarship, "demography" was still a fluid concept that was crystallizing in this same era. Although this new discipline had not yet acquired academic status in most countries, its ambitious projects assumed an increasing role in political agendas. Under the lens of demographic analysis, the nation became more than a symbolic body manifested primarily in common social practices.[6] Many scholars aspired to pin the "nation" down in the concrete numerical terms of their statistical analysis: this "collective body" could be counted, measured, and otherwise examined in the process of becoming subject to theoretical generalization at both the individual and the collective levels.

History of the Military as History of Knowledge

Around the turn of the century, the military and militarism served to catalyze the development of demography as an academic discipline. This relationship, however, was not limited to statistical analysis within the study of demography, which has been underestimated up to the present day, but reflected also the fact that military statistics were increasingly developing as an autonomous field of scholarship with its own heuristics and scientific communities, with its own methods and institutional networks. The goal of this study is not, therefore, to supply a postscript to the history of demography, as most historians of science have not yet studied the history of military statistics up to the present day. Neither shall this book (re)evaluate this data in the sense of a *histoire anthropométrique*, as has been proposed time and again, particularly by French social historians,[7] and I do not want to engage in methodological debates about the correct or incorrect use of historical data sheets.[8] Instead, this study focuses on the production of the statistical material in the context of military recruitment and suggests that historians must consider the contingencies, but also the contestedness, of historical data sets, which do not allow for easy interpretation of statistical materials as social facts. Like any form of knowledge, these anthropometric statistics are the result of a selection process and must be understood as artifacts.

In its development of this selection process, the military played an active role in the development of demographic sciences: it was a unique epistemic sphere,[9] which did not necessarily correspond to the surrounding nation or its demographic knowledge structures and discourse. This sphere could take on a life of its own in which social and political presuppositions could be more or less consciously broken. In the age of European nationalism, this military knowledge played a key role in "modern" forms of defining society. The exchange that transcended borders between the individual European states becomes particularly palpable in this context. In this respect, the military was both an actor and a screen for the reflection of both: the accentuated nationalism and the intensified scholarly exchange between nations.

Of course, the special importance of the military between the latter half of the nineteenth century and the catastrophes of the twentieth century has been addressed before: the historiography of the last twenty years has taken decisive steps to integrate the history of the military into the broader social history of Germany and Europe. The accepted thesis of widespread popular militarism has been tested at the regional and local levels.[10] This research has emphasized the role of the military itself as a conveyor of modernization.[11] Ute Frevert's study shows how strongly militarization can be understood as a complementary process to social modernization, via which the traditional middle classes sought to compensate for the looming loss of social and cultural significance.[12] These aspects of the history of conscription in the late nineteenth century have garnered some attention in recent years, especially in the context of contemporary debates that highlighted the historical development of compulsory service as a social institution.[13] Given this interest, historians have a fairly large body of historical scholarship on the subject of compulsory service at their disposal, though significant gaps remain for some localities and for social and cultural historical topics. It is still quite unclear how conscription was perceived in rural areas and small towns, which means historians must rely on literary sources and autobiographical statements of prominent individuals. Such sources generally present rather limited insight into regional and local militarism and their countermovements.[14] Recent studies have examined the decisive role of military service and its importance in the development of social and cultural constructs of gender. The image of the "masculine" soldier was established via social practice and initiation rites common in the military. The medical examination of potential recruits created a dividing line along which academic inquiry transformed and normed the civil body into a body fit for military service.[15]

This for the most part exhausts the present state of the research on this topic. Despite a soaring interest in the history of the human body,[16] historians mostly treat the body of the soldier as something distinct—an object of Tayloristic management practices,[17] an object of national mourning and cultural commodification.[18] But the construction of the military subject—that is, the soldier and his body—remains largely a desideratum. In short, when historians consider soldiers, they do so as members of "the military" rather than of "society." This then obscures the links between military history and vibrant fields of "social," "cultural," or "knowledge" history.[19] Instead, historians address these topics from the perspective of "military" history, which often implies completely different historical approaches and considerations.[20] The social processes within the military thus typically remain a sort of sealed black box, even though the army represents a specific sphere in which social knowledge was created and transmitted.[21]

The present volume intends to address this gap but makes no claim to adequately fill it. It concentrates on the question of statistics, a question in which historical scholarship has shown great interest in recent years.[22] It should do more, however, than address the question from the perspective of the institution or an academic discipline, for that would do justice neither to contemporary questions of the discipline of history of knowledge[23] nor to the problems scholars faced in the late nineteenth and early twentieth centuries. Lacking diverse social and political contexts, a study of the history of statistical methods in the military would remain incomplete and difficult to understand. Of special importance is the implementation of general compulsory service far into the nineteenth century. This is the key step in creating a clear correlation between the male population of a country and the size and composition of its military. The military became thus more than just the focus of demographic debates; it was itself an object of study. This had far-reaching consequences, particularly in regard to the examinations of potential recruits: these examinations were increasingly a venue in which potential recruits, officers, doctors, and bureaucrats met and the rationales for their actions became entangled in many ways. The examinations, which have been basically ignored in the historiography, present an especially promising object of study for those interested in the history of science and knowledge.

The History of Knowledge as a History of Social Constructs

There is hardly any sphere more clearly "masculine" than the military around the turn of the twentieth century. The French humorist Alphonse

Allais greeted the committee at his examination in the 1870s with a jovial, "Bonjour, Messieurs-Dames" ("Good day, ladies and gentlemen"); this violation of the norm resulted in his immediate fame.[24] The examination was dominated by "masculine" concepts as no other social institution was. The examination of potential recruits serves a unique role as a hinge between knowledge systems and social practice, and this is nowhere clearer than in the social attributions of gender assigned in the military. The presence of women in this exclusively masculine environment could only be decoded as public ridicule of the status quo or as a violation of the norm which would be instantly recognized as such by all those involved.[25]

Compared to the rhetorical construct of "fitness for service," the concept of "military strength" relied much less on gender-specific concepts. Prior to World War I, speaking about the "population" did not involve a strict dichotomy along lines of gender. In the eyes of many contemporaries, the question of the nation's strength involved both women and men. Demography was one of the few academic disciplines in which women were—to a limited extent—able to play an active role.[26] Cultivating and preserving the nation's strength, including especially that of the future generations of soldiers, was a question male scholars recognized as being equally pertinent to women and men. The construct and constant social reproduction of a masculinity fit for military service in knowledge discourses must therefore be considered from a historical perspective as more than the establishment of something self-evidently masculine. Instead, it was the result of an ongoing renegotiation of gender relationships via the interpretation of statistics and elements of knowledge.

Historiography has shown convincingly how powerful social constructs within scientific and statistical discourse live a life "in which they gain authority," to borrow the words of Ian Hacking.[27] The story told here is preceded by a certain number of powerful constructs, and, in return, it generates others. In the second half of the nineteenth century, Darwin's new models of biological evolution broadened understanding of physical evolution, but also led to new descriptions of the abnormal, the backward, and the degenerate. New psychological research, such as French psychiatrist Bénédict Augustin Morel's *Traité des dégénérances*, seemed to underpin and generalize these theories for the human psyche and to define degenerate human behavior.[28] Both disciplinary approaches converged in a strong interpretation of social degeneration, as opposed to the emerging idea of physical and social progress.

Toward the end of the nineteenth century, degeneration was probably one of the most powerful ways of interpreting the social changes that statistics made visible to a larger audience. Indeed, the various ways in which degeneration was a topic in every debate about demographic dynamics in many late nineteenth-century European societies is striking; this allowed for a significant flow of knowledge between different disciplines—or rather, scientific fields in the making. Scholars have shown how emerging fields like criminology in Italy and France were quickly understood with regard to the "law of large numbers," calculating the probability for deviant behavior for every individual, and scientists throughout Europe quickly echoed these new scientific paradigms.[29] This new way to think about the "social" not only related the individual to a larger group, but also made the individual body accessible for new forms of politics.[30] Atavistic characteristics and physical attitudes increasingly became the subject of scientific observation. Through the chronological coincidence with Darwin's theory of evolutionary biology, these new forms of body analysis merged into powerful new scientific paradigms that were to explain society by analyzing its momentum of development, its historic place, and its supposed future missions.[31] All this crystallized around concepts of race, which were still oscillating and scientifically unproven, as scholars sought new methods to make observable what so many contemporaries believed to be obvious biological facts. As has been argued convincingly, colonial encounters were a central motivating factor in the scientific quest to develop new scientific forms of self-description based, at least in part, on the presumption of racial superiority.[32]

However, the new biologistic interpretations of society's fate not only engendered optimistic ways of understanding biological evolutions, but also paved the way for a pessimistic view of the future of national societies.[33] Francis Galton's theory of regression toward mediocrity offered an explanation for an inevitable decline of biological dispositions in society. This belief in a natural degeneration was a powerful paradigm for the analysis of comprehensive statistical material in the late nineteenth century. Military statistics were no exception here; on the contrary, they seemed to offer a particularly rich reservoir of evidence about the living population. They seemed to prove the degeneration of the average, with scientists ignoring the fact that the term *regression* itself is meaningless so long as it is not paired with a frame of reference. Theories of degeneration flourished toward the fin de siècle—in Great Britain and France, but also in Italy and Germany and many other European nations—their roots in claims regarding moral decadence and becoming more like deterministic visions of social decline and biological degeneration.[34]

One can interpret the quest for physical fitness, or the psychological normalization of the later nineteenth century, as a response to the threats of a biological and cultural degeneration, as has been done in the French case.[35] However, there are significant problems with this historiographical narrative of the dissemination of degeneration theory and scientific racism. The question of whether scientific racism and theories about the evolution of society informed racist public discourses is misleadingly one-sided in the sense that scientists are never immune to the discourse of their time and were themselves influenced by the ideas of decadence and decline that pervaded their social context. In a more general sense, instead of focusing on the origins of racism and the degeneration theory, it makes sense to accept that these sentiments could only gain credibility through circular actions of communities of knowledge that were often small, localized, and rooted in specific social constellations unrelated to the fate of society as a whole. Army recruitment offers a particularly interesting insight into this dynamic because it involved new communities of lower- or middle-level military experts as well as new "objects"—the recruits—who were examined in very local social settings. This blurred the clear line between scientists and their "objects" and replaced the historical analysis of "scientific diffusions" with the understanding of their embeddedness and the circular processes that were at the base of new knowledge production.

Within the history of the military and statistics, a complex of interesting historical complexities emerges in which rhetoric, scientific concepts, and social practices are woven together so tightly that it is impossible to conceive of them separately. The recruit as an object of scholars' attention is unimaginable without the dimension of the public "discussion about him," just as the question of the collective strengths of the people is incomprehensible without the social construct of the military sphere. It is in this correlation that the sociology and historiography of academic scholarship find one of their most interesting fields of study.

Such perspectives have recently brought scholarship's inherited positivist relationship of an "objective" stance toward those subjects of its study into question.[36] The process of defining this academic phenomenon was just as central as the question of how the object examined was adapted to conform to the research methods in a sort of *looping effect*,[37] a question which posed a series of fruitful new research perspectives for the history of demography. In addition to these questions involving the dynamics of the scholarly methodology itself, questions were soon raised about the social frame of knowledge. Scientific communities are part of a society, the norms and values of which they do not determine.[38] Knowledge circulates, however, beyond the academic field; it is subjected to negotiation, adaptation, representation, and modification. These processes have in recent years led to new insights and topics within research on the history and sociology of knowledge. Again and again, these insights have highlighted the difficulty of distinguishing between an object and its depiction. The scientific fact itself, the object of scholarship, is far removed from that which can be conveyed to a large audience. At the colloquial level, scholarship morphs into *popular scholarship*. To perceive of an object of scholarship and its public representation as two separate instances is certainly one possible method of portraying the differing logics of the social groups involved.[39] As was widely criticized, however, this leads to too strong a dichotomy between the academic and public spheres and to a linear understanding of the increase in academic insights.[40] Historians of knowledge have thus increasingly dealt with processes of epistemic negotiation, in which an object is defined by its representation. To put it more directly, no knowledge can be simply portrayed without being itself transformed by the portrayal.[41]

As a decisively heterogeneous field of scholarship, demography is ideally situated to examine and call into question the dichotomies outlined previously. As an object of study, the population is particularly impressionable, integrating in a way the very knowledge that is garnered about it. This becomes evident not only in the process of structural adaptation but also—and even especially—at the moment of statistical analysis and data compilation. For demography, this was, for example, the census—or, in the case of conscription, the examination of potential recruits—as an instance of appraising the population and accordingly the nation as such.[42]

In regards to the period in which demography became an established academic discipline, with the discourse and practice that entails, it should not be assumed that there was any sort of preestablished or certain frame with which to define *population*. Instead, the discipline sought to collect the relevant information, to make this accessible, and to establish categories for its compilation.[43] A study of this developmental phase makes increasingly clear how ephemeral the character of the discipline was: population as an object of academic attention only became conceivable with an adequate mode of representation. It was shaped in this original conception by the techniques and persuasive power of these modes of representation—for example, by demographic maps.[44]

In 1894, in Budapest, at the eighth International Congress of Hygiene and Demography, Georg Mayr, a renowned statistician from Strasbourg, outlined the purpose of the discipline from his perspective: statistics and the social sciences were ultimately nothing other than the science of mankind, which could be addressed at the individual or collective level. The purpose of demography was to make "mankind" as accessible at this collective level as biological and medical research had at the level of the individual body. "Admittedly it is thus far only a fraction of the Earth's population over which there is any sort of statistical command, but the advances in this field for statistical elucidation are unstoppable."[45] Such analogies of individuals and the collective were popular and aroused the expectation that the "collective body" could soon be examined and treated.[46] Theories of physiological degeneration could thus also be transposed onto social contexts, and no longer only in a rhetorical sense. Research proposals and institutional academic goals used these new paradigms for orientation. Professional statisticians now aspired no longer only to collect information and make this accessible to other scholars. Instead, they should themselves contribute to the scholarship and facilitate the interpretation of social change as a sort of *social physics*, to borrow the phrasing that the French social scientist and politician Emile Cheysson (and before him Adolphe Quetelet) had repeatedly adopted in the late nineteenth century.[47]

Statistics and demography quickly became part of the academic techniques with which modern societies define and describe themselves. It would be a mistake to assume, however, that they were immediately granted any influential role in modern state politics.[48] The knowledge that many states and empires had of their "populations" was limited,[49] and the interest in expanding this knowledge was quite varied. Statistical knowledge practices had to prove themselves first: demographic experts fought for legitimation of their discipline by displaying competence in regard to political issues.

Research Methods and Topics to Be Addressed

In consideration of the marginalized position of statisticians and self-declared demographers before 1914, this book consistently uses the word *transnational* instead of *international* to describe the points of contact between these experts beyond national borders. For a long time, representatives of the national government were uninterested in the question of the population, and there were no international deliberations about demography, much less its political implications. Individual scholars, rather than state officials, sought to exchange ideas beyond national borders and fought for an audience for their specific research questions. This "professional middle class"[50]—to use Paul Weindling's term—had its own social dynamics and respective autonomous professional identity that it frequently sought to defend. The members of this class forged channels of communication via numerous professional organizations, specialized journals, and, most prominently, international conferences, which flourished in the years before World War I.[51]

Research on the history of the discipline of demography has in recent years focused increasingly on these early social networks and channels of communication between demographers.[52] The increasing significance of the academic discourse over the potential recruits would be meaningless were it not for the exchange between professional groups of statisticians, economists, anthropologists, and, most significantly for the topic at hand, military doctors.

From this perspective, it is also clear why the specific relationship to the nation is a frame of analysis in this book. In the discussions about the potential recruits, the nation meant everything and nothing. In the academic discourse of scholars, it seems to have played no role for long stretches of time. Specialists exchanged ideas at international conferences about their methods and referenced each other's work as though the national borders did not exist. In nearly the same breath, however, this discourse—at times even from the same experts—could be interpreted as so nationalistic as seemingly to preclude an effective transnational exchange. Over and over again, scholars at international conferences noticed that conversation with colleagues from other countries was hardly possible because research agendas varied fundamentally from one nation to another.

This study is especially interested in the dynamics and modalities of transnational academic discourse, which provided the foundation for a specific, if totally heterogeneous, knowledge concept of social-statistical self-description. It does not aim to compare individual European states with each other but rather to outline the circulation and interconnections of knowledge concepts.[53] A recruitment situation in Appenzell can be placed alongside the collection of statistical knowledge in Rome or height measurements taken in Norway, so long as these are all considered part of a larger process of the development of an academic discipline.

It would make little sense, however, to describe a uniform "European" development, because this would necessitate an essentialization of the concept of Europe. There were in fact differences, some of which were quite significant, between the observed cases. These differences did not always occur along national boundaries, however. Often they were particular to individual regions or localities. The administrative differences between

Berlin and Württemberg in regard to the conditions of recruitment and the collection of information on potential recruits could be greater than the difference in attitudes of French versus German military doctors about intrusions in their professional sovereignty.

This study seeks a specific transnational perspective on military statistics and applies this on a variety of levels with a European dimension: at the discursive level, it integrates the history of academic analysis of military statistics into the broader European history. This concentrates on European actors who do not reflect solely a national viewpoint. The Austro-Hungarian military doctors spoke about the various populations within the Danubian monarchy and yet did not refer to all of these to the same extent. The discourse concerning the center of the Habsburg Empire was much more intense than that over its periphery. This was certainly also true of representatives of the Russian Empire. On the other hand, demographic and anthropological attempts at self-definition could be an expression of a process of national integration, as happened in Norway and Italy, or of the redefinition of the border between France and Germany.

At another level, this study aims to differentiate as precisely as possible the groups of actors and classify these according to varied national contexts. This is not possible to the same degree for all countries. The study focuses on three countries and the social dynamics there. These cases may not be representative, but they are pointed and clear: the German Empire (primarily after the unification in 1870); the Second Empire and the Third Republic in France; and, finally, Switzerland, where the new constitution in 1874 created a unified military system for the first time. This selection was due primarily to the body of source material on questions of military statistics and examinations that makes such a scholarly inquiry possible. They also shed light, however, on other striking aspects of the inquiry. Germany and France, for example, were not only the two largest central European nations with comprehensive compulsory service, but also the two countries in which the growth of nationalism can be observed most distinctly. In the debate about military strength, Switzerland looked to the military realities and experiences of its neighboring states, as it had in many other cases before. The relationship to the German-Prussian military system played a key role in the emergence of new military practices.[54] At the same time, many uniquely Swiss traditions were preserved. Transnational circulation went hand in hand with the reinforcement of regional and national peculiarities. The Swiss system of a militia army led to numerous specific practices, meaning that Switzerland serves as a sort of refractory mirror against which the characteristics of the other nations become even more apparent.

In addition to the question outlined earlier about regional dynamics, there was another critical aspect of the question of fitness for military service and its relationship to demographic knowledge: the colonial question. In light of Europe's developing colonial empires, the concept of military fitness evolved again. It became obvious to some military doctors that the universal definition of military fitness that had been formulated with great effort was not in fact so universal. The criteria for service in the colonial territories had to consider other challenges. This was especially true of resistance to tropical diseases and the extreme danger these posed to troops deployed in the colonies. Although the colonial aspect is not an explicit topic covered in this study, it is an important element to understand the context and resonance of the European debates. This is why the discussions about the military strength of the nation at times intensified and changed meaning often.

In contrast to the relatively difficult definition of geographical boundaries, definition of the chronological framework for the study is relatively straightforward. Two parallel and related processes provide a point of departure: the gradual implementation of universal conscription and the thematization of military statistics in these transnational academic circles. Both of these processes became clearly visible beginning in the 1860s. They inspired a number of projects that helped determine how military statistics were discussed and considered, though only some of them were ever realized. The outbreak of World War I in 1914 provides a clear breaking point for the present study: the war abruptly ended any number of scholarly ambitions. The statistics were no longer accessible but were instead considered a matter of military secrecy and guarded accordingly. International conferences were for the most part canceled. In addition, the war blurred the clear relationship between the population and the military. The soldiers were no longer recruited from a homogenous age group, and the criteria for new recruits were relaxed.[55] In the case of Germany, this remained so even after 1918. The Treaty of Versailles restricted the reinstitution of an army drawn from the masses. This was a prerequisite, however, if the numbers collected via military examinations were to have any statistical significance for a broader demographic study of the society at large.

Structure

This study is built around the "recruit" as an object of scientific attention and attempts to place him in the context of academic rhetoric and practice to trace his gradual "demographication." First, in chapter 1, this book examines how statistical knowledge of the potential recruits was collected and in which forms statisticians and economists recorded it and derived a "correct" practice of statistical analysis. This can be particularly well seen in the question of determining the national military strength within the German empire, a question that occupied science, politics, and public dialogue in the late phases of the empire like no other. Debates surrounding the degeneration of the military population were intrinsically linked to the perception of modernization as an economic problem and a biological threat to the nation. This context is crucial to understanding how the discussion of recruits' physical condition was embedded in broader political debates.

The problem of state and social political interventions that were triggered by studies of military statistics are the topic of chapter 2, which outlines the aspirations for advances of the social state and general welfare that were associated with statistics concerning medical services—namely, the medical treatment of members of the military. For military statisticians and doctors, this presented an opportunity to participate in political debates about the role of the welfare state. They especially hoped to find new international methods for data collection and analysis; this also illustrates the limited ambitions of many scholars.

Chapter 3 describes more closely the fields of scholarship involved in the creation and use of military statistics. Beyond the fields of statistics and administration, this information was of especial interest to military doctors who had come of age in this era as the position was institutionalized and professionalized. These were the doctors who were primarily responsible for the examination of potential recruits, even if the regulations did not always make this clear. The conflicts between statisticians and doctors stemmed from their divergent professional interests.

The methods and social situations of these examinations, which formed the foundation of the academic practice, are addressed in chapter 4. Physical criteria were not fixed categories but were negotiable in their practical and contextual interpretations at each instance of their application in physical examinations. If this potential for negotiation is considered, it becomes clear in hindsight—as indeed it was already in the eyes of many contemporaries—that the supposedly objective "data" must be viewed in another light.

The last two chapters clarify how individual bodies melded into the "great whole" of national welfare and what dimensions of interpretation thereby emerged. The way these dimensions intersected in the concept of "military fitness" is a further subject of chapter 5. It is in this intersection that the sum totals of the statisticians were confronted by the individual bodies. The ideals of physical stature that arose in this milieu had very real implications for questions of child-rearing and schooling and for programs intended to prepare and condition youth for future military service. Thanks to these broader implications, even those debates that began within academic circles often ended as discussions of nationalistic significance. With the colonial expansion of the European powers, however, the spatial component of the definition of military fitness became evident.

Chapter 6 addresses the specific biological-anthropological interests that accompanied the statistical compilation in nearly all European countries after the 1880s. The statistics collected at examinations were appraised in regard to their biological meaningfulness. The formulation of a "racial map of Europe" based on scholarly evidence relied on the interpretation of the information gathered at these examinations. This anthropometric, racist interpretation remained only one possible frame of interpretation, and many military doctors and statisticians either had little interest in it or even adamantly rejected it. Within circles of racial research, however, the collected statistical knowledge was considered to be of extraordinary significance because its origins in the "military" made it especially relevant and trustworthy.

1 Computing Military Strength: The Development of Recruitment Statistics

Primarily, however, the populace is the basis for the security and defense of a people against enemy attack which is so necessary. Security is an essential element of the outer felicity. ... It thus necessarily follows that [the ruler] must see to it that the number of his subjects increases, which thereby increases their protection and security. The larger the number of a people becomes, the greater their peace and security, and with these the felicity of the state also grows.[1]

When the cameralist Johann Peter Süßmilch penned these lines in 1761, his sovereign and sponsor, Frederick the Great, was embroiled in a seemingly hopeless situation, in a "justified but most difficult war." The Seven Years' War, which had raged since 1756, was consuming Prussia's resources and pushing the country to its limits. This was true in an economic sense, but also in terms of the number of human casualties, among both the military and the civilian population. There was no possibility of lasting peace in sight, and the problem of the "felicity of the state" was evident at all levels. Süßmilch based his reflections on a well-established analogy, which can be expressed bluntly as *Total population = military strength = degree of security*.[2] Beyond this utilitarian purpose, however, cameralism assumed that an increase in the size of the population—and thus in those subject to the Christian sovereign—ultimately served the purpose of praising the Divine.

Süßmilch's mercantilist logic is still clear today: more is simply more. His elaborations, however, express a paradox that cannot be dismissed as trivial: the size of armies in the early modern period and well into the nineteenth century bore no clear or direct correlation to the size of the population—which, for that matter, no one could have computed exactly.[3] Military conflicts in this age were locally or regionally limited and affected relatively few people. Even given that they could be devastating for those areas, they did not necessarily negatively affect the rest of the territory's populace.[4] The soldiers involved were usually not drafted from the populace at large but were instead mercenaries, often imported from other territories. The equation of military strength with population size was thus less obvious than one might think. The question is further complicated if one considers the general population's state of health—which, given the dearth of statistics available, was difficult to determine. Only in the course of the nineteenth century did a number of political and governmental reformers begin establishing a clearer relationship between the size of population and military strength. Scientists and politicians were faced with the challenge of determining techniques for statistical analysis that could predict the requirements of the army and reliably estimate its strength. The debates their efforts sparked in the nineteenth century reveal the extent to which these statistical methods were woven into political and social discourse.

Conscription and Demography

There were two preconditions that led to a correlation between the size of the total population and that of the army: first, the institution of universal conscription, which initially in theory and later in practice affected the entire male population, and, second, a statistically accurate survey of the population, which enabled such a draft in the first place. The revolutionary wars of the early nineteenth century and those principles of general conscription that were formulated in this context facilitated the development of what was initially a speculative discourse into a mathematical discipline that employed empirical methods.[5]

The scientific discipline of statistics and the institution of conscription evolved in distinctly separate spheres. Although the military draft was implemented in most European nations over the course of the nineteenth century, its introduction varied greatly from country to country. In addition, the theoretical legal basis for conscription often concealed stark contrasts in its practical implementation. Immediately following the introduction of the earliest draft—in France—there were numerous legal exceptions. For a long time, the army simply did not need as many soldiers as could theoretically be recruited. For that reason, until 1872 a lottery determined who was drafted for compulsory service (approximately one-sixth of the eligible men in any given birth year).[6] The *bons numéros* were completely freed from service, while the *mauvais numéros* were called to serve for a period of six years (until the 1860s).[7] Social practices quickly developed that impeded a fair draft in which all citizens had equal odds of being called upon for compulsory service. With the release of the first law concerning compulsory service in 1818, it was possible for an individual who had been drafted to pay a substitute (*remplaçant*) to enter the military in his stead.[8] Within two years of this law, a new form of insurance had developed: parents could, for a relatively small premium, insure their newborn children against the later fate of having their number drawn in the draft.[9]

The principle of *general* compulsory service was further undermined by the introduction of the process of *exonération* (in 1855). Instead of paying a substitute, wealthy citizens could exempt their children from compulsory service by paying a special tax to the French state, an option that more and more citizens used. With these additional funds, the state could hire its own soldiers. Recruitment procedures in postrevolutionary France thus began to resemble the mercenary system of the *ancien régime*. Until the foundation of the Third Republic, these conditions meant that there was no direct statistical correlation between the size and strength of the military and that of the population. The topos of equality for all citizens—which, at least in the political rhetoric,[10] played an important role in postrevolutionary France—was not reflected in the actual burden of military service, expressed in more lofty terms as the *blood toll* (*impôt du sang*). Increasing awareness of this inequality and discussion of new legal parameters, which after the 1830s also drew heavily on statistics, made the question of equality regarding the draft an increasingly important issue.[11]

After gaining access to the first body of data concerning the actual demographics of those affected by the draft,[12] politicians in the short-lived Second Republic (1848–1851) debated the question of whether and how a more general equality of conscription could be effected. On October 10, 1848, French Minister of War Juchault de Larmocière and the bourgeois liberal politician Adolphe Thiers exchanged verbal blows in a heated debate. Thiers insisted on maintaining a constitutional right to buy an exemption from military service, whereas the minister of war favored legal action to treat all French citizens equally and eliminate such possibilities of evading the draft. In the subsequent Second Empire, the aspect of equality in regards to the draft played a subordinate role; ironically, it was the government under Adolphe Thiers at the beginning of the Third Republic that ultimately abolished such exemptions from military service as part of the military reforms of 1872.[13] Only toward the end of the nineteenth century did the concept of a five-year period of service become widely established in principle, and even then its implementation varied widely.[14]

The ideal of a general duty to perform military service spread throughout other European countries, with the notable exception of the United Kingdom.[15] In each case, however, the process of implementing such a duty was quite lengthy[16] and often reflected the socioeconomic diversity of these societies. In nearly all cases, an egalitarian, fair system of conscription remained mostly a rhetorical claim. In reality, these countries almost all established models that largely exempted those classes that fueled economic and industrial development from the draft or at least granted them significant concessions.[17] Especially in those countries with the most expansive territorial claims—for example, the Russian czardom and the Hapsburg Empire—large segments of the populace were critical toward military service to varying degrees.[18] This rejection was also related to the fact that in multiethnic empires, different ethnicities were recruited into the military in varying degrees.[19]

Despite the best efforts of the central governments, the implementation of general compulsory service often remained a purely symbolic goal.[20] Even during its implementation, obviously divergent expectations became evident, reflecting in part the different political attitudes of the actors involved.[21] In the German countries, conscription was introduced due to the Napoleonic ordinances. Introduced in Prussia in 1803 and in Bavaria in 1805, the draft proved to be anything but an instrument of social equality. It resulted rather in a heightened social heterogeneity.[22] The (at times) extremely long periods of service—up to eight years—dramatically reduced the percentage of male citizens actually drafted. In addition, the common process of selection considered factors of social class.[23]

The question of to what extent general recruitment from all men of an eligible age was even a good idea was the subject of much discussion in the military. It was little disputed in such circles, however, that longer periods of service and lower fluctuation of personnel favorably influenced military efficiency. This militaristic pragmatism stood in opposition to the noble goals that not only the Prussian political theorists but also the military's own politicians had formulated in their reforms in the early nineteenth century in regard to the foundation of general conscription and its pedagogical potential for the populace.[24]

No European country managed to establish complete equality in the draft prior to World War I. Although the topos of equality—which remains an ideal even today—played a role in the political rhetoric before the war, it only gradually became a central principle of public discourse.[25] Exceptional privileges for members of higher social classes existed in many countries—for example, shorter periods of military service. In Prussia after 1814, graduates of preparatory schools (*Gymnasien* and *Realgymnasien*) had the option to perform "voluntary, one-year" service. Over the course of the following hundred years, this regulation was also introduced in the other German lands and developed into an undisguised privilege for the members of certain professions.[26] Ute Frevert has demonstrated that, following the unification of Germany, the "voluntary, one-year" service in the German Empire served to reconcile the growing bourgeoisie with the supremacy of the Prussian military state. It also created a social incentive system that involved both symbolic and economic capital.[27] The sons of the wealthier farmer class, however, enjoyed similar privileges. It thus appears that conscription in Germany, as in France, served as a social mechanism to transform these traditional privileges for the context of the modern state.

In rural areas, widespread nepotism hindered an egalitarian implementation of the draft for all citizens. In addition, there were active attempts to exclude certain undesirable social groups from military service, including members of specific political movements: in the German Empire, following passage of the Anti-Socialist Laws, this meant those in leadership positions in the social democratic and anarchic groups.[28]

Despite all these restrictions and exclusions, the correlation between the size of the military and that of the population increased as the model of the national army became predominant. The military reforms starting in the 1850s and the successive shortening of the military periods of service were increasingly discussed within the context of the demographic situation.

In the future, it was thought it would be necessary to calculate as closely as possible the effects various political projects would have on the size of the army. In the 1870s, France created a new *premier bureau—effectifs*, an office that answered directly to the general staff and specialized in statistical analysis. The extrapolation of such data over extended time periods was the central mission of the new institution—or, as the reports claimed, a matter "of great interest for the French state."[29] These calculations were an opportunity to formulate goals for the recruitment of new soldiers. In the 1870s, the birth rate in France fell,[30] and in 1905 the standard term of military service was shortened to two years (following the German example).[31] These two factors inspired a flood of calculations regarding the size of France's future military.[32] It was feared that the army would increasingly suffer, in terms of both quantity and quality, as a result of the population's decline. Two objects of scientific statistical study— the size of the population and that of the army—that had been more or less unrelated at the turn of the nineteenth century were now clearly intertwined.

How to Count Soldiers: The Best Practices of Recruitment Statistics

Although the establishment of military intern departments for statistical collection and analysis after the mid-nineteenth century rekindled discussions about draft statistics and facilitated the use of these in technocratic contexts, the army had already long been an object of statistical discourse at this point. This was especially true for the calculations to estimate the relationship between the number of eligible potential recruits and the requirements of the army. On this point, individual scholars in France were already at work in the early nineteenth century to define the "correct" composition of the military and to develop an adequate formula for determining the general population's fitness for service. The administration of the French army system under the ancien régime and the Restoration did not in principle rely on such statistical analysis. Instead, the system divided the country into individual regions for conscription, called *cantons*; the general staff subsequently informed these regions each year of the number of recruits they were to "deliver." How the individual cantons chose to draft their candidates was basically left up to them.

As one might imagine, this cantonal system led to an obvious inequality in regard to the draft; it threatened to divide the country along not only social but also regional lines. One of the first statisticians to systematically address this problem was Taillepied de Bondy. In his opinion, developing a scientific method to calculate an appropriate relationship between a geographic area and a fixed numeric goal for conscription served to counter a deplorable state of affairs. His suggestion to base the current number of conscripts on regional demographic development over the previous decade was intended to produce a fairer estimation of the demographic potential of particular regions.[33]

Whereas Bondy's interest in interregional equality led him to advocate changes to statistical approaches and the military, his successors soon developed new priorities. Boudin highlighted how limited the information gleaned from military statistics had been up to that point. In the context of political reforms after 1848, he argued that criteria for a more detailed statistical profile of the country should be defined. In his eyes, statistics related to conscription were intended as a mirror of social inequality and thus also as a tool to improve public social policy.[34] This essentially marks the beginning of the welfare state's interest in the analysis of military statistics, although it still lacked both adequate methods and the development of a scientific discipline.

Prussian statisticians had a more functional logic in their study of the military. A bureau of statistics was founded in Prussia in 1805, and one of its central tasks in the course of Prussian reforms was to collect information concerning the "class and movement of the civil and military population with their characteristic properties (including the professions and employment of the population) in addition to evidence of immigration and emigration, that is increases and decreases in [the number of those holding] national (and/or Imperial) citizenship."[35] Both the second director of the new office for statistical analysis, C. F. W. Diterici, and his better known successor, Ernst Engel, performed this duty by composing comprehensive reports on the recruitment of soldiers for the reserves—that is, on examinations and recruitment.[36]

Statisticians and military officials were in close contact. The former, however, were hardly autonomous actors; their work was influenced by the military. Statisticians' central task was not to *generate* information, but to gather it. Given the lack of consistency over time or from region to region in the criteria and methods of measurement, the statistical material available to them allowed for little more than a numerical calculation of the number of those drafted and was hardly conducive to any more meaningful scholarship. After several years of analyzing this statistical material, the Bavarian physiologist Thomas Bischoff concluded that a comparison of the individual German states was basically impossible due to the inconsistent units of measurement. According to his estimation, the statistics available at that point resulted in no "certain truth and [no] well-founded comparison in regards to the development, relative health, or fitness for service of the general population in the various [German] states."[37] The methods of measurement and individual examination procedures were too diverse to allow for comparison within Germany, and they also differed significantly from those in other European states. Bischoff was one of the first to openly address a significant aim for the supposedly uninspiring collection of statistical material and the methods of measurement employed, noting: "Until these methods are better regulated and consistent, the numbers which are calculated will have no potential in regards to the general development and state of health of a people."[38]

The phrase *biostatistical results* itself reveals a new biological interest in information collected within the military, an interest that can no longer be understood as solely national. It was in precisely this sphere of the military that mutual observation, but also intensive strategic networking and cooperation between military actors beyond national borders, was especially formative. Various European states published statistics related to military recruitment quite early. Here, too, France was the forerunner, having published its annual "Comptes rendus sur le récrutement de l'armée" starting in 1819. These reports, which at first were limited to an overview of the number of troops within the military regiments at a particular moment (a "stock figure"[39]), became more extensive over time.

Only in the 1860s, however, did the overviews in several European countries become so detailed that statisticians could use them for international comparison. In Spain, the Office of Statistics published its first collection in 1860, a collection that included data for three previous years.[40] Similar publications appeared in this period in the Netherlands, Belgium, and Sweden, although the latter two nations had released their first studies in the early 1850s. The Saxon military doctor Fröhlich formulated the positivist, optimist understanding of statistics as a scientific method: "In this way material is being collected quickly which is able to provide a mathematical foundation for the judgments passed in the examinations."[41]

In some countries, however, the first problems soon surfaced. Studying the Austro-Hungarian Empire proved especially difficult because the diverse nations, kingdoms, and other administrative areas unified in the empire had their own independent agencies to collect statistics, and these had no unified method to do so. It was only possible, therefore, to produce a statistical summary based on a number of individual studies, but this too was complicated by the fact that the number of new recruits to be provided by each country varied depending on political agreements and negotiations. As a result, they employed different systems for the draft, which made a uniform statistical calculation difficult. Starting in 1870, the general staff doctor Hassinger published a statistical report about conscription within the Austro-Hungarian Monarchy in the Austrian journal for military medicine *Der Militärarzt*. In the same year, the third division of the technical and administrative military committee under Weikard's leadership began publishing an annual *Yearbook of Military Statistics*, which included the heterogeneous statistical collections.

In a similar vein, Switzerland introduced a uniform system for conscription to replace the previous regional regulations in 1875.[42] The new criteria included for the first time a physical examination according to a nationally uniform set of questions, and these results became available the following year in the annual "Report on the Medical Examination of Potential Recruits."[43] It was not until the 1890s, however, that the most important elements of this report were regularly included in the *Schweizerische Zeitschrift für Statistik*.

Nearly all the nations in Europe moved to reform their respective militaries in the latter half of the nineteenth century. These changes frequently aimed to streamline the process of conscription to better work within the national administrative structures and thus to provide, at least in geographic terms, a fairer draft system. From the beginning, these reforms involved statistical compilation and accurate calculations as important elements.

A Transnational Trend

It is no coincidence that interest in military statistics began increasing in various European countries simultaneously, but rather an indication of growing ties between statisticians, especially those working in a military context. In 1853, statisticians—primarily those working within government administrations—met in Brussels for the first International Statistical Congress, which had been organized by the Belgian scholar Adolphe Quetelet.[44] These scholars recommended that in the future every state should report regularly, at least on the absolute size of the military and its proportion relative to either the state's general populace or the number of men capable of military service.[45]

Ten years after this first meeting, these statistical conferences had become regular occurrences. The director of the Prussian statistical office, Ernst Engel, invited the congress to meet in Berlin in 1863, which was its fifth convention. Several attendees here drew attention to the *Assenthierungsgeschäft*—that is, the statistical numbers collected via military examinations of potential recruits. Why this question was accorded such importance in the run-up to the congress in Berlin is the subject of speculation. Ian Hacking has pointed out the extent to which German statisticians especially strove to compile comprehensive records instead of applying the laws of mathematical probability.[46] This Prussian logic of "holistic" statistical methods demanded by definition the largest and most complete collection of information pertaining to the numbers of soldiers drafted and the respective proportions of those deemed fit for service. The possibilities that such a wealth of information from these inspections represented seem to have been especially attractive to Engel, who actively sought to encourage a general analysis of these military statistics leading up to the conference in Berlin.

In a curious development, the impetus that finally led to a deeper analysis of these statistics within Europe came in the end from the United States. Engel invited a member of the American Statistical Association, Ezekiel B. Elliott, to present statistics compiled within the US military at the conference in Berlin. Since the outbreak of the American Civil War in 1861, the US Sanitary Commission had compiled numerous statistics on the morbidity and mortality of combat troops. These reports included not only detailed tables on casualties and causes of death on the battlefield, but also statistical tables of soldier height. Elliott analyzed a number of these overviews to prepare for the convention, first with his colleagues within the Sanitary Commission in Washington and then with Engel in Berlin. This first military statistical study of the US army (of the Northern states) was published the same year in Berlin for the convention, impressive evidence of the level of international networking already taking place in this field.[47]

Elliott explained that, although he could compare a few individual statistics with those compiled for the European countries, "the collection of facts of this nature in regards to the armies is quite limited." It is not clear whether Engel intended for his American guest to be a source of inspiration for the European statisticians or whether the dynamics that ensued were the result of something else. In the end, it was the German doctor Rudolf Virchow whose report served as the second starting signal for an improvement of military statistics' standing. Virchow saw reliable, meaningful military statistics as a key to establishing scientific standards for the emerging discipline of anthropology.[48] His remarks succeeded in sparking a wave of efforts in other European countries to collect the relevant information for their respective armed forces.[49] Those numerical overviews that had been compiled up to this point for the European armies and their systems of conscription were to be significantly expanded: in addition to statistics regarding illness, the various categories used in the examinations were to be included in the official statistics in such a way that the various criteria could be combined and compared.

National Trends

The growing trend toward international conferences, which was increasingly noticeable in the last third of the nineteenth century,[50] served as a catalyst for various attempts to co-opt military studies as a scientific discipline. There was a certain contradiction in the simultaneous rise of nationalism and the transnational dimension of the growth of statistical studies. The transnational exchange among experts was repeatedly consumed and dominated by nationalistic dimensions, especially after the turn of the century. An international congress in Berlin in 1907 renewed the discussion of conscription statistics. The chief German military doctor, Otto Schjerning, along with others, opened the International Congress of Hygiene and Demography (the successor of the International Statistical Congress after 1878) in the capital city of the German Empire. In his opening speech to the assembled demographers, Schjerning emphasized the importance of data collection via the military for the further development of their discipline: "All those factors which influence birth and death rates and the state of health of a nation also affect the composition and strength of the national army."[51]

The conference in Berlin included a section dedicated to "conscription statistics,"[52] which was in large part an initiative of a circle of military doctors in Berlin, especially Heinrich Schwiening, a captain in the medical corps who was already known for his statistical studies.[53] Both the speakers' panel and the audience was composed not only of German—more precisely, Prussian—scholars but also of French specialists in the field of military statistics; in addition to Schwiening, the renowned German statisticians Karl Ballod and Georg Evert, who had succeeded Ernst Engel at the Prussian office of statistics, were present in the audience, as was the head doctor of the French medical corps, Adrien Granjux. Whereas the Germans primarily presented arguments against the previously claimed drop in absolute numbers of new conscripts, the French scholars reported on political impediments to the work of the conscription commissions and the problem presented by decentralized data collection. A statistician from Leipzig and representatives of the Pan-German League complained that the more comprehensive statistics available for conscription in Switzerland and Austria were hardly being addressed at the conference. In addition, very few scholars from other countries had attended the conference, and none of these were among the presenters. The Belgian scholars were unhappy with the generalizations made by their French and German colleagues.[54]

The way this section unfolded illustrates the general peculiarity of military and conscription statistics in the last decade before the outbreak of World War I: the debate, which increasingly involved only Germany and France, concentrated on the numerical question of the absolute numbers of combat troops available to both powers.[55] Within both the German Empire and France, fear of a reduction in the number of men fit for military service was rampant, for this was seen as being inevitably linked to a weakening of the military and political regime.

In France especially, these social anxieties had become deeply entrenched in the proceeding forty years. Long before the victory of German forces in the Franco-Prussian War of 1870–1871, the French had feared an impending population decline.[56] The head military doctor of the French army, Jean-Charles Chenu, had warned in 1867 that the French population "was not growing to the extent that it should."[57] In his opinion, this decline was reflected in the number of soldiers eligible for the draft. Chenu, however, did not consider the two figures to be congruent. The unfolding discussion over the decline in the birth rate put the concept of general conscription and even more so the army itself on the defensive: Did the draft keep young adults from having children while the men served their compulsory service? And was the high mortality rate in the army not another factor responsible for the decline in the size of the population? Chenu could refute these hypotheses with the statistical material available to him. The defeat of 1870 also fundamentally changed the discussion surrounding the military. It soon became the focus of the demographic debates, which increasingly dealt with the proportional superiority of the German Empire compared with the incipient Third Republic.[58]

Six years after Chenu, Georges Morache, a professor at the academy for military medicine—the Val-de-Grâce—published a text on questions related to conscription and population. He, too, felt obligated to defend military practice against accusations in the press, but his defense was already dealing with another issue: he sought to challenge the alleged birth-rate crisis itself. He could use the statistics compiled in conscription to counter the overly negative projection of the development of the French population. The results of the examinations, he claimed, revealed that not only had the number of new recruits not fallen, but that recent candidates were stronger in terms of physical fitness.[59] Essentially, the skewed debate stemmed from the general public's mathematical fallacy: the soldiers serving were a smaller percentage of the total populace due to the longer life expectancy of the general population. The ominous predictions that were circulating in France were shown to be the result of a misinterpretation of the statistics.[60]

The discussion of how to interpret these French statistics remained heated until the outbreak of World War I. The French officer Frocard, the second in command of the cabinet of the Department of War, felt obliged to speak out in 1911 against the dire predictions for the future based on the size of the military: "In broad circles of the French public—and unfortunately also within the military—the size of the military is accorded such importance that within France there is presently a downright panic due to the slight reduction in our forces."[61] This fear was completely unfounded in his eyes, for in principle the number of soldiers was growing steadily, if slowly.[62] Such appeasements, however, mostly fell on deaf ears.

In 1913, the French government reinstated the three-year term of compulsory service. Exemptions were henceforth limited to members of the *grandes écoles*. Members of the lower classes were drafted without restriction, as were seminarians studying for the priesthood (*"curés sac au dos"*[63]), who had previously been granted a right of exemption.[64] In the negotiations leading up to these new legal regulations, Minister of War Eugène Etienne had pointed out to French President Raymond Poincaré that the improved general health of the French populace resulting from numerous improvements to hygiene more than compensated for the relative decline in the birth rate.[65] Due to these factors, the size of the army varied less under these circumstances than many observers had first predicted.

The French military had already prepared strategies to counter the relative decline of the population. In the Franco-Prussian War of 1870, the military leadership had already called in troops from the French colonies as reinforcements for the regular combat forces.[66] This strategy was not restricted to the colonial regions but also used in the department of Algeria, where a regular one-year term of compulsory service was introduced in 1875. This was the first time that compulsory military service had been required outside of France itself, even if it was significantly shorter than the service expected in the home country.[67] Until 1914, however, it was not possible to systematically enforce universal conscription in Algeria because there was no system of documenting possible male recruits.[68]

The expansion of colonial rule necessitated the deployment of so many soldiers that the safety of the French homeland itself seemed at first to be in danger.[69] Politicians and military officials, however, began discussing the demographic resources of these regions around the turn of the century. In the years leading up to World War I, the strategy of recruiting soldiers from outside of France's borders was increasingly linked to the issue of the declining birth rate. The army's Department of Conscription composed a catalog of possibilities for countering the declining birth rate in 1911. The central element here was a plan to send three thousand soldiers per year to France and thus reinforce the French troops.[70] This was expected to have the positive side effect of helping to integrate the territories, because this measure would lead to "that element of Algeria which is least French [being] melded with the block of the nation and transfer to them the French mentality."[71] In demographic terms, too, the colonies were seen as a possible tool with which to compensate for fluctuations in fertility. Within the German Empire, on the other hand, such deployment of colonial resources was explicitly rejected.[72]

The low birth rates in the home countries were still seen as a central threat to the ability of the nation to defend itself, however. In France, the declining birth rate was even presented as a question of the country's very survival. Organizations like the Alliance nationale pour l'accroissement de la population française, founded in 1896, campaigned for a change in mindset among the population by emphasizing the dangers it perceived.[73] To save France, the organization indicated, *every* married couple should produce four children.[74] The impending danger was more than anything of a military nature. The German archrival to the east, of which the army—thanks to demographic advantages—far outnumbered the French forces (*five* German soldiers for *every two* French soldiers), was not the only threat; Italy's population was *also* growing, and some argued that Italy threatened to challenge France's claim to Provence and territory in Tunisia.

Figure 1.1
France vs. Germany: a problem of birth rates
Source: La patrie est en danger (Paris: Alliance nationale pour l'accroissement de la population française, 1913)

These debates in France over "depopulation" had a traumatizing effect on the country, though they hardly reflected an adequate understanding of the actual demographic situation. No one summed these fears up better than the most influential of the French demographic specialists of the prewar period, Jacques Bertillon. As the president of the Société de statistique de Paris since the 1880s, Bertillon had made a name for himself not only in academic circles but also within the general public. The foundation of the Alliance nationale had been mostly his idea.[75] In his classic work, "La dépopulation de la France," published in 1911, he claimed: "The fatal point is that in other countries it is not only those who are unfit who can be excluded from service, but also those who are mediocre; they take only the best men. In France, to the contrary, even the unfit and mediocre are drafted for the relief services."[76] Even if the inequality between the birth rates of individual European countries was far less dramatic than the scenarios many authors outlined, it increasingly drew attention. Bertillon concluded: "The reality today is that the simple man is the only one who truly comprehends the military consequences of the low birth rate. It is rare, nonetheless, that the public can correctly judge this development with all its grave repercussions, even if they are well informed."[77] The rivalry with the German neighbor remained a central framework of the statistical analysis, both within the scholarship and the political discourse. There were attempts in both realms to instrumentalize the Franco-German antagonism for their own purposes.

Divergent Interpretations of Military Strength

The question of military strength did not remain in any way confined to this context; beyond France it also developed an impressive, if slightly different, influence. In the German Empire, for example, demographic extrapolation was carried out far further into the predicted future. Warnings backed by statistics only became audible in the last years before the war in the theses of Julius Wolf and other scholars, who pointed to a likely decline in the birth rate, putting Germany in a similar position to France and presenting an existential threat to the survival of the nation.[78] By that point, however, the problem of population development and its correlation to the nation's military strength was already deeply seated in public consciousness. The question of whether the German Empire could maintain combat troops of a sufficient quality and quantity in the future led to a debate no less heated than that in France, but driven by different motives. One of the first texts to inspire and feed on this widespread fear of depopulation was Georg

Hansen's *Die drei Bevölkerungsstufen* (Three Stages of Population) in 1889.[79] Hansen, a statistician in Munich who worked partially with historical data, used the results of communal census data from Leipzig and Munich to back his claims of a structural regularity in the development of German industrialized society. In three stages, the population developed from relying on an agrarian subsistence economy to a society of social estates in which resources and wealth had been stockpiled, which finally ended in the inevitable impoverishment of the new urban proletariat. Hansen's research itself did not have a groundbreaking influence among the general public, but it did change the paradigm for many demographic studies because it connected debates about social hygiene with questions of social structure studied by economists.

This correlation between the economic development of the nation and the hygienic conditions of the populace evolved into a distinct feature of the German debate around recruits as a mirror of general demographic trends. German economists calculated the economic potential of recruits and argued on this basis that the nation's fate was dependent on the healthy recruit. They opened the debate over agrarian versus industrial states and pursued it in depth in their most influential organization, the *Verein für Socialpolitik* (association for social policy, i.e., a professional association for economists in Germany). An agrarian economist and professor at the Agricultural University of Berlin, Max Sering, provided a sort of "translation" of these demographic scenarios into economic research problems. Three years after the publication of Hansen's study, Sering referred to the basic idea of urban degeneration and warned his most faithful audience, the *Deutsche Landwirtschaftsrat* (German Federal Committee for Agriculture), of the consequences for the development of "German military strength."[80] Sering's two main causes—the fight against the liberalization of the agricultural markets to favor imports on the one hand and the internal colonization of the German Empire, especially east of the Elbe, on the other[81]—combined particularly well with Hansen's scenario of degeneration. For, assuming that agrarian Germany should become less important and that the German society should develop into an urban industrial society, what consequences would that be likely to have on the ability of Germany to defend itself— that is, on the "military strength" of the German people?[82] Sering's answer was simple: he reiterated Hansen's theses showing that the "quality" of soldiers would decline as a result of the physical degeneration of the German people. If Sering's suggestions themselves were not alarming enough, in 1892 an anonymous text strengthened their effect by presenting his theses in a polemic manner and reaching a broader audience: "Because ... the rural populace ... makes up the core of our replacement troops, its relative decline is simultaneously an endless weakening of the military strength of our fatherland."[83] These vague statistical predictions were accompanied by a whole range of pessimistic cultural assumptions.

These theses about degeneration can only be understood against the backdrop of violent political debates, of which they formed a functional part. Degeneration theory was not a biological fact here but necessarily fit into the political discourses that had very different political motivations. Sering was engaged in a battle against the political push for free trade, which German Chancellor Leo von Caprivi implemented between 1891 in 1893 in the form of a new system of moderately liberal trade treaties—especially with Russia and the United States.[84] A group of those fundamentally opposed to these new trade policies coalesced among not only agricultural elites but also scholars working on agricultural topics. A clear position on the side of the agrarian lobbyists and for the interests of the farmers' association was certainly not the "common sense" of the Verein für Socialpolitik. Instead, it was Sering's involvement in the issue that mobilized the professional association and polarized the members in the coming years, dividing those with protectionist and economically liberal tendencies.

Lujo Brentano, a political economist in Munich, quickly became a central member of the latter party within the society. At first, the two parties' disagreement was one of ideological perspective and concentrated on the question of economists' position and role within the political system.[85] It did not involve concrete differences of opinion or approach.[86] The controversy over Sering's prediction of Germany's endangered military strength, a prediction he presented as being objectively based on statistics, changed the character of the debate. It grew into a fundamental clash of scholars in which both the tone and the implications of the discussion shifted. What had been a difference of opinion on questions of economic policy became, bit by bit, an argument increasingly focused on the military.[87]

In 1895, a nineteen-year-old student in economics and legal studies, Robert René Kuczynski, participated in the Economics and Social Political Summer School of the Verein für Socialpolitik in Berlin, where he witnessed the growing conflict within the association. Kuczynski attended lectures by Johannes Conrad and Max Sering about the threat that the dwindling of the agrarian population posed to the German nation, the question of the pauperization of the populace, and the necessity of both external and internal colonization to preserve the nation's strength.[88] Eugen

Philippovich and Lujo Brentano, on the other hand, taught courses on international trade ties and the advantages of liberal trade policies for large segments of the populace, as well as the need to restructure the traditional agrarian state east of the Elbe.

Kuczynski did not comment in his notes about which of his teachers' arguments he found most convincing,[89] but he soon chose a camp. Only one year later, he began working on a dissertation in economics at the University of Munich under Brentano's supervision. Kuczynski's dissertation, almost certainly at Brentano's suggestion, aimed to critically revise the arguments of Hansen, Sering, and Otto Ammon, an author and self-proclaimed socioanthropologist from Karlsruhe.[90] Kuczynski was to test the theory that claimed a correlation between industrialization and decline in the number of new recruits by examining the statistics; he hoped thereby to undermine the thesis of the degeneration theorists. He wrote first to numerous cities and municipalities to request the results of their most recent censuses and then analyzed these in light of Sering's claims.[91]

Kuczynski soon discovered multiple gaps in the statistics and data available. On the one hand, many cities and regions had only recently begun to comprehensively collect this information, which meant that it lacked statistical depth. On the other hand—and this was more critical—Kuczynski observed that the available information hardly allowed for definitive analysis because of the categories used. In fact, Kuczynski could not consistently determine the origins of the residents counted in any of the cities in his study. He had similar problems addressing questions about the social and professional profile of the populace: the statistics provided for no definitive conclusions about anything other than a person's current seat of residence. It was impossible, for example, to determine whether those living in rural areas were actively engaged in agriculture or members of the rural proletariat.

The publication[92] of Kuczynski's thesis can be interpreted as an open declaration of war between these two camps of scholars. Sering's theses were based on the idea that it is statistically possible to clearly separate rural and urban populations to appraise their effect on military strength, a point that was challenged by Kuczynski's arguments. Ammon's theses came under an even harsher attack, for he had claimed to have observed a concrete degeneration of physique related to the transition from a rural to an urban population. Kuczynski's hybridization of these categories raised doubts about Ammon's supposedly clear evidence to support his biologistic argument. Kuczynski's supervisor, however, seized the opportunity to further caricature his opponents' arguments.

In the context of advising the Bavarian parliament on the allocation of the military budget, Brentano discussed the recent statistics for recruits across the entire kingdom.[93] Parallel to these negotiations, he also presented his findings to an assembly of Munich's *Volkswirthschaftliche Gesellschaft* (Society for Economics).[94] He incorporated his student's research into his own argument: given the shortcomings of the available information over a historical period, it was not possible to differentiate or extrapolate the development of the population along these lines. Using statistical material stemming from the censuses of businesses taken in 1882 and 1895, Brentano claimed that there had been a recent reversal of the ratio of urban and rural recruits: whereas the majority of recruits in 1882 had come from the countryside, thirteen years later the majority had been employed in industry. Because the army had remained constant in terms of absolute numbers, however, Brentano concluded that the industrialization of the society had in no way negatively impacted the national military strength. The invalidity of arguments to the contrary would become clearer, predicted Brentano, as soon as laws had been passed to improve occupational safety and to prohibit excessive exploitation of workers in industrial settings.[95]

These arguments went back and forth between the camps, and the statistical debate became more and more heated as it involved a number of normative and moral claims about the future form of society, all of which played out very publicly in the press.[96] The newspaper *Neue Preußische Zeitung*, popularly known as the *Kreuzzeitung*, became the mouthpiece of the camp of the national conservatives and agrarian lobby; their attacks against "the liberal city folk" did not stop short of anti-Semitism. The paper spoke, for example, of an imminent "sobering-up of the Philistines" and "the 'Jewish' liberal truth," which would stop laughing soon enough.[97] According to the calculations, the German military strength was greatest in that region of Germany that was most sparsely populated, the East Prussian region of Gumbinnen, where approximately two-thirds of the adult male population was suited to military service.[98]

Brentano, meanwhile, continued to lobby for the opposite camp[99] and attracted a group of lobbyists—for example, the *Schutzverband gegen agrarische Übergriffe* (Association for Protection against Agrarian Incursions), founded in 1896, which made a simplified version of Brentano's arguments its own.[100]

As the available statistics became more extensive and detailed according to age group, the question of at what age and in what phase of development a social or even biological degeneration could be observed grew in significance.[101] The series of numbers used were often static, and factors like the migration between cities and countryside and among the various regions of the German Empire had not been considered. Even the conservative newspapers had to admit that the methods of data collection used obscured any details of migration patterns. Was the populace in industrial regions necessarily "industrialized"? At first, the necessary questions about the milieu and living situations could only be answered based upon the categorization of occupations among the populace.[102] The debate developed its own dynamic: with every new volley, the statistical arguments on both sides eroded. As a result, the discussion that had originally been sparked by Otto Ammon over social patterns and questions of racial hygiene became increasingly important. These tended to idealize rural life and its positive effects on evolution.[103] Many members of the liberal camp, however, could not support this line of argumentation.[104]

Robert René Kuczynski, for instance, initially had not participated in the controversy his dissertation had helped to spark. Following a successful doctoral defense, Kuczynski had traveled to Washington, DC, to conduct research at the Bureau of Labor Statistics. He returned to Germany after several months, where he was confronted with this smoldering debate, which had not gone out because it was being stoked regularly by the *Kreuzzeitung*.[105]

In his examination, Kuczynski focused on statistical precision and believed that accurate calculations could bridge the ideological divide. He took up the laborious task of carefully studying the abundance of literature that had been published in the 1890s.[106] Despite these best efforts, however, he was unable to put a final end to the debate. The topic of military strength, having become firmly entrenched in the realm of public discourse within the empire, could no longer be put to rest by mere scholarly exchange.

Statistics, Media, Audiences

When the imperial government under the direction of Bernhard von Bülow implemented a massive increase in protectionist duties for agricultural products after December 25, 1902, the sensibilities of the statisticians were in no way assuaged.[107] In principle, the agrarian lobby had achieved its goal; further propaganda in support of an agricultural Germany was hardly necessary. The spirits that had been summoned, however, could not be easily laid to rest in the years to come. The general public remained aware of the topic: the *Landwirtschaftsrat* (German Agricultural Council) continued putting out propaganda, and other publications raised these issues as well. Within the public debate over military strength, the dichotomy between an

Figure 1.2

Propaganda postcard published by the German Agricultural Council, undated [after 1909]

agrarian and industrial state had been so often reiterated that it became an ingrained pattern of thought.

As a result of the high degree of mediatization surrounding the debate, the view of those who were pessimistic about the potential military strength of the nation dominated public opinion; their political demands toward the government had been more or less met. The members of the more liberal camp, on the other hand, found themselves increasingly on the defensive.

Numerous local societies and civilian groups embodied this antagonism between the rural and urban populations. In the Kingdom of Württemberg, the *Wirtschaftliche Vereinigung* (Economic Union) suggested in early 1908 that soldiers in the army should be instructed in agricultural techniques to better support the future generation of farmers. This petition was approved and such instruction subsequently introduced.[108] Three years later, the *Sozialharmonische Verein Stuttgart* (Society for Social Harmony in Stuttgart) made a similar suggestion in the Reichstag. It was an attempt to weaken the existing ban on abortion. The society argued that urban "degeneration" would be accelerated via the impoverishment of families with many children, threatening the general health of the populace.[109]

These lines of attack are evidence of the numerous difficulties faced in formulating a scientific definition of an industrial society. A large number of scholars in the social sciences, economics, and natural sciences felt called to address these questions. Brentano was to a certain degree responsible for widening the scope of the debate: in one of his first contributions to the discussion, he had linked the question of fitness for military service to his standard research topics—namely, the welfare of the working class and legislation for social welfare.[110] Reforms to the system of public welfare were in his view the only way to curtail the excessive physical exploitation of laborers.[111] As evidence of this, Brentano pointed to studies of fatigue that had been conducted in the Italian Alps by a prominent physiologist in Turin, Angelo Mosso[112]; this research addressed the way industrialized society perceived itself from an entirely new angle. On a similar note, Arthur Dix had already placed the debate within a broad anthropological context in early January 1898, when he asked where, given a constant number of individuals, vitality was the highest.[113]

Many of the studies that played a role in the debate over the national economy until 1914 used statistical analysis as the basis for anthropological, medical, and physiological observations. Once interest in these questions had been aroused, scholars began expanding their focus beyond the conscripts as sole object. In the eyes of the military doctor Georg Bindewald, the military fitness of the individual potential recruits represented an "official governmental seal for the masculine individual, [confirming] that he belongs in the hereditary line of the populace, which guarantees a healthy continuation of our people." He was thus "the warrantor for future healthy generations."[114] The military strength of the populace of the whole was nevertheless not only a question of the male youth, but came to express more generally the state of general health.

Bindewald argued that military strength could be enhanced by limiting the employment of women because, with their reproductive function, they provided a crucial element of military strength.[115] The introduction of this transgenerational dynamic into the debate affected the relationships between gender and age groups, and the category of military strength had conclusively been added as a core concept of demographic analysis. It was the impetus for research on the development of public health, and it simultaneously provided an apparatus for the study.[116] In the search for an explanation for the urban population's (hypothetical) inferior fitness for military service, the focus shifted to questions of nervosity, mental illness, and suicidal tendencies.[117] These various lines of interpretation made the debate over military strength a point of reference with paradigmatic implications for the broader society.[118]

Beyond the realm of scholarly discourse, however, the debate over military strength had another effect on political and statistical practice. When the first fears surfaced in 1892 about the decline in military strength, Bavaria was the first German state to respond. The Bavarian parliament commissioned a statistical study, which was published in 1897. The report was fundamentally flawed, however, because the statisticians responsible had failed to ask potential recruits about their origins; as a result, they could say very little about migration patterns, a topic that dominated the debate in the years following.

The debate had other political effects as well. In 1901, the Reichstag approved a large-scale study in which not only the birthplace of the conscripts—and whether this was urban or rural—was to be recorded, but their respective occupations, as well.[119] This study was a direct response to the controversy over military strength, especially in recent publications by Kuczynski and Brentano. Both men had suggested that a more precise answer to the questions raised would require a detailed examination of social circumstances and living conditions, which they hoped could be deduced in part from occupational data. Once again, however, the information gathered was evaluated in principle based solely on the place of birth. The studies actually did find some discrepancies related to the numbers

regarding military fitness: those born in rural areas were 1.8 percent fitter than the total average, whereas those born in cities were 3.3 percent
below the average.[120] The additional information concerning occupation
seems to have been hardly considered, perhaps due to its complexity and
the fact that it was recorded separately by the respective civilian chairmen
of the conscription commissions. The seemingly neutral statistical tables
that had been produced as tools for civic administration had become politically charged elements of a public debate.

Transnational Trends of Nationalized Topoi

There had been relatively few attempts to make international comparisons
in the course of this long debate over the military strength of the German populace. Hardly ever had a controversy within statistical scholarship
sparked a similarly public debate within the media as that which resulted
from this disagreement between the agrarian lobby and liberal economists
about military strength. Hardly any other controversy, however, remained
so confined to the national context. Although the German discussion did
involve the debate over depopulation in France and the English theories of
urban degeneration that had been circulating since the 1840s,[121] virtually
no one attempted to compare German data to that of other countries at a
statistical, empirical level. One reason for this was certainly the problematic
nature of the available statistical material. As difficult as it was to compile
usable statistics for Germany, it was even more challenging to find data
for any analysis at an international level. Furthermore, neither of the two
camps was particularly invested in a systematic international comparison.
In the end, the debate remained rooted in a self-referential national frame.
The bone of contention was not the substance of the recruits themselves
but rather the appraisal of the superior or inferior position of one's own
country within the context of competing political concepts around the
turn of the century—namely, whether one was optimistic about progress
or critical of modernity.

It was only in the period immediately preceding World War I that isolated
scholars began challenging these starkly nationalized conceptual limits of
statistical studies.[122] Two of the main participants in this debate, Brentano
and Kuczynski, now recognized the necessity of stepping back from the
national contexts to compare German statistics with those of other countries, especially in regard to the still unanswered question of how potential
recruits' occupations were related to their fitness for military service. Their
research profited from one of the earliest transatlantic funding programs

of the Carnegie Endowment for International Peace. In 1912, they signed a contract with the new institution, which sought to "promote a thorough and scientific investigation and study of the causes of war and of the practical methods to prevent and avoid it."[123] With their research, Brentano and (especially) Kuczynski hoped to gain insights into the "influences of changes in occupations of a people upon the composition and efficiency of armies and influences of the changes in the composition of armies on the economic life."[124] They planned to focus first on a comparison of statistics from Germany, Austria, and Switzerland, and then in a second step to address statistics from other European countries. The contract had to be prolonged after one year because the scope of the project proved to be so complex. With the outbreak of World War I, however, the project was brought to an abrupt end: circumstances changed overnight, and access to the data was cut off.

It was not only in Germany that at least a few scholars began adopting a wider perspective and attempting international comparisons in the first decade of the twentieth century. The dynamic of the German debate had aroused interest in a number of other European countries as well. In Switzerland, there had been efforts for some time to create a statistical basis for such debates, which had been conducted in part in the *Schweizerischen Blättern für Wirtschafts- und Sozialpolitik* (Swiss Journal for Economic and Social Policy).[125] A similar interest was pushed upon Swiss statisticians when a doctoral student of Sering's, Walter Abelsdorff, set up Switzerland as a model in opposition to a Germany suffering the symptoms of industrial degeneration.[126] This monolithic image of a rural Swiss populace clearly contradicted the perception of much of urban bourgeois Swiss society, which distanced itself from such remote mountain regions. Before and during the war, scholars of medicine were especially motivated to begin such research on the likely effects on Swiss military strength resulting from changes in recruitment among the rural and urban populations for Switzerland.[127]

The discussion of recruitment numbers as an end in itself—in other words, the best practice for documenting them—was a transnational rather than an international problem. The negotiations did not obliterate national borders but rather transcended these borders while remaining conscious of the significance of these numbers for the fate of the nation. It thus is not surprising that this issue was raised again and again given the polarized public opinion leading up to 1914. Statisticians and military doctors continued playing the "numbers game,"[128] but arguments based on numbers alone increasingly disappeared from the discourse. The number of soldiers in the military was dependent on so many variables that it was practically impossible to prove a continuous proportional ratio to the size of the populace as a whole. The attempts to view a populace based on its "military strength" in a more differentiated way, however, had other repercussions. The supposedly neutral and objective calculation of army size resulted in inconsistencies, which scholars in various fields noticed. The inequalities between nations, between rural and urban populations, or between social classes all demanded a new interpretative approach given the newly discovered "draft equality." A new series of problems came to light, which, in the decades leading up to World War I, became permanently associated with potential recruits as an object of scientific study.

2   From Pathologies to Topographies: Statistics of Illness within the Military in New Social Contexts

During the Crimean War, in January 1855, three thousand British soldiers died in infirmaries, mostly of avoidable infectious diseases, even as the work of the nurse Florence Nightingale reached its peak. After noting that soldiers in British hospitals were nearly twice as likely to die as their French counterparts, Nightingale felt compelled to alleviate the situation, and she began working on a series of suggestions for improvements.[1] She began by compiling statistics on their causes of death. While Nightingale worked during the day with other nurses to improve hygienic conditions in the hospital, she spent her evenings analyzing the information she had collected.[2] With her findings, she contributed to the research of the Royal Commission on the Sanitary Condition of the Army.[3]

After the war ended, Nightingale sought to make those in positions of political and military leadership aware of the pressing need for improvements in this area. She drew some of the most famous diagrams in the history of statistics, called "Nightingale's roses" or "Nightingale's coxcombs." They clearly showed the percentage of soldiers who had died during the war of infectious disease, rather than anything that had happened on the battlefield.[4] Nightingale sent the first such graphic, which had caused a considerable stir in the general public, to Queen Victoria in 1858.

Immediately upon her return from the war zone, Nightingale had compiled statistics showing that, even during peacetime, soldiers' morbidity rate was twice that of the general population due to the inferior hygienic conditions in the barracks. Nightingale's efforts led not only to improvements in conditions within the British Army—albeit too late to prevent the devastating effects of bad hygiene during the Crimean War—but also to her being the first woman accepted into the Royal Statistical Society. In subsequent years, she played an important role in public health reforms in Britain.[5] In her *Notes on Nursing*, published in 1860, she summarized her study of statistics for the general state of health services thus:

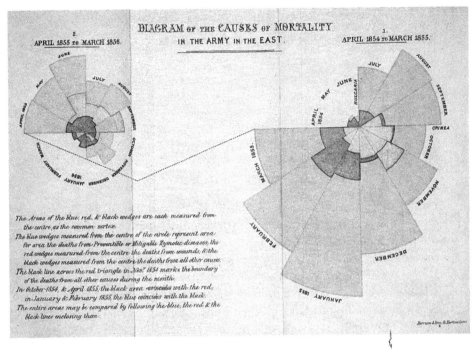

Figure 2.1
Florence Nightingale's diagram

Were they instead of having the person examined by the medical man, to have the houses, conditions, ways of life, of these persons examined, at how much truer results would they arrive! ... We know, say, that from 22 to 24 per 1,000 will die in London next year. But minute enquiries into conditions enable us to know that in such a district, nay, in such a street—or even on one side of that street, in such a particular house, or even on one floor of that particular house—will be the excess of mortality, that is, the person will die who ought not to have died before old age.[6]

The story of Florence Nightingale clearly illustrates the connections among the field of military statistics, the hygiene movement, and social reform. In her extensive treatment of the military, she also displayed growing interest in the army as a "reflection of society," a view she shared with a growing number of scholars, statisticians, and politicians throughout Europe. It was this interest that made her an international expert in the field of medical statistics. In her statistical studies, she convincingly adjusted the scale of her observations accurately from the fairly tangible setting of the military and made projections for larger medical questions about society as a whole. Of course, these observations were of direct importance to the military in wartime. After the war, however, she used the military as a lens to study the general populace. The recognition paid to her by statisticians testifies to the fact that her arguments seemed sound even in this wider context.

The Military as a Reflection of Society: The Project of Comparing Morbidity Statistics

Statistics on morbidity—whether those collected within military or civilian contexts—were very important because they were the prerequisite for protecting against individual risks in the sense of "social physics." Knowledge of "living conditions" was necessary to calculate and control probable risks, an idea that had already been central in the work of the statistical coryphaeus, Adolphe Quetelet, in *A Treatise on Man and the Development of His Faculties* (1842).[7] Based on this concept, morbidity statistics were part of a normative, determinist school of statistics that dominated statistical research in different countries[8] and raised hopes that scholarship could help to improve social policy. Although the idea of a collective safety net as a foundational principle of public social policy gained in popularity in the second half of the nineteenth century, the academic and statistical foundations for the concrete formulation of such policies were greatly lacking. Demographers and statisticians called for the collection of statistical information on morbidity and accidents on all claims filed by those insured; this information would enable a new appraisal of occupational hazards. Comprehensive data on the social circumstances of the entire population did not exist and remained an unachieved ideal for quite some time,[9] but the statistics available for the army and marines served, at least to some extent, as an alternative.[10]

Their expectations that social policy should increasingly be shaped by scientific research did not necessarily reflect the realities of social policy in these respective countries.[11] This was most clear in the case of England: Nightingale's research and a number of other studies analyzing such statistics presented a stark contrast to the relatively weak tradition of social policy in many aspects of the English (and British) political tradition.[12] Although Britain had, in an attempt to improve hygiene in impoverished and working-class neighborhoods, begun collecting "vital statistics" in the 1840s and 1850s, this was not to be confused with a systematic program to reduce risk.[13]

Nightingale was the most prominent but not the first statistician to become interested in morbidity statistics in the army. The French military had begun compiling more careful and detailed statistics on illness within its ranks after its at times traumatic experiences during Napoleon's campaigns. As part of the military reforms under Louis XVIII, starting in 1819, the *comptes rendus sur le récrutement de l'armée* was compiled. Although this initially included little more than the number of those inducted and discharged from the military, it significantly allowed for the calculation of the higher rate of mortality as compared to the civilian population.[14] In 1833, the French military doctor Louis Benoiston de Châteauneuf published a study of military statistics collected during the 1820s in which he concluded that a soldier was nearly twice as likely to die as a civilian in any given year.[15] The doctor in charge of caring for the mountain infantry, Jean Boudin, also published a study on medical statistics within the military.[16] Both studies suggested that more detailed statistics were necessary because soldiers' illness rates within the military also varied: In the first two years of service, there was a higher rate of illness and fatal accident. After this, especially among those who had reached at least the rank of noncommissioned officer, the morbidity rate was actually lower than that of the civilian population.[17] It was these more nuanced observations that challenged politicians and the military leadership to consider the conditions in the barracks and the risks involved in their maneuvers and to compare the situation of the French Army to that of its counterparts in other countries.[18] Boudin emphasized the importance of such information for the formulation of public health policy. From this perspective, the military was primarily an interesting case study: "One of the most important tasks of public health is without doubt to process scientific information in order to help lawmakers formulate fitting legislation."[19]

The far-reaching hopes that many scholars had for the possibilities represented by the military morbidity statistics remained unattained for quite some time. In addition to the early studies on the French military, which remained partial and incomplete, in 1840 the Office of the Surgeon General released a first comprehensive report—albeit just for the United States—on military medical statistics.[20]

In the field of military statistics, a few guiding aspects of interpretation crystallized quite early: (1) the interest in a wide-ranging statistical determination of individual risks within the context of public health policies for the purpose of better understanding the populace via statistics;[21] (2) an intrinsic interest of the military in the improvement of its own situation; and (3) the transnational comparison with other countries, which included questions of national prestige and vehement fears concerning the ability of these nations to defend themselves. Each of these three aspects created its own dynamic in which both political and scientific interests were closely intertwined. Prior to World War I, such statistical expectations were only partially converted into concrete changes to the political system in the sense of "social engineering," but they were nevertheless formative in helping to identify points at which social policy might intervene in the future.

"National prestige" came to play an important role in the "success story" of medical statistics, one that is critical to historical understanding. While the correlation between the spheres of politics and the military usually occurred within the frame of the "nation," statisticians approached these questions from another angle: at international conventions, they repeatedly expressed the need for a system of medical statistics collected in the various European armies which would allow for comparative studies, and they succeeded in making changes to the statistical practices in individual countries. Long before the political leadership of these individual nation states had recognized the problem, statistical experts were engaged in a lively discussion of comparative medical statistics that transcended national borders.

Here, again, the fifth International Statistical Congress in Berlin in 1863 was a sort of catalyst. In preliminary meetings to prepare for the convention, the recent statistical studies in the United Kingdom and Nightingale's new ideas were an important topic. Ernst Engel, the director of the Prussian statistical office, was in many respects the "soul" of the conference. He reported that "statistics reflecting the state of health of the troops in general and within the hospitals in particular, according to the recommendations made by Miss Florence Nightingale," belonged to the "unsolved or only half-solved questions" left after the previous conference in London in 1860, a sort of "homework" to be addressed by the attendees in Berlin.[22] Engel argued that attempts at international statistical study could no longer be limited to efforts to standardize the questionnaires themselves. In his eyes, the task of an international conference on the subject was instead to create permanent organizations that were also able to carry out their own statistical studies.[23] This went beyond a nominal standardization of the categories for such studies to mean that methods of measurement also should be adjusted for consistency.

The congress in Berlin proposed ten fields that were meant to cover various aspects of statistical study, from insurance statistics to the administration of national censuses. The seventh of these fields was dedicated to the "state of health and mortality of the military population in comparison with that of the civilian population."[24] In other words, the field of mortality and illness statistics in the army had been included in its rather limited catalog of statistical methods and areas of study that made up the core of statistical expertise and the discipline's growing attempts to address questions of social life in a scientific manner. Since the foundation of the International Statistical Congress in 1853, it had been the scholars' goal to generate knowledge in these selected areas that would facilitate the development and improvement of public health policy. Rudolf Virchow, who was also present at the congress, was certain that the medical statistics of the army "together with the conscription statistics" represented the "foundation of an in-depth knowledge of the corporal development of our nation."[25] This undertaking was codified in the attempts to "hygienize" the public and private spheres that were so formative in the last third of the nineteenth century.

The rhetoric of the project to create a body of standardized international military medical statistics was quite developed, and numerous studies repeatedly commented upon this need, but significant obstacles to the practical implementation of creating this specific statistical genre remained. As late as the 1880s, the statistical offices in individual countries had not acted upon the emphatic plea of the 1863 Berlin congress. The demands for the creation of an international commission for military statistics went unmet. The Austro-Hungarian military doctors were the only ones to publish relevant studies in the late 1860s,[26] and the Austrian military doctor Wiekard was the only representative of his discipline who traveled to St. Petersburg in 1872 for the international congress.[27] Although representatives of other countries did begin to make similar efforts in the 1870s,[28] the statistics available on illness within the military remained deficient in the eyes of many scholars.

For many of the largest nations, there was practically no information available at all, including the German Empire. The head military doctor in Saxony, Wilhelm August Roth, described the surveys published for other countries as "awe-inspiring publications" that made the reader painfully aware "that such studies for Germany will presumably remain wishful thinking for some time to come."[29] Roused by this crushing judgment, the Prussian Ministry of War strove to rectify this situation,[30] but only the Kingdoms of Württemberg and Saxony joined them in their attempts at standardized data collection. The Bavarian military was not included at all in the statistics.[31]

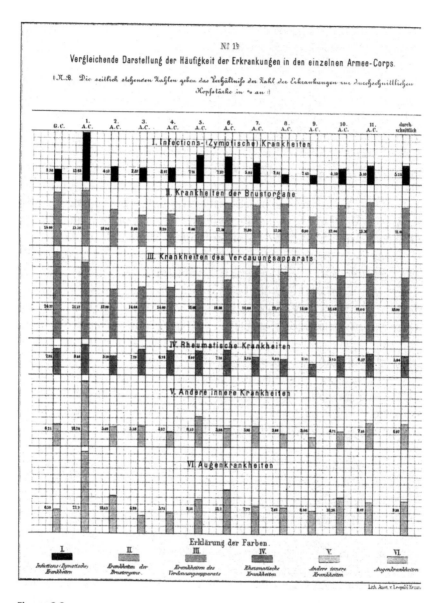

Figure 2.2

Comparative overview of the frequency of illnesses in the first medical statistical report of the Royal Prussian Army for 1867

Modalities of the Transnational: The Ambitious Failure of the Proposal to Collect International Military Medical Statistics

It took nearly thirty years for the general expression of interest in military medical statistics in these international contexts to find some realization in a few first concrete steps. The basic idea of an international collection of statistical information related to illness and injury within the military was revived once again in Berlin—not at a statistical or demographic congress per se, but rather at the tenth International Medical Congress, which took place from August 4–9, 1890. In section 18 on military medicine, the American military doctor and later social statistician John Shaw Billings renewed the suggestion that a standardized system for collection of military medical statistics should be created based on standardized nosological classifications and nomenclature of illness. His French colleague George Schneider went one step further and called for a standardization of the recruitment statistics in terms of the medical data collection. This proposal was so well received that the assembled military medical professionals agreed to create a provisional commission to implement the suggestions at a practical level. The committee consisted of representatives of Great Britain, the United States, the German Empire, and France.[32]

Their spokesperson, the British military doctor J. Lane Notter, reported for the first time only four years later at the subsequent medical congress in Rome.[33] The French representative, Antony, even presented the first concrete suggestions—for example, the standardization of time periods used in the measurement process and the question of how the sickness levels of soldiers should be defined. This groundwork having been laid, the assembly moved to establish a permanent commission in place of the provisional one. This group met for the first time on September 3, 1894, in the military officers' club in Budapest as part of the seventh International Congress for Hygiene and Demography. The new commission was composed of representatives of all eleven states involved: Austria-Hungary, Russia, Prussia, Bavaria, Saxony, Italy, France, Belgium, England, Denmark, and the United States. By 1910, the Netherlands, Norway, Spain, and Serbia had also joined.[34] In this introductory phase, the participation of individual countries was very much dependent upon the initiative of individual military doctors. Indeed, the original circle of interested military doctors was first and foremost a quite closed social network and much less a decision-making body guided by governments. The representatives of these various states committed themselves in the future to completing a standardized set of ten tables in addition to conducting their own statistical reports; the details of these tables were yet to be determined, but they were intended for publication in the appendix of the corresponding national reports. The first of these tables was, in keeping with Schneider's suggestions, to show results of the examinations that were considered relevant for statistics on illness.

This set of tables and the criteria for completing them were to be made available to those countries not directly participating in the commission so that they too could be involved in a comparison of national militaries. The response to these appeals, however, was often guarded. Switzerland is a good example of simultaneous cooperation and refusal. The confederacy had compiled internal medical statistics for the Swiss military since 1875[35] and remained true to this principle: although it implemented methods outlined by the congress in Budapest, it did not publish this specific information,[36] which meant that the reports of the commission could not consider such information.[37] It was not until 1910 that the newly appointed chief medical officer of the Swiss army, Hauser, lobbied the Bundesrat to facilitate publication of these reports.[38] After 1911, more than twenty years after the founding of the commission, the Swiss army finally published a regular compilation titled "Illness during Basic Training," which complied with some but not all of the commission's recommendations.

In those countries that were participating, adjusting the related statistical practices was quite slow. The first nations to do so were Austria-Hungary and the United States. Many others followed their example, in some cases with a quite significant delay. The principles that had seemed so straightforward when the commission approved them proved much more difficult to enact in reality, especially in regard to the medical statistics collected during the conscription process. Some countries summarized the results for the entire nation. Federal countries like Italy, on the other hand, grouped the results more or less separately by province; depression statistics were sorted according to the borders of its governorates. The separate statistics of the individual German states with their regional variances in methods of compilation were the source of considerable confusion. The United States had segregated according to the categories of "negros" and "whites," which made this data practically inscrutable for comparison by European military doctors—and Great Britain did not even have general conscription, so it was clear from the outset that comparisons with the other countries made little sense. This list of statistical difficulties, mistakes, and misunderstandings is practically endless. The secretary of the commission who was responsible for the standardization, the Austrian military doctor Paul von Myrdacz, lamented these shortcomings in a long essay in the Austrian military medical journal *Der Militärarzt*.[39]

These challenges were being addressed after 1894, but progress was slow. At first, the standards of the international commission were implemented neither in France nor in Germany; the commission, which generally convened every three years in conjunction with the International Congress for Hygiene and Demography, repeatedly urged compliance, but there was considerable reticence.

In Prussia, Saxony, Württemberg, and the rest of the German lands, except for Bavaria, the situation changed around the turn of the century. In 1895, several military medical institutions merged to form the new Kaiser Wilhelms-Akademie für militärärztliches Bildungswesen (Emperor Wilhelm Academy for Military Medical Education). This prestigious school provided a central location for the training of future doctors to serve in the German military. The new academy was, however, responsible for more than just the education of new field doctors. The medical division of the Ministry of War, which was overwhelmed by the task of compiling military medical statistics, used the opportunity to rid itself of this responsibility. Starting in 1898, the national statistics were compiled within the academy, which had a department dedicated to this purpose.[40] The academy was also responsible for the publication of these statistics starting around the turn of the century, and in 1902 it succeeded in compiling not only the German statistics but also the information called for by the International Commission for Military Medical Statistics, although the statistics for Bavaria continued to be published separately.[41] The work of and pressure exerted by the international commission, in addition to the pressure created by the newly formed institution, led the Ministry of War to take the issue of conscription statistics more seriously. The more favorable institutional context meant that the relevant statistical practices became entrenched for the first time.

In 1907, another international convention, the Congress for Hygiene and Demography, took place in Berlin. There, it became clear that since the previous convention the field of military statistics had achieved a fully new standing in Germany. In advance of the congress, the Ministry of War had informed the Foreign Office about the importance of the international commission.[42] After a period in which the commission had been less active than in the initial phase, the congress presented an opportunity to give these statistical studies more room in Berlin. The director of the Kaiser Wilhelms-Akademie, Otto Schjerning, opened the convention.[43] German Chancellor Bernhard von Bülow explicitly invited the delegated military doctors to the meeting of the international commission that was to take place during the congress.[44] Individual countries tried to outdo each other with the number of delegates they sent; France alone sent twenty-one doctors for the different sections of the congress, including two representatives for the international commission.[45] Once again, hopes were high that military medical statistics might become a central instrument for demographic research. In his opening address to his assembled colleagues, Schjerning highlighted the "medical report of the army and navy," pointing out that it was "important for demographers as well."[46]

At this point, the difficulties of statistical compilation had been minimized to the extent that Germany and France, the largest nations involved, had begun releasing this information for their militaries. The commission assigned Myrdacz the task of finally using the collected information to produce a first report, which was completed for the subsequent meeting in conjunction with the International Congress for Hygiene and Demography in Budapest in 1909.[47] Myrdacz, in a most neutral manner, presented a variety of comparative results concerning the state of health and the frequency of various illnesses in those countries that had submitted such information. He did not, however, consider a great deal of the statistical material available, including the medical statistics collected in the process of examinations and conscription, which the commission had fought long and hard to acquire.[48] The statistical material was too inconsistent, as had been the reaction of the nations involved, some of which had refused to provide the relevant information. Individual countries had proven quite reticent in providing details of physical characteristics. The numerous debates on the strength of the armies in an increasingly militarized atmosphere had made countries wary of sharing such information, which had never been an issue before. Those representing the discipline of military medicine were increasingly confronted with the political interests of the ministry; this conflict was soon resolved at the expense of the scholars in favor of stricter confidentiality of military information. Just a few years before the outbreak of World War I, individual states did not hesitate to publish statistics regarding their forces. On the contrary, the publication of such information was viewed, at least by the statisticians, as a mark of academic prestige.

The problems, however, went deeper: in the eyes of many servicemen and military doctors, the very character of the examinations for fitness for military service themselves was at risk. According to traditional military logic, this moment was characterized by positive selection rather than the negative compilation of statistics on illness; the latter might even require more extensive tools and certainly more time.[49] It was here that clear divergences became apparent between the statistical ambitions of the military doctors attending the international congresses and the working practice of the military conscription commissions.[50] The conclusions of the commission, in the words of the report by Myrdacz after twenty years of study, were sobering:

> The field of international military medical statistics, in its current form and direction, does not fulfill the expectations hoped for to the degree which would be in accord with the effort invested. It has thus far not been possible to achieve the aims for consistency in international reports, and mutual comparisons of the data is only possible with many caveats and restrictions, which undermine the certainty of any conclusions which can be drawn. This all means that the principles and methods of military medical statistics require a fundamental overhaul which can only be undertaken by an ad hoc convention of an international military medical commission summoned for an extended period with members who are intimately familiar with the workings of the statistical apparatus within their own militaries.[51]

Such a reorientation based on closer cooperation of the individual countries' representatives could not be realized before World War I. A comparison of medical statistics within the European armies remained an ambitious project, and its fragmentary implementation did not have the explanatory potential that many scholars had anticipated. What were the reasons for this relative failure?

First, the discourse that had developed in some countries around the question of military statistics did not overlap with the realities of international statistics; the frames of their interpretation were quite divergent. In other words, national and international statistics in many ways did not complement each other. Furthermore, the social discourse of crisis within individual countries tended to crumble at a transnational level. The German debate over whether the urban or rural areas were more important as the conveyors of German military strength could not be confirmed in the medical statistics: neither in the sickness rates nor in regard to rates of hospitalization or morbidity could the statistics guide the discussion in a conclusive direction. The large German cities—Berlin, for example—ranked somewhere in the middle for morbidity rates in the report of the international commission. The fact that Russia had the lowest rate of illness when compared with the other European powers was the source of considerable consternation: the common expectation of an "East-West divide" in questions of sanitation was an established stereotype that was already influential in public debates. The British dread of degeneration[52] or the French *anxiété* about a declining population within its own borders were not substantiated by the numbers.

Second, the information available was extremely inconsistent in regard to how it had been gathered, and this created misunderstandings due to both the diverse methods of the survey and the geographical scope. For example, Great Britain's mortality and morbidity rates were at the top of the list, but the colonies had been included in the calculations. The country had been understood not as a European nation but as a colonial empire, and comparisons with other states, the armies of which were involved to a much lesser degree in colonial campaigns, were rendered inconclusive. This was even more the case because troops in the colonies around the turn of the century were much more likely to die due to exposure to numerous tropical diseases.[53] The "tropics" thus quickly became a very special place on the pathological map of "colonial Europe." Those units stationed in the colonies were documented most carefully, but these medical records frequently followed their own logic related to specific pathological threats.

In the German Empire, statistical reports on the health of the Imperial German Navy were issued regularly between the foundation of the empire and World War I; these were independent of the medical statistics for the much larger army.[54] The statistics for the navy, however, included a separate category for "tropical diseases"—especially malaria and typhoid fever, but also yellow fever and heat-stroke; the report compared these results with instances reported by other colonial powers.[55] This special form of statistical compilation that included "colonial" illnesses was much less concerned with statistical regularity based on "large numbers," which were often unavailable in the case of the colonies, where even the small contingents present could not always be systematically assessed. The comparison of the scant statistical material available for the European colonial powers only grew in importance as a result, however, and opened another sphere of transnational statistical comparison of its own,[56] which intensified the highly complex questions concerning the comparability of medical statistics.

Military Numbers and Social Intervention

In the nineteenth century, both statisticians and military doctors began routinely using military medical statistics, whether for international comparison or limited to individual regions or units, as a tool for scientific study. What knowledge did they hope to gain from these statistics? Which process of learning was inspired by the construction of such transnational statistical knowledge? Military officials harbored great hopes that studying these statistics would help to minimize the significant dangers posed by the lack of sanitation in the context of industrial urbanization. Early results—for example, advances made in the United States during the Civil War—reinforced the optimism of military doctors and statisticians:

The smaller rates of mortality observable, as compared with those of the other protracted wars cited, are believed to be due in no small degree to the organization, almost before the army had assembled, of systematic methods of inquiry, as to the condition and necessities of the soldier; of advice as to the best means of preventing the recurrence of evils, which—discerned by the light of the published experience of other armies in active service—were believed seriously to threaten the efficiency of the new and inexperienced forces ... Thanks to the searching investigations and efficient labors of the Herberts and the Nightingales ... new experiences of mortality from disease and of suffering were not needed to show the general character of the dangers which would beset the soldier; but the impending evils could, to an important extent, be anticipated, and, not unfrequently even before their presence was clearly manifest, proper means of prevention and remedy be applied.[57]

Knowledge concerning soldier morbidity was steadily increasing. In the course of implementing measures to improve public health and hygiene, many military doctors in the 1860s sought to use their statistical knowledge of life in the barracks as a "control case for all new hygienic institutions" and as a "guideline for all enlightened public administration."[58] The barracks as a site for increasing hygiene became a central focus of reforming intervention. At the same time, they often became the stage on which dysfunctional relationships among the various actors played out. This raised the question of who was ultimately responsible for the soldiers' health: the state, the military administration, the local commanders? Or was it the military doctors, who were gradually liberating themselves from the traditional military hierarchy?

In a polemical essay, an anonymous German military doctor demanded that the state intervene to improve conditions in the barracks, which should be a place for the safekeeping of the healthiest male members of a generation "and should never be old monasteries." The state could not, in the author's opinion, stand by given the current state of affairs:

Yes, the poor state! It can't protect the barracks, in which its military strength is set up against the laws of nature, against the contamination of the soil; it cannot try to remove the well from the [vicinity of] the fecal material, or even to adapt modern latrines, and to thus maintain the soil, water, and in part even the air in an uncontaminated state. ... And if it cannot, and the military strength then falls victim to this *non possumus* [i.e., inability to act] in the struggle against these laws of nature and suffers and becomes physically atrophied, then natural disasters, war, and divine plague are semiofficially and euphemistically blamed for these evils.[59]

Instead of this fatalistic stance, the author favors active intervention based on statistical knowledge: social engineering within the barracks.

In France, this question was addressed in the 1860s, first at the rhetorical level and then, with the military reforms of the new Third Republic, at the practical level. In 1862, the French military, looking to the precedent set by the English and Russian armies with their more detailed morbidity statistics, instituted a broad reform of the taxonomies and classifications used in compiling its statistics. These changes ensured a standardized and streamlined computation of the numbers of soldiers affected by disease and injury,[60] and this information provided the foundation for sweeping changes to health care and hygienic practice in the barracks.[61]

The historian Jean-François Chanet has described this process in the 1870s as a "battle of hygiene" in and around the barracks, which went much further than the measures to improve general hygiene in the society at large in the early nineteenth century.[62] In many places, the measures to reduce mortality in the barracks became a compelling argument for the renovation of old buildings and the selection of locations to erect new barracks. Having just suffered a defeat, the young republic was resolved to strengthen its military with the changes implemented in 1872 and 1873. The campaign against common diseases played a symbolic role as evidence of the credibility and effectiveness of these reforms.[63]

For this point, then, the interaction between the discourse in the realm of public administration and that of the medical experts and statisticians becomes clear. Civil administrations—of municipalities, garrisons, and local regions—often were aware of the health risks present in the barracks. The French Corps of Engineers was, generally speaking, the first to intervene at this local level and provide for more hygienic conditions—for example, by installing sewer systems.[64] The steady growth of the French army necessitated the construction of new barracks in the 1870s. Consideration of various barracks constructed during this time reveals that, in this context, mayors and prefects instrumentalized hygienic standards for the purposes of their own arguments. They frequently found support among military doctors, who saw these questions as an opportunity to develop their profile as autonomous professionals even as they were engaged in a battle for recognition within the military hierarchy due to a lack of professional structures.[65]

In the end, however, the transnational dimension of morbidity statistics suggests that the source of this discourse on military hygiene lies beyond the statistics themselves. The movement to improve hygiene was especially efficient in making transnational, national, and local connections even before these were commonplace. The barracks and everyday life of the soldiers served as a sort of "black box," which statisticians could unlock in the interest of social engineering. In 1909, Edouard Lachaud, a doctor and representative of Corrèze, published a book called *Pour la race: Notre soldat, sa caserne*, which clearly illustrates how interwoven these various levels and discourses had become in the subsequent years. Although Lachaud himself was a radical republican socialist, his book reads as an amalgam of efforts to implement modern hygienic practices, nationalist themes, and hints of the nascent scientific racism that resulted from these. Lachaud was certain that scientific and political priority should be placed upon "making and expanding all those improvements by which our neighbors have surpassed us in regards to military medical statistics, because we have not succeeded in making similar progress."[66] This task was all the more pressing because "all countries of the world, without exception, are growing, [while] France alone is flagging, shrinking, getting smaller and seems to be on the path to oblivion."[67] At least the advances in hygiene in the barracks and the consideration of international epidemiological research had led to the elimination of the latent excessive mortality rate in the military. If the military was to be the last defense of the shrinking nation, it was, in the eyes of Lachaud and many of his contemporaries, necessary to do everything possible to prevent its collapse. This was even more the case once the military was seen to play an important role in battling epidemics, for as part of the early warning system, certain diseases were required to be reported within the military and these reports forwarded to the responsible authorities.[68] The improvement of public hygiene within France had become, as in England, an issue of national importance. The question of military hygiene and the new measures taken in the barracks created new fields of political action and intervention.[69] Earlier than in many other areas, it was possible here for the emerging French welfare state to test its own powers of intervention.

Medical Statistics, Geognosy, and the Geographical Distribution of Symptoms

Many of the consequences of the compilation of military medical statistics were unintended but enduring. Such information made it possible, for

example, to divide a land into zones with similar pathological characteristics. To define clinical pictures that were not limited to specific periods
(epidemic) but rather to regions (endemic), scientists required settings for
their research that allowed them to differentiate by region. In his directions
for conscription in 1870, the Saxon military doctor Fröhlich had already
outlined how the "terrestrial circumstances"—especially altitude and soil
type—influenced the stature and health of potential soldiers. It was to
be assumed that those living in regions with limestone-rich soils dating
to the Jurassic or Triassic periods were likely be either extremely light or
extremely heavy and thus unsuited to serve in the military.[70] There was,
however, hardly any substantive evidence to back these claims, statistical
or otherwise. It was hoped that conscription statistics or regional morbidity statistics might open further avenues for addressing these theories. Two
countries became especially important in this discussion: Austria-Hungary
and Switzerland.

Within the multiethnic Hapsburg territories, the question of internal
differentiation of several factors of the population predated the transnational debate on such questions. In 1861, two years prior to the recommendations of the international congress in Berlin, the Imperial and Royal
Ministry of War founded an independent bureau of statistics, which was
initially intended to assist in the plans for mobilization. As the necessity
for comparative medical statistics became more clear, the bureau assumed
further responsibilities, including "the military statistical description of the
Austrian kingdom and its neighboring countries" and the "comparison of
the cultural development of the general population with the lives of soldiers and the mutual effects of these relationships."[71] The military doctors
did not hesitate to make sweeping, bold interpretations: the authors, for
example, suggested that physical development of the population in Ven-
ice was stunted and that the population of Galicia was slowly dying out
due to excessive alcohol consumption. (This was in fact the only region of
Europe for which the authors believed they observed a decline in the population.) The sketchy statistical material and the variables that were difficult
to define did not hinder the staff surgeon general of the Austro-Hungarian
Army, Hassinger, and his colleague, Pundschu, from essentializing and gen-
eralizing in this manner.[72] In the case of Austria-Hungary, the morbidity
statistics played an important role in differentiating among various groups
within the empire and reinforced national self-identity within a crumbling
empire.

Aside from epidemic illness, diseases of the eye, and injuries, the most oft-
cited reason for declaring potential recruits unfit in the Austrian heartland

and Tirol in 1869 was "idiocy and cretinism."[73] The diagnosis was much more common in these regions than it was, for example, in Italy or other lowland areas within the Danubian monarchy, which suggests an endemic factor in the mountainous region of the Alps. In principle, this had been known for centuries, but it was the widespread compilation of military medical statistics that allowed for the first studies of this phenomenon.[74] *Cretinism*—in other words, chronic goiter or thyroid dysfunction—was thus emerging at the end of the nineteenth century as an endemic concept with still unanticipated repercussions.

These symptoms, however, did not reach their apex in Austria but in neighboring Switzerland. In both the earliest phase of calls for the compilation of international morbidity statistics and in the subsequent phase in which the International Commission for Military Medical Statistics sought to achieve this goal, the Swiss military administration had not been involved in these efforts. This was primarily the result of Switzerland's decentralized military structure. One year after the constitutional reforms of 1874, Switzerland implemented a more consistent system of recruitment. Up to that point, the criteria for conscription and the compilation of the related statistics had been left up to the individual cantons, which were also obligated to meet certain quotas of new recruits.[75] In subsequent years, regular reports on conscription statistics were published, albeit not by the military itself or by the offices of the leading Swiss military doctor, the *Oberfeldarzt*, but rather by the Swiss Federal Bureau of Statistics.[76] The statistical information included in these reports did not meet the requirements of the calls for an international compilation of military medical statistics. As a result, at least at an institutional level, Switzerland was not integrated into this transnational discussion before the outbreak of World War I.

In principle, however, the information was available—but there was a problem of compilation and accessibility. This created a deficiency that a few individuals were able to exploit as an opportunity to develop new scientific methods. The increased frequency of goiter in particular regions necessitated explanation from the very beginning.[77] Military doctors quickly developed the impression that geographical factors made the population in these areas more susceptible. Josef Hürlimann, a military doctor in Zug, was one of the first to study the data collected as part of the "health examinations of potential recruits"; he surmised that this illness was somehow related to infant nutrition via breast milk or cow's milk. Degeneration thus became a phenomenon that particularly affected rural regions: "If we go to the Canton of Schwyz, that of Obwalden or Nidwalden, in the valley of the Emme, in the lowland cantons of Aargau and Lucerne, to Frutigen, in the Rhône valley by Visp, everywhere, we find animal races characterized by their beauty or productivity; fat oxen, productive cows, often proud horses—but also many miserable, weak, goitrous conscripts."[78]

Another doctor, Heinrich Bircher, also began a systematic study of the statistical material on potential recruits in Aargau. Bircher, who during his education as a military doctor had registered as a volunteer for the German Army in order to study injuries during the Franco-Prussian War, was active not only in the military but also in the political sphere throughout his life.[79] For his first major medical study, he relied primarily on conscription statistics to outline the distribution of "endemic goiter" in the country.[80] In many respects, for the Swiss case, he did not succeed in drawing clear boundaries or confirming the supposed biological boundaries that military doctors had proposed in other countries,[81] because in Switzerland the "mingling of the races is too great."[82] He pointed even more emphatically to goiter as endemic to Switzerland, a problem second only to general physical weakness as a reason that potential soldiers were deemed unfit to serve in the Swiss army. These two reasons were far and away the most significant, and Bircher was certain that "without these exclusions ... the army [could] include an entire extra division."[83] In a display of scholarly tenacity that stretched over many years, Bircher extracted data on the goiter endemic in Swiss military zones from records of conscription examinations and overlaid these maps with those displaying soil type and elevation of the individual regions. In the areas where Bircher's geological argument based on the type of bedrock was not entirely adequate, he extended his argument to consider the water quality, as well. In areas where the population drank directly from the Rhine or its tributaries, goiter was less common.[84]

It was not Bircher's intention, however, to suggest that these pathological diagnoses reflected a general crisis for the country. He was vehemently opposed to the thesis of a generalized degeneration of society. He attempted to disprove the arguments of those who were pessimistic about Switzerland's future military strength with an experiment in which he borrowed old suits of armor from museums and asked members of the Swiss army to wear them. The results were clear: the Swiss soldiers were taller and stronger than their ancestors; the armor was too small.[85] With this "proof," Bircher sought to undermine an overly simplified concept of degeneration that had dominated debates abroad. For Bircher, the concept of degeneration was not a matter of cultural criticism,[86] but rather a question of political differentiation: "The cause of this inequality is ... the significant difference of the

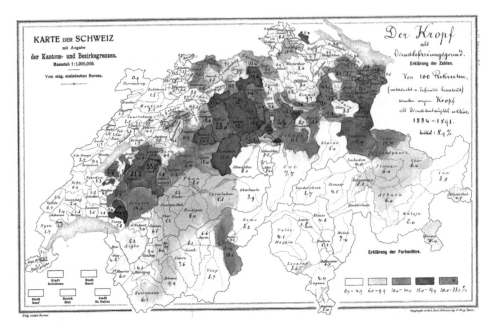

Figure 2.3

Goiter as reason for being freed from military service (MedHist Archiv Zürich PN 10.1
50), undated [ca. 1892]

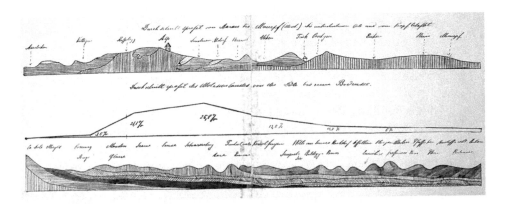

Figure 2.4

Profile of the Canton of Aargau, ca. 1880

population in the various regions regarding their physical characteristics and also their qualifications as soldiers."[87] The "disproportional relationship [of the] percentage of candidates judged fit, service time, and conscription targets"[88] in individual conscription zones was noticeable here. Given the circumstances, it was advisable in his opinion to reorganize the army and redistrict the military zones. The endemic analysis of the country was itself therefore highly politicized. The maps with which Heinrich Bircher outlined the frequency of endemic goiter or flat-footedness in Switzerland in the 1880s were based on new statistical material that had not previously been used in this manner. The interpretation of pathologies and the military organization developed a relationship of mutual dependence.

The "substance" of the conscripts seemed here to generate a new level of evidence, which meant that sources of mistakes and uncertainties that had plagued previous statistical methods could be avoided. On the other hand, they influenced the official statistical collection such that, as early as 1906, the Oberfeldarzt and the military department were compiling independent surveys and studies on the number of those affected by flat-footedness and thyroid dysfunction (goiter).[89]

"Endemic goiter" was stylized as a broad indicator of "cretinous degeneration." Instead of being regarded as a purely somatic hypothyroidism, the diagnosis evolved to include a sort of mental "feeble-mindedness," which played an especially important role in Switzerland in the early twentieth century.[90] Changes in examination techniques and diagnoses changed the clinical picture and soon made it into a sort of code, first within the discourse concerning Swiss fitness for service, and later in regard to the Alps and even mountainous areas more generally. In the early twentieth century, there was an increasing number of studies in mountainous regions of Germany, Austria, and Italy in which "cretinism" became engrained as a criterion for consideration of potential conscripts. The unsystematic malaise of many mountainous regions had developed into a defined somatic disorder that could be statistically localized. Here, too, the statistical knowledge of the military was used as an instrument to describe geographically defined characteristics of the population. This highlights divergent interpretations: as reflected in the debates about military strength, this disorder was considered characteristic of the weaker rural populations—which in Switzerland, unlike in other European countries, remained in the majority. These problematic rural areas represented the primary areas of intervention by Swiss doctors in the next decades, while other countries were worried about the negative influence of urban life.

Switzerland was not the only country in which such endemic studies were conducted based on military medical statistics,[91] but it was the country in which this perspective had the most enduring influence on the image of military medical statistics by "pathologizing" large areas of the country. Such discussions and methods of study contributed to a new facet of demographic research that became quite important around the turn of the century: the demographic map. The map was an ideal method for conveying geographical information related to studies of endemic diseases and offered an impressive form of visualization.[92]

3 In the Realm of the Experts

"Scientifically speaking, the examination [of potential recruits] can be seen from two perspectives: on the one hand there is the question about the fitness of individual recruits for military service, and, on the other hand, the question about the general well-being of the nation."[1] These two perspectives, outlined by the anthropologist Gustave Lagneau after France's defeat in the war against Prussia, were soon revealed to be two sides of the same coin. Researchers interested in military statistics had always been open about their divergent backgrounds and motivations. Regardless of the reasons for their interest, however, they all required trustworthy and "good" statistical material which had been collected in a consistent manner. In the end, this depended on the records of the conscription examinations kept by personnel responsible—in general, the military doctors themselves.

The two most important elements of military statistics, conscription statistics and medical statistics, were both the product of a number of examinations and individual decisions, whether these took place before the countless conscription commissions or during medical examinations in the barracks. The more attention was paid to the questions of fitness for military service and military strength, the louder the voices became warning that these numbers should not be considered objective. In the French discussion concerning the relationship between the declining birthrate and the size of the army, for example, the military doctor Frocard was certain that "the correlation between those obligated to service and the birth rate does not allow for any precise deduction of the methods used by the examination commissions and can therefore not be used to appraise these methods."[2] About the same time, Alfons Fischer, an anthropologist working in Germany, also relativized the significance of the supposedly objective debate over military strength: "Before we turn to the correlation between military fitness and the industrial state, we must agree on a meaning of the term "military fitness," which is by no means used consistently.

Whether or not a candidate eligible for the draft is classified as fit or not depends namely on the judgment of the responsible authorities. They see things differently, however, depending on the time and place [of the examination]."[3]

The debates over fitness for military service did actually lead to the formation of new groups of experts in various countries. To be more precise, they led existing professional groups to become involved in the scientific debates and to defend their own interests therein. The question of how statisticians and doctors negotiated the knowledge surrounding the army and the practice of conscription highlights the space in which these professional groups compiled such statistics. An examination of these new experts suggests that the question of military statistics evolved into a question of professional autonomy and the public display of scientific expertise.

Statistical Uncertainties and Complex Procedures of Conscription

During times of war, no one questioned the necessity of military medical professionals, but during peacetime, their professional identity was threatened. In many countries, military doctors remained integrated into the command structure until the nineteenth century; they were subordinate to the respective heads of their companies and were released from regular duties for special assignments—for example, the medical examination of potential recruits. The implementation of general conscription in many European countries and the resulting changes to the importance of the examination of potential recruits were, in addition to the more frequent deployments in colonial areas, the most important elements contributing to a greater autonomy of military medical divisions.[4]

Assessments by military doctors had been instituted since the establishment of standing armies toward the end of the seventeenth century. It was only with the introduction of general compulsory service, however, that conscription became an established military, and soon also social, institution consisting of much more than the medical assessment. In fact, in many European countries, it was a matter of principle that the conscription commissions were composed equally of civilians and military personnel, whose job was explicitly defined as unrelated to the physical examination of the young men, but rather to ensure that all eligible young men were registered correctly and that their social situation was known.[5] The actual medical examinations, on the other hand, were carried out by so-called experts, military doctors who had been delegated for this purpose but had no actual say in the commission's final decision.[6] The decision about fitness for service in the army—as defined by nearly all European states—was supposed to be democratic—or at least a decision in which both public administration and the military played balanced roles.

The recruitment itself proved to be a lengthy process, employing a considerable number of individuals for nearly six months, in which diverse statistical and medical procedures were intertwined with issues of civil and military law. The decisions made by the conscription commissions (*Rekrutierungsräte*, as they were called in the German Empire) could only be appealed before one higher commission, the *Oberrekrutierungsrat*. This body was similarly balanced, and the civilian representatives were adamant about maintaining their independence from the military.[7] The structure of these commissions was thus heterogeneous and fragile, requiring a constant series of reforms, to varying degrees.[8] The diversity of bureaucratic regulations and guidelines for the final decision nearly overwhelmed the individual members of the conscription commissions, especially considering that most members sat on the committee only for a few years. An impressive number of handbooks are evidence of this fact, as are the many reports of unsolved problems, which emerged in the course of the commissions' work in the countless conscription locales that had been provisionally set up in local church halls or taverns.[9]

In the German Empire, the process of conscription typically proceeded along these lines: from the beginning of the year into the spring, the civil authorities and chairmen were to see that the individual localities compiled lists of all those men eligible for conscription between twenty and twenty-two years of age.[10] These lists became the "conscription roll," a long list of names and civilian data for these young men, with columns for adding the results of their examinations.

Between March and April, the candidates were appraised, disregarding the actual need for new conscripts. Theoretically, then, this first examination of potential recruits included all the male citizens in the defined age group. It was conducted in a relatively central location, and placards, posted on official buildings like schools or taverns instructed the men to report at an appointed time and place. Only after this examination were those potential conscripts deemed fit for service assigned draft numbers, which were called up later according to the needs of the army. In other words, many of those deemed fit for service were not in fact drafted.

The process was concluded by the so-called Aushebung, in which the commission traveled from place to place within the district. The potential recruits were examined once again, though somewhat superficially: some twenty conscripts at a time were called, naked, before the commission, which then had to reach the final decision very quickly. In those cases in which a young man appealed the decision of the conscription commission, a further, more in-depth medical examination was conducted. This system was designed to prevent erroneous decisions before the recruits were assigned to various divisions based on the requirements of the individual branches of the military. During the summer months, the newly drafted soldiers were to appear before their new units, where they were examined one last time in the barracks, though this examination was not part of the conscription process per se.

"The journey of conscription is no junket,"[11] was the underlying message of the reports from members of the commissions. The trips typically lasted for six weeks, and the members during this time had to deal with strenuous working conditions while under considerable time pressure. This applied to the chairman—usually the head of the local government, the chief of police, or chief local magistrate—but also to the military chairman (often the local commander) and to a lieutenant and four civilian members.[12] The last in this list was the military doctor, who in the draft itself—as in the initial examination of recruits—served only in an advisory capacity.[13] To the extent possible, the members of the commission were to come from the local districts and communities in which the draft was being implemented. It often fell to the civilian chairman to provide for a smooth implementation of the procedure in the individual localities. These duties were not limited only to organizing physical space for the examination and deliberations, but also had other implications for maintaining local order:

When it becomes known that examinations or conscription are planned, both the civilian and military [authorities] have a common vision of boisterous streets full of drunk young men prone to fisticuffs and arrest. ... Certainly it can be said, however, that the behavior of those required to appear, who are not yet subject to military laws, reveals how much influence the military and civilian chairman of the substitute commission have in their respective districts. There are districts in which those obligated to appear have for years the experience that when one appears before the commission, one responds to the command "at attention" by standing absolutely still, that one maintains exemplary behavior throughout the process, and that when the procedure has concluded, one calmly returns home.[14]

The civilian chairman's responsibilities, however, extended beyond these social components: following inquiries by the German Reichstag, after 1902 he was responsible for entering the trade and birthplace of all those to be examined into the roll of names.[15]

In many cases, it appears that the task of compiling this information nearly overwhelmed those assigned the task. Around the turn of the century, statisticians with the most diverse political and ideological interests uniformly deplored the quality of the statistical information gathered by these civilian chairmen as completely inadequate.[16] Indeed, the chairmen hardly ever had any training in this field. A detailed outline of the questions posed—for example, place of birth of the parents or other indicators of social standing—would have been crucial for the statisticians, but, due to the limitations on their time, the chairmen were not able to provide these. In addition, it was acknowledged that the classifications were only general due to the restraints on their time. The places of birth, for example, were only categorized as to whether they had "more or fewer than two thousand residents." The regulations called for the information compiled to draw on the statistics gathered in the recent censuses, but this, too, proved impractical when confronted with the practical limitations of time. It seems much more plausible that the recruits themselves reported on the sizes of their birthplaces, which does not improve the accuracy of the information recorded. Ute Frevert has drawn attention to the fact that the decisions made by the conscription commissions regarding the examinations and the draft were often, especially in small rural localities, hardly objective, given the social influence of local elites on the commissions: "The social composition of the conscription commissions insured locals of high social standing a favorable treatment of their sons."[17] These and other social and structural complexities had already raised serious doubts about the accuracy of the information collected around the turn of the century.

Objective Criteria and Conflict among Experts: The Professionalization of Military Medical Services

From a scientific perspective, the diverse interpretations and attitudes of those who compiled the statistics muddied the picture for the neutral gaze of the experts. This became increasingly true after the turn of the century, as the conscription commissions were expected to gather social information in the course of their inquiries. This scientific overdetermination of the information gathered was evident not only in the statistical compilation related to social contexts, but also in the fact that this information—the origins and professions of the soldiers, for example—was implicitly linked to the medical results of the examining military doctors. These doctors were thus often forced to perform their exams under conditions they considered less than ideal and, beyond that, to accept that these conditions could have marked effects on the behavior and disposition of the potential recruits.

As mentioned previously, the military doctors had no direct say in the conscription process; they were considered experts whose recommendations were heard.[18] The situation was quite delicate because the decision regarding fitness for military service rested primarily on the medical appraisal of potential recruits. Candidates who were eliminated for other reasons like family situations or, later, "mental limitations" were typically excluded from the initial roll of names. In the kingdom of Württemberg, for example, the heads of schools reported such cases to the civilian chairmen.[19] The ministries of war did compile detailed lists for the assessment, which were appended to the respective legislation and intended to permit definitive, quick decisions based on a catalog of objective criteria, but the reality was often much different. In 1858, for example, the Prussian instructions for military doctors conducting such examinations stipulated: "In our practical age we ask about the mathematical size of the individual body parts without letting ourselves be led astray by perceived size. This is an inevitable step, since mathematical formulas are the ultimate aim of any natural science." The instructions concluded, however, with a caveat: "The appendices to the conscription laws provide a general foundation for the examination of those eligible for the draft and the assessment of their suitability for service in combat, but it remains to the discretion of the individual doctors to decide whether and to which degree other afflictions not included in these lists impair service."[20]

In the end, the definition of norms, averages, and exclusion criteria set by the state took shape in the independent judgments of the military doctors on the ground, a point about which the doctors, regardless of nationality, were all quite emphatic from an early date. It was doubtful, claimed the doctor Fröhlich, whether one could ever define "certain guidelines" that encompass all aspects of "the human body's suitability for military service. Such guidelines are until now only vague sketches and in some areas do not exist at all."[21] As long as such guidelines are lacking, Fröhlich argued, the doctor has no choice but to reach a reasonable judgment himself. The French doctor Emile Duponchel came to a similar conclusion in his reflections on objective criteria for the diagnoses of physical weakness. Much time had been invested in the search for an objective, "less elastic foundation for the assessment of physical weakness. It would certainly be ideal if this diagnosis could be reduced to a simple calculation." This goal was unattainable, however, because there was no possibility of definitively describing physical weakness.[22] A few years later, the Italian military doctor

Ridolfo Livi addressed the purpose of statistical limits for the commissions' decision-making in a more general sense. The aim of the examinations, he said, was not to look for an "average type" or to find the strongest individuals, but rather to exclude the weakest candidates: "The conscientious and experienced observer will be able to develop a detailed picture of a [potential] soldier's suitability for service based on the totality of outer appearance without the quite convenient aid of looking quite mechanically at a prescribed scale."[23] In his handbook for the procedure of conscription, Livi's German colleague, Otto Kunow, recommended that military doctors rely not only on the official criteria but also consider their own measures, because fitness is "very dependent from conscription district to conscription district on the characteristics of the populace and the development of the respective cohort."[24]

The military doctors' reflections on the basis of their own decisions reveal an undeniable paradox: despite their considerable self-confidence, the administrative structures meant that it was not the doctors who were responsible for the final decision. Their "expert" opinions were granted only an advisory function in the decision-making of the conscription commissions. In a review of Kunow's book, one critic pointed out precisely this problem, suggesting that future conscription rolls should include an additional (fifteenth) column to record whether the commission's decision was in accord with the recommendation of the medical experts.[25] This was similar to the procedure that had been implemented in France in the 1890s.[26]

The exact relationship of scientific expert discourse to principles of civil law and administrative practice can only be inferred from the impressions of this process recorded by those involved. This dimension is particularly well documented for France, where the methods of the conscription commissions were the target of considerable criticism. On the one hand, the lower birth rate compared to Germany was commonly known. On the other hand, the military leadership saw the weakening of the conscription criteria due to the falling birth rate as a threat.[27] Within the context of the military reforms of 1893, this pressure was initially felt in the form of a higher rate of conscription, which was achieved not by universally applying the criteria for conscription but rather via a principle of "relative fitness," according to which the criteria could be adjusted according to suit the army's needs and the concrete situation given the geographic and social situation. This prompted ongoing debate between the French Ministry of War and the military leadership and the *premier bureau*[28] regarding the proper formulation and enforcement of such criteria for conscription. Following the reforms, an increasing frequency of cadets granted medical discharge and the subsequent belated drafting of new soldiers had resulted in significant costs, which the ministry was unwilling to simply absorb. This led to pressure on military doctors to enforce the criteria for conscription more rigidly, regardless of the effects this might have on the decrease in the conscription quota.[29] Whether or not the military doctors changed their approach to the examinations, they were certainly subject to harsher criticism than before. Furthermore, the number of fully qualified doctors in the French army was so low that it was sometimes nearly impossible to follow the procedures to the letter.[30] This was due in part to the disproportional number of military medical professionals dispatched to French colonies.

These specific factors led to a charged discussion among French military doctors about their own tasks and their role in the *conseils de revision*, the conscription commissions. These debates reveal how these committees actually worked. In a polemical essay over the function of the conscription commissions and the advisory capacity of the military personnel, Alphonse Dumas told his readers in 1891: "You have understood correctly: this commission demands broad theoretical and practical knowledge, but science has no representative [on it]."[31] Dumas, however, like many of his colleagues, was aware of a contradiction between the legal guidelines and the practical reality of conscription. Regardless of the official rules, the judgment of the experts was accorded disproportionate importance in the decision-making—and indeed, it was often the only real factor.[32] Generally speaking, the French commission had to appraise sixty potential recruits per hour. In large cities, however, especially Paris, the number was significantly higher; here they were examining up to one hundred per hour. The civil members of the commission were sometimes trained to perform some measurements to relieve the *médicin-expert* of some duties; the pressure during the examinations was so intense that the doctors switched shifts every hour.[33] The situation became increasingly problematic; shortly after the turn of the century, a doctor from Corrèze reported in a letter to Edouard Lachaud, himself a doctor and representative in the national assembly, that doctors had a mere thirty-one seconds per candidate.[34] This certainly did not mean that doctors spent precisely this amount of time on each potential conscript. Dumas described the normal procedure from his experience: the doctor began in the morning with an excruciatingly thorough examination of the patients, but, as the day progressed, the constraints of time became more and more intense, so that in the end the remaining two-thirds of the candidates had to be examined in less than one-third of the day.[35] Although the experts were under

Figure 3.1
Pierre-George Jeanniot, *Le Conseil de révision*, 1895

extreme pressure to pronounce judgment about each candidate's suitability, the members of the commission who would reach the final decision in reality had absolutely no chance to ask for a justification of this
recommendation.[36]

Due to this lack of time and the demands made on each individual member of the commission, the examination was a process plagued by frequent
mistakes.[37] In some French military districts, more than a few French military doctors seem to have capitulated to the demands represented by the
examinations; internal calculations of the military leadership suggested a
lack of three hundred military doctors in France.[38] The legal representative
of the military doctors, Alphonse Dumas, filed complaint after complaint
around the turn of the century about the burdens that were increasingly
discouraging doctors from volunteering for service in the army. Civilian
doctors often were called upon to take over these responsibilities and support the military structures. In many corps of the army, Dumas argued,
"the work of the conscription commissions poses a constant threat" to the
functionality of the medical services.[39]

Despite the demands on their time, many military doctors did not see the situation as purely disadvantageous for their profession; nearly all the statements emphasized that the existing system provided for absolute independence from the military hierarchy, but also from the social context.[40] This autonomous decision of the military doctor was increasingly polarizing.[41] The question of whether the size of the army or each individual's fitness should be decisive forced the doctors to take a social political position. Their profession became the center of attention of seemingly bureaucratic decision processes and increasingly often of the media, as well.[42] The military doctors played a crucial role in answering the question of whether the strength of the French nation was only nominally a topic of debate or if the relaxing of certain criteria for inspections represented a qualitative weakening.[43]

The military doctors aggressively confronted this increased pressure from all sides. They viewed the politicization of these issues not only as potentially disadvantageous, but also as a means of achieving greater professional recognition. In the last two years before the outbreak of World War I, the doctors' status in the commissions was the source of considerable unrest among French medical physicians. The discussions stretched over a longer period and found expression at the meetings of the Société de médecine militaire française and in the professional journal of the French medical doctors.[44] The military doctors had adopted the discourse of crisis concerning the declining birth rate, but they also emphasized the significance of the rigid decisions of the commissions.[45] At the same time, the doctors themselves insisted that the process should remain primarily a civil one, because this structure, in the opinion of Doctor Rouget, allowed the military doctors to exercise their full influence:

If one demands that their [the doctors'] vote is decisive, this would undermine the principle of *cedant arma togae* and attempt to place the military element over the civilian element .... I myself have had the opportunity to participate in an examination of potential recruits in Paris where two presidents made a recommendation at the beginning of a meeting which contradicted my expert opinion. It was completely sufficient, when the meeting had ended, to ask—quite within my rights—the military director, who participates as inspector, to note in the minutes of the meeting that the expert opinion contradicted the final decision [of the commission]. The commission's decision was immediately amended.[46]

Why, then, should they do anything that might be seen to contest the outer appearance of a republican, democratic process, when they were ultimately controlling it anyway? Rouget's colleague in Cambrai, Solomon, was in full agreement with him on this point. In his opinion, in 999 out of 1,000 cases, the commissions were following the experts' recommendations; the only members who played an important role were the president and the doctor.[47]

In 1914, the guidelines were changed so that military doctors were to have more say in the process in the future. Henceforth, in addition to formally dissenting from the decision, the examining doctor was entitled to send potential recruits for an extra examination by an outside civilian doctor in cases of disagreement. Here, too, Rouget—as a specialist for statistics and medical practice in the military—warned of a further dynamic that devalued the expertise of military medical personnel, because the truly important part of the medical appraisal of an individual's fitness for service should remain, in his opinion, under the control of the conscription commissions.[48]

Between the late 1860s and 1900, the status of military doctors changed in nearly all those militarized Western European nations. They were removed from the regular hierarchy and formed their own military medical corps.[49] Professional associations and unions strengthened a new professional identity, as did a proliferation of journals and specialized publications.[50] The drafting of new conscripts, as the field of expertise of military doctors, played an important role in this process. It was not only an opportunity for military doctors to display specific competence on the basis of scientific innovation,[51] but, beyond that, a way to make their professional discourse politically relevant.[52] It is, therefore, hardly surprising that military doctors pressed for greater professional autonomy in the debate over the compilation of military statistics. This was, on the one hand, a matter of distancing themselves from "civilian" doctors and, on the other, of asserting their independence from military command structures. Such strivings for independence often found expression in the foundation of military medical institutions.[53]

In the German Empire, military doctors in all the large garrison towns came together to found new professional organizations for this purpose, starting in the 1860s.[54] With the foundation of the Kaiser Wilhelms-Akademie für militärärztliches Bildungswesen in Berlin, with its statistical activities, the military doctors created an institutional mouthpiece to promote their interests in the political sphere over the long term.[55] The close contacts between the academy and the military doctors' association meant that both the personnel of the two organizations and the issues they addressed overlapped in many ways. The director of the academy, for example, got the ball rolling for the statistical studies completed by Heinrich

Schwiening, the head of Berlin's professional association for military medical personnel.[56]

French military doctors were slower to organize: on September 9, 1906, they formed the Société de médecine militaire française with a "purely scientific aim." Structurally, they drew heavily on the preexisting school for the training of military doctors, Val-de-Grâce, and they were ultimately subordinate to the French Ministry of War.[57] Those who had initiated the association's foundation saw it as part of a process of professionalization that put it on par with a number of other medical and scientific professions: "The necessity of staying informed day to day of new developments within the field of medical science and to check these means that every individual discipline within this field is compelled to found its own scientific society, in which these new or revived questions can be examined in open, free, competent, collegial discourse."[58] Unlike in the German Empire, where the statistical activities of the new institutions for military medical professionals had supplanted even the ministry's statistical bureau for the compilation of illness statistics, in France the military leadership and Ministry of War retained responsibility for the statistical analysis of the conscription results.

Professional Autonomy and Public Interest: The Field of Medicine versus the Discipline of Statistics

The fact that experts were given de facto authority in the decision-making process was thus a core element of military doctors' professional identity. As their trade was increasingly professionalized, this was taken for granted.[59] However, though the relationships within scientific circles and toward military and state administrative organizations were now clear, there were still unsettled questions between statisticians and medical researchers about the rights to use the statistical material.

Over several decades, the "usability of the results of the conscription process" for statistical purposes became a bone of contention between statisticians and military doctors, who were engaged in a real struggle over control of the information. In the first comparative study on the quality of military statistical material, Bischoff had warned in the 1860s that the Prussian material especially was hardly useful in any biostatistical sense because it was simply too detailed.[60] Because the doctors had been so eager to record individual realities and clinical pictures, they had, in Bischoff's opinion, failed to use the level of abstraction necessary to allow for comparative analysis. Some years later, Bischoff's colleague Kratz found that the advice of the military doctor was, "furthermore, increasingly successful the more mathematically it was construed."[61] Ultimately, in his words, "the reporting of the military doctors" corresponded to "the tendering of accounts by the economic administrator"—a role that, in his opinion, in no way did justice to the military doctors.[62] Given the importance of the statistical material at their disposal, however, it was only fitting and proper that they be forced to compile this information in a statistically competent manner: "The state must make more such demands of its military doctors: and, because as a large 'military organism' it cannot deal with individuals—as perhaps the head of a family or even the director of a factory might—but rather only with numbers, the role of the military doctor in the said relationship is that much more important in terms of its meaning and repercussions."[63]

Kratz himself was a military doctor and viewed the demands he made of his colleagues as a means to the end of making the field of military statistics the domain of military doctors. The lively debates in subsequent years changed the perception of the supposed opportunities for cooperation between professional military personnel and statisticians. Conflicts emerged that involved both the compilation of information and its use. The debate in several European countries over how the responsibilities and authority in regard to the conscription statistics should be shared between the Ministry of War, statistical bureaus, and the professional organizations of military doctors reflected in truth a deeper question about how such information should be handled at all.[64]

Especially in this early phase of systematic information gathering, it was not the governmental authorities that played the central role in this process of negotiation. Military doctors actively argued for the relevance of their information for social and economic policy. The Austrian *Allgemeine Militärärztliche Zeitung* provides ample evidence of this in its argument for hygienic reforms within the military based on the statistical material that had been gathered: "The army is a burden on the taxpayers which consumes a good million and which doubly drains the national economy. This burden is heavy, and it is easy to forget that the army is of the citizens' flesh and blood."[65] This clearly reflects an ongoing conflation of topics of political and national allegiance with the supposedly neutral statistical material.

In neighboring Switzerland, military doctors posed as voices of caution as well in the interest of the general populace's well-being. As shown in chapter 2, the endemic situation in Switzerland provided a decisive impetus in the discussion, which grew into a sort of permanent conflict. Following the introduction of the medical examination of conscripts in the federal military reforms of 1875, a central statistical agency was, by decree of the Swiss Federal Assembly, to compile the information gathered in the course of those examinations.[66] The divergent interests of the two professions soon became obvious, and the situation was more charged because the two groups answered to two different governmental ministries: the Department of the Military was responsible for the army, and the Bureau of Statistics answered to the Department of the Interior.[67] Furthermore, the structure of the conscription examinations was exceptional in Switzerland: unlike in other European countries, the military doctor served here as chairman of the conscription commission and his vote was decisive.[68] Although the practical weight given to the doctors' opinions differed little from the doctors' influence in the other countries, this privileged status in Switzerland lent the profession a more influential role in the public debates on questions of national military strength.

Within a few years of the military reforms of 1875, the military doctors' associations increasingly petitioned to prevent the statistical agency from utilizing this information.[69] They were especially uneasy about the regular reports issued by the agency under the title "Results of the Conscription Examinations."[70] The Swiss surgeon general suggested that such attempts to optimize for statistical purposes information that had been gathered in the military were doomed to failure because this had not been the intrinsic purpose of the military doctors:

I have to most emphatically revolt against the tendency of only wanting to conduct statistical analysis using fully perfect material. Any such material—even the very best—has its imperfections, partly from the exception of individuals (e.g., sick candidates who do not appear), partly from mismeasurements, partly from mistakes in the recording which can happen even to the most practiced and industrious personnel. Imperfect material can also be worth analyzing and can produce results (if not definitive, then at least by providing numbers for future comparison) which make the work worthwhile, as long as one handles and calculates the numbers solely as that which they are.[71]

In 1888, the Department of the Military investigated the grievances and made inquiries of the Swiss surgeon general, who confirmed the complaints. His answer clearly demonstrates the complexity of the conflict: "It is quite apparent that the Bureau of Statistics prefers to prepare pedagogical results and that they treat the sanitary statistical material critically in a spirit far removed from Christian love and often lacking the relevant competence."[72] The statistical bureau had, in other words, already made similar accusations against the military doctors, whose methods in the examination of potential recruits could not be precisely recorded for statistical study. Although

the military medical personnel may have been considering their own interests in the statistical analysis, they first and foremost did not want to be
told how to practice their profession by the statisticians. The statisticians'
treatment of the military doctors was quite problematic in the opinion of
the Swiss surgeon general, however, because it easily sparked defiant reactions of the military doctors so that

during the draft, the doctors limit themselves narrowly to their military assignments
and stoically disregard all further statistical or demographical demands. If we want
to criticize the statistical bureaus from the perspective of the military's demands,
the list of sins of omission would be quite long, and if the Federal Assembly commissioned the statistical analysis of the results of the statistical examinations, it did
so at least not only in the interest of demography but rather also in the interest of
military administration. Where, for example, do the reports include statistics on discharges for physical weakness in the different corps? Or according to military rank?
It certainly would not hurt for the military department to admonish the statistical
bureau.[73]

The Swiss surgeon general took a clear stance because the statistical analysis
seemed important enough to him that it should not be simply blocked; the
potential for insights based on the reports was high, but the vastly divergent interests in this knowledge created the structural problems:

Don't these reports provide the basis for valuable demographic statistical studies, to
say nothing of their value for the military administration? The demographer quite
rightly asks how many instances of goiter occur for every hundred potential recruits
in a particular district; for the military, however, the primary question is how many
of these hundred cases are declared unfit for service as a result; the cases of goiter
in those who were excluded for other reasons are less interesting. Certain statistical studies will always rely on these summary reports [of the military doctors],
because they include some information that the surveys of the statistical bureau
do not.[74]

The result of all these efforts was thus flawed statistical material for
which the military doctors and statisticians each blamed the other. The
focus of the criticism—as, indeed, in France, Germany, and other European
countries—was on the methods with which the information was compiled.
At the same time, this criticism was linked to specific elements of the Swiss
political system. One of the statistical bureau's suggestions for improvement was to stipulate that in the future potential recruits should be examined in their own language; statisticians hoped that the questions relevant
to the statistical surveys thus would be answered more precisely.[75]

The question of language was part of a deeper conflict between the
central compilation and the localized administration of the individual

cantons. Although the procedure had theoretically been standardized by the reform in 1875, the results varied greatly from canton to canton. The cantonal representatives viewed this as a reason to doubt the central compilation because their own studies often reached conclusions other than those reported by the central statistical bureau.[76]

Although these conflicts are visible at the level of the medical examination results, they become even clearer in the question of the pedagogical test of potential recruits, which was a part of the inspection of potential recruits conducted only in Switzerland for the purposes of appraising potential recruits' levels of education.[77] A number of the predominately rural cantons were concerned that their results in the reports of the statistical bureau were well below the national average.[78]

The distribution of educational opportunities and institutions thus became a further topic of debate. The representatives of the Canton of Appenzell, for example, complained to the statistical bureau that these figures regarding the level of education could hardly be compared across cantons. Due to the greater accessibility of schools in urban regions, residents of these areas had much greater educational opportunities. The rural population, and especially those who lived in the mountains, were thus underrepresented in the good results. Young men with the potential of achieving better reports, furthermore, tended to migrate to more urban areas, where they helped to improve the results of these regions.[79] Multiple cantons joined in Appenzell's complaint.[80] The pedagogical tests of potential recruits actually were only conducted in the schools and thus had a very high potential to reinforce controversial social patterns.[81] Neither the question of migration within Switzerland nor that of each individual's socioeconomic status was adequately considered, because the statisticians in Bern were more concerned with the practical implementation of their test.

This added a further dimension to the conflict: it was not just a struggle over the statistical versus medical use of the available information but rather over the demarcation of the central government and the local cantons. As a result, these statistics were regarded as potentially explosive; they represented a potentially dangerous resource that, around the turn of the century, was to a certain extent subject to official surveillance.

In spring 1893, a draft officer, Sacc, sought access to the results of the pedagogical test of potential recruits for his physical inspection of potential recruits in the French-speaking region of Switzerland, but the president of the pedagogical commission of the second division refused his request.[82] Sacc was the only conscription commissioner in years who believed that the pedagogical results were significant in the appraisal of the physical potential of recruits. In fact, the man responsible for the examination of potential recruits in western Switzerland, Scherff, had filed repeated complaints to the statistical bureau that the effort involved in gathering the relevant information for the conscription commissions was too much for his division. These complaints had not, however, led to the escalation of the situation. Only after Sacc's indiscreet treatment of the pedagogical statistics had resulted in some reports and tables being printed in *Liberté*, a newspaper in Fribourg, did Scherff refuse him access to the information. In this conflict situation, the army leadership resorted to drastic measures and did not hesitate to take their case to the Swiss Federal Council, the collective head of the Swiss government that oversaw the Department of the Military. The responsible councilor ruled in favor of the chairman of the pedagogical commission (Scherff) and against the conscription officer (Sacc). In a decree from June 6, 1893, the department forbade the publication of the statistical material by any party other than the statistical bureau.[83] The Department of the Military maintained this monopoly over the statistical material in the following years, although Scherff and a Bernese teacher, Reinhard, were commissioned after 1905 to produce an annual analysis of the material and to prepare a brief report.[84]

The reason for this strictness became evident in 1907. After pedagogical experts had discussed the previous year's results, the representatives from the Canton of Jura passed along the secret information to the local newspaper, *Le démocrate*, which published it immediately.[85] The title page on June 13, 1907, included an overview of the results of the pedagogical examination of potential recruits listed by canton. The seeming supremacy of the urban cantons was evident in the report; the inner Swiss cantons and Graubünden were at the bottom of the list.[86] The results, which could easily be considered indicative of the intellectual capacities of the Swiss populace, were highly politically charged. This permanently changed the way the statistics were handled and had lasting effects on the practice of conscription.

It was not only the relationship of the examining doctors to the question of the statistical compilation which changed; rather, the discussions led to a more restrictive access to military information in general, which had implications for academic research as well. In 1897, a few years after the decree of the military department, a doctoral student from Basel, Oswald Heer, attempted unsuccessfully to gain access to the conscription statistics, which were generally kept secret.[87] After 1912, all statistical overviews, including the military doctors' records of the conscription proceedings, were marked "confidential."[88] It was difficult and often even impossible to gain access to this material.[89]

As specific as this line of argumentation first seems to the situation in the Swiss Confederation, it is also reflective of a more general conflict of social modernization. In the Swiss case, the friction was within and between certain levels and bodies of government, but more generally speaking this friction stemmed from an antagonism between urban and rural areas. This antagonism became manifest in Germany in conflicts between economists, lobby groups, and the general public, whereas in Switzerland there was more friction between governmental bodies themselves. As a result, statistical material represented a body of national knowledge to which access was increasingly carefully guarded.

Due to the professional, regional, and social heterogeneity of the Swiss Confederation, the problems here were recorded in more depth than in other European countries. In regard to the right to use and publish military statistics, however, similarly ambivalent situations can be observed in other countries as well. The growing scientific interest in such questions led scholars to compile more information for publication.[90] For a long time, many of the involved parties from the administration viewed the military statistical material as simple objective numbers. Until the end of the nineteenth century, European governments did not generally perceive a need to control the publication of such information. As the information became more politically charged, however, the relevant expert circles became involved in attempts to monopolize the resources for their own purposes. The state also became gradually more interested in this material and in exerting control over the information.[91] The numerous efforts to institutionalize the gathering of such statistics, including the establishment of international organizations and conventions, were thus limited: in some cases in the years leading up to the war, military doctors and statisticians were not able to present their statistics freely and participated at times unwillingly in such costly transnational meetings and conventions, if at all.[92]

This meant there was a certain amount of tension between statistical science and the actual medical act of the examination of potential recruits. Both acts regarded the potential recruits to a degree as the object of scientific study, but from two different angles. The overlapping of their scientific interests created an ambiguity that seemed contrary to the frequently proclaimed aim of scientific accuracy and precision. Adolphe Quetelet, for example, calculated for French military doctors in 1846 that the only deviation in the conscription examination results from the probabilistic distribution was in the field of minimal height, which was defined at 157 centimeters. A remarkably large number of potential recruits were just a few millimeters below this limit.[93] Such a statistical discrepancy could only be interpreted as a willful exclusion of potential recruits who would otherwise have been judged fit for military service. This seemed to be evidence that military doctors were consciously protecting potential recruits. The scientific accuracy of those using statistical methods to point out mistakes or even conscious malpractice by medical professionals opened a new field for conflict, which became characteristic of the relationship of the two groups.

The discipline of statistics, for its part, remained a hybrid method well into the twentieth century, which was characterized most distinctly by pragmatic implementation in the interests of the state administration. Most of the statisticians who were involved in the discussion were not employed by universities but rather by governmental offices, and they were only sporadically interested in further developing the discipline. The lack of institutional and academic connections led to widespread disciplinary defensiveness toward other professional groups. The discipline of statistics, wrote Hermann Hassinger, would retain its credibility "only as long as not every layperson tries to profit in this area, but it rather remains reserved for educated specialists."[94] These processes of professional definition and defense suggest an explanation for why military statistics, especially conscription statistics, were often jealously guarded; their confidentiality not only served the state but was also in the interest of numerous professional groups, especially statisticians and military doctors.

4 Measuring European Soldiers

When European countries introduced the concept of general compulsory service toward the end of the nineteenth century, their militaries struggled to address the problem of efficiency in the examination of potential recruits. The basic question was how to appraise as many candidates as possible in the shortest span of time. The doctors responsible for these examinations were not inherently interested in studying the exceptional cases; they sought precise standards with which to determine whether candidates were or were not fit for military service. Statisticians themselves claimed at the international conferences that they were less interested in understanding deviations and exceptions than in the question of the "average man," as outlined in the studies of Adolphe Quetelet, the doyen of their guild.[1] As the Saxon military doctor Fröhlich pointed out, however, it was not possible to do one without the other: "All statistical compilations based on examination results are, moreover, in vain, if the boundaries of fitness and unfitness—the foundation of any comparative study—are unknown."[2]

The overarching paradigm that underlaid both the examination for recruitment and, even more so, the elimination of those deemed unsuitable for military service found expression in the definition of these "boundaries." In the eyes of many military doctors, the discussion of how to statistically define suitability and unsuitability transcended national boundaries. Within the context of this medical discourse, the question of fitness and the methods of examination necessary for its efficient determination seemed to present a purely technical dilemma, on which medical doctors were working irrespective of national borders.

However, conscription developed into its own realm of social experience that shaped the process of the examination itself and influenced the collection and compilation of statistical information and measurements. The present study cannot adequately address the social history of this process, but it is necessary to address the social contexts that shaped the medical decisions and the anxieties and hopes of the doctors and those examined. This had a significant influence on the relationship between scholars and their "scientific objects," the potential recruits.

Juxtaposing the diverse scientific expectations with the social realities in which they were carried out reveals the weak foundations of many contemporary statistical and demographic studies. All too often, the authors of these studies ignored or concealed these uncertainties. Such studies require a transnational perspective on the circulation of scholarly concepts and methods and the way they evolved in light of local contexts.

The Plasticity of Physical Weakness in Scientific and Political Contexts

In those countries that enforced general compulsory service, the expectation during the recruitment process was that all eligible citizens should perform such service. The examination of potential recruits was intended primarily to identify cases in which a candidate's fitness for military service was questionable or required further consideration and to eliminate those candidates who were deemed unsuited for service. This exclusion was based on a whole range of illnesses and disorders for which separate statistics were compiled. In all European countries, however, the most frequent reason for eliminating candidates was general "physical weakness," which accounted for half or more of all declarations of unsuitability. The diagnosis was intended to avoid physically overtaxing soldiers in such a way as to cause long-term damage after their term of military service. However, the fundamental problem for military medical professionals was that there were no clear criteria for this diagnosis. While the individual experts reached this conclusion at their own discretion, the military doctors and the statistical agencies strove for an objectifiable definition and explicit limits.

Such a definition had in fact been mandated by governmental decrees instituting compulsory military service, and increasingly, extensive manuals were issued in which the reasons for exclusion from service were to be as clearly and unambiguously outlined as possible.[3] French doctors and publicists especially suspected that the criteria for recruitment were subject to political manipulation and intensive negotiation, which raises the question of to what extent such limits—or even the concept of "fitness for service" itself—were objective categories. On several occasions, French doctors reported publicly that the criteria for the examination had been manipulated in accordance with political expectations regarding the ideal size of the military. Under the influence of these political factors, the criteria for the examination varied in regards to vision[4] or minimum height, the latter of which ranged between 1.52 and 1.7 meters over the course of time and various conflicts and crises in the nineteenth century.[5] In fact, the criterion of height was adjusted downward so radically that the French Ministry of War concluded in 1901 that such an isolated number was essentially meaningless and abolished it completely. Swiss Surgeon General Alfred Mürset suggested that such differences in fitness resulted not from the varying methods of examination but rather, in Switzerland's case, from the "pressure of fiscal decrees" that have "constant regrettable repercussions."[6] During peacetime, the state tried to reduce costs by limiting the size of the army and thus raised the minimum standards for conscription. The military, on the other hand, had a radically different position: it strove to maintain clear criteria and steady numerical growth. In the end, however, the argument of rising costs associated with maintaining too large an army outweighed the arguments of military personnel and significantly affected the process of conscription.

Soon conscription—and, more precisely, the elimination of potential candidates—was a factor in the economic calculations of national budgets. As the Swiss example shows, these economic arguments were often more significant than the definition of an abstract "national military strength" or the enforcement of the principle that all were equal in regard to the draft. Supposed and actual mistakes made during the examination process were perceived as economic problems. In those countries with general compulsory military service, there was an awareness that the process of recruitment could have detrimental economic consequences.[7] The critics also pointed out the expenses of providing medical care in the barracks and military hospitals and the loss of human life due to the infamous higher rate of mortality within the army. Alphonse Dumas, for example, criticized the French system of recruitment; he suggested that the drafting of "many sickly candidates, with their corresponding dispositions and diathetic tendencies" had led to "filling our hospitals and exhausting their budgets, without being of any use." Furthermore, "in the end, [these sickly recruits] die, although they could have led full lives and started a family" had they never been drafted.[8]

Arguments like this, based on a sort of "economy of human beings,"[9] were sparked by the situation of conscription and became the object of political controversy—and not only in regard to national military strength. As Jakob Vogel has shown, in the aftermath of the Franco-Prussian War of

1870, more attention was paid to the social costs of war. The Bismarckian welfare state sought to balance these costs with its strivings toward social harmony.[10] In consideration of statements by French contemporaries, these arguments can seemingly be expanded to include the social costs of conscription and the maintenance of a standing army. It was not only the social costs of war that were an issue; critics also pointed to the costs of maintaining a standing army during peacetime, especially the increased mortality rate.

This was also the basis upon which the doctors conducting the examinations argued for maintaining stringent methods and limits with which they hoped to protect their authority over the interpretation of the resulting statistics. They feared that the categories used to measure fitness for service could be co-opted by the states or the military leadership as mere variables in their calculations. The Swiss military doctor Heinrich Bircher emphasized how political attempts to manipulate the physiological appraisal of potential recruits could backfire. In Switzerland, shortly after the introduction of reforms in 1875, doctors had quite loosely interpreted the state's guidelines and norms. In fact, the surgeon general had recommended that they not adhere "too fastidiously to the instructions."[11]

Creating Indicators

Doctors were generally at the very least ambivalent about the guidelines and norms set by the state. For their own purposes, however, they went to significant lengths to develop workable criteria and quantifiable medical and physiological guidelines for determining potential military strength. The measurement of height as a standard was established quite early and presented no practical problem for the doctors conducting these examinations. Experts agreed, however, that appraising potential recruits based on height alone was unsatisfactory. Shorter individuals sometimes proved fitter for military service than other, taller individuals. In the 1850s, chest circumference was added as a criterion in an attempt to better predict fitness for military service and identify "physical weakness."[12] A combination of height and chest circumference was intended to form the basis of a fixed index. This supposedly objective relationship proved to be more complex in the practical application by military doctors, however, than initially anticipated. At the Statistical Congress in Berlin in 1863, where the compilation of the medical examination results was also a topic of discussion, the military medical division asked the staff surgeon general of the Prussian army, Friedrich Löffler, to devise a method for measuring chest circumference and computing an average that could be implemented as a new, international standard for determining fitness for military service.

The initial results were disappointing: "Dr. Löffler undertook this task with noticeable reservations and admitted with commendable abnegation that future scholars might find better methods than he had."[13] The question of whether the measuring tape should be placed above or below the nipple when taking such measurements remained unanswered, which distorted the results.[14] In addition, no standardized procedure stipulated whether such measurements should be taken while the candidate was inhaling or exhaling. As a result, the official statistical compilations were unreliable: for statistical purposes, therefore, only data sets personally compiled by individual doctors could be considered useful.[15] Both the lack of guidelines and their inconsistent implementation marred the uniformity of the results: "The actual placement of the measuring tape is usually not addressed, but consistency in the positioning of the hands and fingers, and even in the doctor's posture, are important factors in placing the measuring tape, tightening it, following the candidate's inhalation as consistently as possible. Only if measurements are taken in such a consistent manner will it be possible to compare those taken by multiple examiners, which at the moment is quite pointless."[16]

During the 1870s, methods used in military medical examinations were standardized to some extent: chest circumference was measured both horizontally and at a slight diagonal while the candidate slowly counted backward from ten. Measurements thus were taken with both inflated and empty lungs. Nevertheless, there were no uniform official guidelines for the methods used, and a lack of time and qualified personnel further impaired such measurements.

Eventually, the Austro-Hungarian Ministry of War commissioned Carl Toldt to conduct a study to determine whether chest circumference was a reliable indicator of capability for military service. Due to precisely the problems outlined earlier regarding the consistency of measurement, he concluded that this criterion alone should not be decisive. In his opinion, only the ratio of several measurements together could serve as a useful and stable indicator.[17] It seemed increasingly doubtful that "fitness for military service" could be expressed in any single figure.[18] The French doctor Pierre Rigal drew on Toldt's studies, arguing that any attempt to set definitive limits was futile. The appraisal of an individual's fitness required consideration of various factors that added up to a sort of *harmonie constitutionelle*. Due to the problems with inconsistent methods of measurement and appraisal, Rigal suggested including body weight and circumference of the thigh in

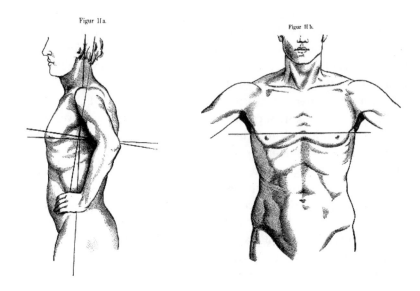

Figure 4.1
Measurement of chest circumference, according to Busch

this computation of "harmony" to minimize the influence of inaccurate measurements and avoid erroneous judgments.[19]

Various doctors tried to "save" the criterion of chest circumference by combining it with other measurements.[20] The Swiss surgeon general, for example, in the round of examinations conducted in the autumn of 1882, called for the measurement of candidates' upper arms.[21] He viewed this as "a straightforward method ... to furnish doctors with a system for assessing musculature. The simplest method is to measure the circumference of the middle of the outstretched left (and thus weaker) upper arm. The calf would have been another possibility, but the upper arm is more practical. The measurement does not take more than three seconds per man."[22]

The Swiss surgeon general was not the only one with the idea of measuring the upper arm as an indication of a man's fitness for military service. He adopted the idea from Fröhlich, the military doctor in Leipzig, who had previously set a limit of twenty-two centimeters. If the circumference of a candidate's upper arm was less than this, the diagnosis of physical weakness was, in Fröhlich's opinion, beyond question. The Swiss surgeon general, on the other hand, set this measurement in relation to height and devised a clear diagram via which military doctors were to define physical strength.

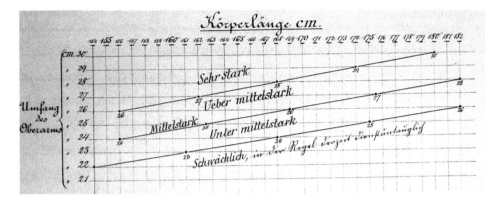

Figure 4.2
Index of upper arm circumference and height by the Swiss surgeon general, 1884, BA
Bern E 27 Tit 5855

Such straightforward correlations challenged not only statisticians but
also other scholars to become involved. They filed protests with the Department of the Military, claiming that reducing the medical examinations for
conscription to a simple formula ran counter to their own efforts for greater
statistical differentiation. The surgeon general defended his plan against
this (in his opinion) unqualified outside criticism with his usual eloquence:
"I have always worked resolutely against those demands from various sides
(the statistical bureau, ophthalmologists, and other medical specialists)
which would burden the conscription commissions with statistical surveys
that serve a general scientific interest but have no military purpose. It was
not for statistical purposes that I introduced the measurement of upper arm
circumference, but purely for the purposes of the military."[23]

The measurement of upper arm circumference may indeed have broadened the foundation for the calculation of an individual's fitness for
military service, but the basic difficulty concerning the inconsistency of
measurements applied here as well. To make their lines of defense stronger,
military doctors did not hesitate to draw on expertise from their colleagues
from abroad to make the case for their professional independence.

The serious doubts about any such measurements meant that they were
often abandoned altogether or, at least, that they were not used in any
unambiguous classification. As a result of the debates, for example, chest circumference was not systematically measured within Austria-Hungary in the
era leading up to the turn of the twentieth century.[24] In Italy, on the other
hand, the statistics were still collected, but primarily for anthropometric

and anthropological purposes.[25] Within the German Empire, the use of this criterion was quite controversial, polarizing not only the military doctors themselves, but also anthropologists who sought to use the results of such measurements in their own efforts to define a universally applicable concept of "fitness."[26] Unlike military officials, however, anthropologists were not looking for an absolutely foolproof tool for use in the conscription process; instead, they sought relatively precise instruments for description with which they could position themselves among other scientific disciplines in the academic discourse of modern industrial society. Not only the results of military conscription examinations but also other statistics suggested that it was doubtful that the use of chest circumference alone as such a measure would allow for valid conclusions.[27]

In 1900, the French military doctor Maurice Pignet generalized a formula he had developed in examinations of potential recruits; his formula, which became known as the *Pignet index*, was subsequently widely used in various physiological and anthropometric contexts. Pignet's formula subtracted the sum of an individual's body weight (in kilograms) plus his chest circumference (in centimeters) from his height (in centimeters)—that is, [height in cm - (weight in kg + chest circumference in cm)]. The larger the resulting number, the more likely that the candidate would be rejected as "physically weak." Based on his own experiences, Pignet set the limit at thirty-five for determining whether a candidate should be declared fit for service as a soldier.

As an indicator of fitness, the Pignet index was the subject of controversy in many countries. The German military did not generally adapt it, but individual military doctors did experiment with the practical implementation of this procedure. Simon, a captain in the medical corps in Strasbourg, used this technique when examining candidates in Baden—much in the tradition of Otto Ammon. Based on statistics already collected in the course of the examination of potential recruits, Simon calculated their ratings according to the Pignet index and came to the conclusion that it was a precise indicator of actual fitness.[28] The chairmen of the military doctors' society in Berlin, Heinrich Schwiening, had also used Pignet's formula for his statistical study of those volunteering for a year of service; his study suggested that the volunteers were fitter on average than those who had been conscripted, but he also observed that too many questionable cases had been declared fit in the general assessment.[29] Many military doctors thus concluded that Pignet's approach was useful only in theory;[30] the error rate was too high for it to be of use in judging fitness for service in individual cases.[31]

Although French and Belgian scholars continued looking for ways to refine the Pignet index so that it could be used in a standardized procedure, such methods were unable to predict individual fitness for service with certainty.[32] Instead of universal limits, the number was "demoted" to an index for recognizing cases of tuberculosis.[33] The basic approach of combining height, weight, and chest circumference remained a central element of the conscription examination guidelines in France,[34] even though it seemed increasingly impossible to devise a method for this calculation. The index itself remained illusory, but in the development of statistically relevant tools for research, scholars had a lasting impact on professional practice.

The Circumstances of the Examination of Potential Recruits

As the discussions had only too clearly shown, military doctors were dependent upon the technical devices used for their measurements and concrete situations in the various locations where they were conducting their examinations. The working conditions of the local commissions were radically different from those with which the responsible senior doctors in Berlin, Vienna, or Paris were familiar. The intense time pressure during the examination of potential recruits was often paired with the fully insufficient physical space of the "local conscription headquarters," usually set up in taverns or other public buildings. The lighting in such establishments was typically deficient, and often no separate room was available for the examination of more problematic cases[35] or for the examination of family members, as was required in the German Empire for cases of hereditary illness.[36] Eye charts could not be hung at the right distance, and the hearing test could not be conducted in a separate room of at least eight square meters, as the guidelines stipulated.[37]

The technical equipment presented even greater problems. One of the reasons that weight was not considered in the assessment in France was that not all conscription headquarters had access to an appropriate set of scales. The responsible Ministry of War opposed the expenditure of time and money it would entail,[38] although it did consider requiring local communities to provide livestock scales. In the end, it seemed easier to simply forego systematically weighing candidates.[39] The rules were finally changed to require a set of scales for conscription examinations in 1904,[40] but this was three years after the measurement of candidates' height had been discontinued, so even after this change, it was not possible to combine the two measurements.

In all European countries, military doctors were outfitted with the utensils required for standard examinations of potential recruits[41]—but they were responsible for the care and maintenance of these tools. The Swiss surgeon general issued rules in the early 1880s that suggest the challenges this presented for medical personnel:

Every measuring tape which, when held to a wooden measuring stick, has stretched one centimeter or more should be ... replaced. Worn out springs in the devices for length measurement should be replaced. For repairs which you believe to be beyond your authority, you can contact me for special instructions. ...

Eye exams are to be carried out near, or across from, a window in a well-lit spot; the measuring rod should be placed in the same spot where the candidate is to stand for the eye exam; the president, commission, and secretary should sit next to this spot, not scattered in all four corners of the room.[42]

He was not the only one struggling with these technical issues. Throughout the entire second half of the nineteenth century, physicians complained about inadequate or imprecise instruments. They were also confronted with the problem of a still incomplete conversion to the metric system.[43] As a consequence, the guidelines issued by central administrations could not be applied in many local contexts. Technical standards of measurement and the proper use of the tools that were available were thus the subject of much discussion among physicians. In the quest for improving their methods, they exchanged information across national borders and worked implement improvements in their techniques in a truly transnational project.[44]

In regard to the question of measuring chest circumference, the reticence of many military doctors can be inferred from their resistance to the standardized examination procedures: "Chest circumference is to be measured exactly in accordance with the instructions. One needs not concern himself with the question whether other methods of measurement might be better, but rather one must conform to the guidelines."[45] Considering the limited technical capabilities, it was fully unrealistic to expect that new mechanical or technologically advanced procedures for measurement, like the recently developed technique of radioscopy, could be widely implemented as some contemporaries hoped.[46] Even if such a procedure might have offered a solution for many specific problems with conscription examinations in regard to the time needed and the precision of the results, they remained out of reach due to the limited resources available.

In addition to the test of general fitness for military service or physical weakness, the conscription examinations considered a second factor: the identification of illness in the candidates. Compared to the controversy surrounding the indications of individuals' physical strength and weakness, the guidelines in this case were quite rudimentary. The methods for these pathological examinations were more or less left up to individual doctors, who were to recognize symptoms with their "expert eyes" and more closely examine anyone who aroused their suspicions. Unlike in the case of the physical measurements, the methods for this part of the examination were not clearly defined, and the guidelines only applied to cases in which there was some question or doubt. The doctors' examinations focused on identifying weaknesses of vision or hearing, respiratory illnesses (especially the widespread tuberculosis),[47] sexually transmitted diseases (for which there was a detailed catalog),[48] and, in the more remote mountainous regions, goiter, along with more general musculoskeletal handicaps.[49] Only those cases of disease that were identified in this way entered the conscription statistics.[50] The numerous illnesses that went unnoticed in this rather superficial examination of the potential recruits were not recorded in the statistics.

In addition, officials in the German Empire considered requiring doctors to report cases of infectious tuberculosis to the civil health officials. Minister of War Karl von Einem, however, successfully opposed this instrumentalization of the conscription process for the sake of the public health. His arguments against the suggestion highlight once again the conflicting interests of the parties involved in conscription:

For the purposes of the military medical examinations for conscription, it is not necessary to come to as thorough a diagnosis of the individual organs and their relationship to the more general well-being as might be required for conscientious treatment of an individual. [The latter] usually requires a quite in-depth inquiry into the individual's personal situation. ... The completely different purposes of a military doctor's examination to appraise the degree of fitness for military service and an examination to assess the necessity of a particular course of medical treatment require in some cases not only different methods but also consideration of completely different factors. Disruptions and complications of the conscription process would be unavoidable if military doctors were required to assume responsibility for diagnosing existing conditions and prescribing treatment.[51]

By definition, the conscription examination of recruits was based on the exclusion of those unfit for military service, but not on any effort to precisely identify or examine a particular clinical picture, much less to heal the individual being examined. Any attempts in this direction were significantly impaired by the material limitations. In addition, the commissions moved from place to place, meaning that not only their instruments for measurements but also their medical provisions were quite limited.

It remained their prerogative to take along materials not included in the standard procedure—including, for example, chemical solutions for urine analysis.[52] It was therefore quite likely that in cases of uncertainty, doctors had little opportunity to develop a more nuanced diagnosis and could only rely on the reports of civil doctors.[53]

Confrontations: Clear Decisions and Social Contexts

Doctors within the military often viewed reports from their colleagues in the civilian sector rather dubiously and were reluctant to rely upon these for their final decisions. Although the civil doctor's opinion was an important element of information for the military doctor, it was "insufficient for a decision, especially because such reports are often vague and the test results inconsistent," according to the French military doctor Albouze.[54] Underlying these concerns was a latent suspicion that external reports were often used in efforts to deceive the commission and that relying on them would open the floodgates of attempts to fake illness or handicap to avoid the draft. There was an institutionalized distrust at various levels of the conscription hierarchy. On the one hand, this was the result of suspected nepotism among the members of the commission. In the context of the examinations, the potential recruits' personal interests ran counter to the general principle that all were equal in regards to the draft. On the other hand, the parties involved seemed keenly aware of the gap between the expectations for medical accuracy and the deficiencies of the concrete circumstances of the local commission headquarters.

The French military doctors Du Cazal and Catrin tried to impress upon their colleagues how important it was to maintain a sense of distance from the potential recruits they were examining. During the examinations, they recommended, the doctor was to speak in such a way that everyone present could hear the questions; the doctor should never speak so softly that only the potential recruit could understand him. In the evenings, he should be careful not to be left alone or to converse with strangers; he should accept no invitations, but rather seek the companionship of his colleagues.[55] It was an incontrovertible rule that military doctors were never to be deployed in their native regions and that the names of the doctors who were to conduct examinations should be kept confidential for as long as possible. The risk was simply too great that potential recruits' families would attempt to influence the results.[56]

The families of the potential recruits were a "dangerous" group for the military doctors nonetheless. Doctors had to deal carefully with attempts at bribery and other indirect strategies to influence their judgment, like the "complaining fathers and ... mothers" eager to testify to their sons' medical deficiencies: "If one becomes weak in a single individual case, in other words if one is 'talked into' anything, the complaints will grow like a hydra, meaning that after this moment of weakness, every petition which one rejects spurns three new ones, and then typically they will appeal via all legal means open to them, including formal calls for mercy."[57] The attempts at deception and complaint could go in both directions: it was feasible both that soldiers might fake bodily handicaps to avoid conscription or conceal handicaps or illness in an attempt to prove themselves fit for service. In any case, the former was presumably the more common scenario in the German Empire and beyond.

The boundary between conforming to such social expectations and consciously faking medical symptoms as a form of pretense—that is, simulating illness—was fluid. Guide books for military doctors presented these as adjacent categories.[58] This was even more the case because most cases of simulating an illness involved illnesses for which somatic diagnoses were difficult. This helps to explain, among other things, why vision was accorded such importance in the research on fitness for military service and later in the final assessment of potential recruits. Disruptions of vision and hearing were considered somatic indicators for modern new neurological clinical pictures and psychological disturbances.[59] They were seen as irrefutable signs of hysteria and epilepsy, which, around the turn of the century, were not only clearly "fashionable illnesses" in the German-speaking world[60] but also among the diseases most frequently simulated at conscription examinations. Many of these symptoms can be mimicked without military doctors being able to prove the contrary. These mental "illnesses of degeneration" were an important element of the discourse of "crisis" in the period of rapid socioeconomic changes in the last third of the nineteenth century. Many civil doctors diagnosed epilepsy as an early stage of a broadly conceived psychopathological concept of hysteria.[61] It seemed perfectly natural to contemporaries that this same pattern could be observed in the case of potential recruits. The typical symptoms of "hysteria" were thus freed from their initial association with the female gender.[62] Conscription and the scientific discourse over such attempts at simulation on the one hand cast doubts on such clear-cut attributions and on the other served to define the healthy, masculine, archetypal soldier in opposition to an ephemeral, ill, unfit potential recruit.

The military thus reflected the psychiatric discourse in which the "hysterical psychopath" was long a dominant image.[63] The literary case of simulation that became most well-known was that of Thomas Mann's Felix Krull. Mann's character was not exceptional in this regard but instead an example of a common social practice against which military doctors were vehemently struggling with anything but complete success. The somewhat antiquated suggestion of several Austrian military doctors to deny those diagnosed with epilepsy the right to marry in an attempt to discourage simulation was not adopted, but it does suggest the growing significance of this test of fitness in a wider social context.[64]

Military doctors, however, feared misrepresentations in the other direction as well. Not only simulation but also dissimulation was widespread as potential recruits attempted to conceal handicaps or illness so as to be conscripted. This phenomenon was a more pronounced problem in the examination of voluntary candidates for military service.[65] This might have been due either to an actual (over)eagerness of the volunteers or, more likely, to the more thorough methods of examination employed in such cases;[66] unfortunately, the historical record does not shed much light on this question. At the same time, at these points, a more differentiated image begins to crystallize of the social context of conscription and recruits' knowledge of their own bodies. In individual cases, for example, it was necessary to more carefully examine a candidate's personality—or, as the guidelines for conscription within the German Empire put it:

The medical officer [must] continuously be aware of this possibility [the simulation of nonexistent symptoms] and meet it with disciplined science, medical knowledge, calm, and caution. More than anything, suspicions should never be mentioned right away; instead one should consider the claims made by the suspect and meticulously examine anything which might be detected. In many cases one will conclude that the complaints are not completely grasped from thin air but rather that the individual examined has, with no ill intent, exaggerated in order to make his weakness as clear as possible. Often their own lack of knowledge and self-interest play a role as well.[67]

In other words, it became clear that the potential recruits being examined were not always capable of deciding whether they suffered from an illness or not. Anamnesis as a method used in the conscription process was ascribed an importance that, at the same time, was limited by the recruits' understanding of their own bodies. This did not always reflect intentional deception.

The military doctors' judgment was a product of a reciprocal relationship with the candidates; their decisions were based not only on "holistic judgment and medical awareness,"[68] but also on trust and distrust.

The interactions of the candidates with the doctors and members of the conscription commissions were, in the end, just as important as the sheer measurements.

From this perspective, an important element of the examination was the candidate's nudity. It was necessitated by the procedure and the requirements for the conscription examination itself, but it also provided some indication of the socially variable, perhaps even nationally constructed, "sense of shame." In France, where the examination of potential recruits had been in principle a public event since the Napoleonic period, the recruits were presented in groups and were completely unclothed. This was the cause of some concern for some potential recruits: "It is necessary to remain calm and polite; otherwise the majority of the young people, who in rural areas especially are intimidated by the circumstances and characterized by a natural reserve, will be incapable of coherently answering the questions put to them."[69]

In Switzerland, the surgeon general had stipulated that those conducting the examinations were to organize them so that the candidates did not see each other and that members of the public especially were not to be admitted during the procedure.[70] In Germany, the official regulations of the Prussian army explicitly allowed for the modesty of the potential recruits and permitted them to keep their shirts on until just before the measurements were actually taken.[71] In addition, the military leadership decreed: "If the unsuitability of a potential conscript is not already evident without his undressing completely, a thorough inspection of his naked body should be conducted with as much consideration for his sense of shame as possible. During the conscription process, the physical examination is to be conducted in the presence of the chairmen [of the commission]."[72] In the public sphere, the naked masculine body at the examination of recruits was part of the visual discourse, which did not always avoid embarrassingly detailed depictions of the nudity itself.

The protests of the anarchists against the state's conscription procedures also suggest that the perceived threat to the masculine body's integrity in the conscription process was one of the central stereotypes associated with the process. For example, in this poem of protest from 1907:

Examination time. So, man by man
in rank and file, young people come.
A grim commander, doctor, corporal
wait to exam them in the hall.
"Strip naked" comes the order, shrill.

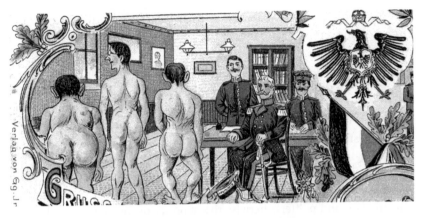

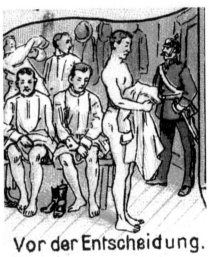

Vor der Entscheidung.

Figure 4.3
Excerpts from postcards depicting naked men at the examination

The Kaiser never asks your will.
And on the scales, far from the rolling greens
the cattle step reluctantly, and bare.[73]

The criticism of the conscription process and the state military are less surprising here than the seemingly instinctive reference to appearing nude before representatives of the state, military, and science and the connection made to the anonymity of living among the masses in the modern industrial society.

It was not only the recruits who were invested in the issue of nudity within the context of the conscription examinations. The members of the commission were often surrounded in their conscription headquarters by "30 to 40 individuals, half of them naked," a situation which they found uncomfortable and even embarrassing.[74]

Whether such discourse was shaped by a degree of irony or not, it highlights the importance of the process of conscription as a rite of passage and a stage upon which social experiences met the scientific discipline of medicine. Even before World War I, conscription commissions frequently complained about potential recruits drinking to excess. This, too, can be seen as indicative of the exceptional circumstances and tension between this rite of initiation and the confrontation with state and scientific authority.[75] Cleanliness and bodily hygiene were routinely addressed in the course of the examinations, which made this an unusual case of the authorities intervening in regards to potential recruits' bodies.[76] The historical record offers little to indicate the extent to which these factors led to generally positive or negative attitudes or whether recruits were generally cooperative or not.

Examining Bodies between the Soma and the Psyche: Tests of the Body and of the Intellect

All these factors contributed to increasing doubts about the clearly defined category of physical fitness and supposedly objective scientific examinations. Instead, many doctors realized that the only way to ensure a fair draft was to consider various criteria, including aspects of a recruit's physical and psychological health, his disposition, and his social situation. The number of additional possible considerations opened virtually endless possibilities for potential criteria for the examination and hypothetical definitions of "fitness" for military service. Again, however, it bears repeating that none of these alternative systems could be implemented prior to World War I. Nevertheless, the debate over their potential alone reflects the complex tensions between scientific discourse and practical implementation.

This is especially clear in the case of Switzerland, where the subsequent scientific interest in the conscription process was stronger than elsewhere in Europe. In addition, the Swiss militia system fostered a particularly close coordination of civil and military institutions. Parallel to the centralization of the "medical examination" of recruits, the Swiss Department of the Military standardized the "pedagogical examination," which had already been tested in some cantons.[77] Especially those potential recruits who had received no advanced schooling were to be examined in the subjects of "arithmetic, composition, reading, and local geography" and questioned as to their civic views.[78] In this way, the mental capacity of the candidates was to be assessed in addition to their physical suitability for service. Two years after the introduction of the pedagogical examinations, in 1877, the first statistical summaries of their results were published.[79] The central message of this report, however, was that any meaningful conclusions were precluded by the failure to record the results in any correlation with the physical data; though some cantons and communities had subjected all the young men eligible for conscription to the pedagogical exam, others had only questioned those who had been judged physically fit for service.[80]

The conditions under which the pedagogical exam was conducted and the personnel responsible were even less consistent than for the medical examination. The statistical bureau had been commissioned with analyzing these results in addition to the statistics collected during the medical examinations, but this was basically impossible given the inconsistencies. The results varied greatly from canton to canton: though this suggested a real qualitative difference in the various educational levels, or even within the population itself, the variance could be traced to the differences in the decentralized school and apprenticeship programs.[81]

Unlike in the case of the medical examination of potential recruits, however, the inconsistencies in the pedagogical examination were recognized from the beginning, which meant that most authors discounted biologistic arguments. The divergent results were attributed instead to social and geographic variables—for example, widespread child labor, multilingualism unique to Switzerland, or poor nutrition in mountainous regions. That debate initially sparked a political controversy over, among other things, the centralization of the school system.[82] Once again, there were conflicting interests in the examination of potential recruits for military service: schoolteachers and administrators hoped for insights on "whether the school system in one or another canton was satisfactory," but those who advocated a more perfunctory examination based on minimal standards had the last word in this case.[83]

Buried within the organization and implementation of the pedagogical examination was not only a political difference of opinion but also a scientific dispute that becomes evident in the question of how to deal with those who were intellectually weaker. Was mental capacity ultimately measurable in physical concrete terms, or could it only be appraised by such active tests of knowledge? Lacking other instruments for the study of "mental weakness," scholars relied upon the results of these examinations for their research. This meant that the question of recruits' educational levels was linked to the inquiry regarding their mental capacities, even if their contemporaries did not explicitly recognize this discrepancy.

After the pedagogical commission had graded a recruit's performance, it forwarded the results to the conscription commission. If a candidate had failed the pedagogical examination, the conscription commission would use this as a reason to not draft the candidate. Twenty years after the pedagogical examination had been introduced, the commission of "pedagogical experts" recommended that the files of questionable candidates, especially of those who were illiterate, should be forwarded to "the medical commission for definitive discharge." According to this suggestion, there would be no numerical grade assigned in such cases; the case instead would be left up to the judgment of the medical personnel. Instead of reclaiming authority on the question of mental handicap, however, the Swiss surgeon general reacted differently: he saw the grading of the pedagogical conscription examination by qualified instructors as the better strategy for identifying "idiots" and "mental handicaps."[84] It is not clear, however, whether these two parties actually disagreed about the best scientific strategy for conscription or whether the surgeon general simply wanted to avoid being held responsible in any way for the (in some cases, disastrous) results of individual cantons in the pedagogical examination. The controversies over cretinism and degeneration within the rural population certainly contained potential political dimensions that should not be underestimated.[85]

The struggle over the fundamental purpose of such a pedagogical examination, which was meant only as a recommendation but was itself hardly able to define minimum criteria for military fitness, continued into the early twentieth century. Military doctors, and subsequently the Department of the Military, soon viewed the examination as useless, but the Swiss federal government insisted upon it. Without a doubt, the examinations served to significantly increase civic knowledge, especially among secondary school students. "Abandoning this institution at the very moment in which other countries are imitating our procedure cannot be justified," the council argued; even if it was not always possible to clearly define the criteria, the examination provided "good indicators for the conscription officers."[86] The integration of military institutions such as the examination of potential recruits into civil society's conception of itself was a process facilitated by scientific and statistical interests.

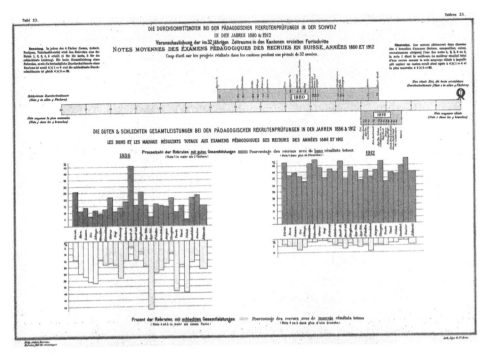

Figure 4.4
Overview of the results of the pedagogical examination, comparing the Swiss cantons

With the pedagogical examination of potential recruits, the Swiss military relied on a criterion for conscription that was unique within Europe. In other countries, however, there were repeated demands to include potential recruits' intellectual capabilities in some form in the assessment. In the neighboring Kingdom of Württemberg, the Oberrekrutierungsrat considered similar examinations in an attempt to at least reduce the number of illiterate soldiers within the army.[87]

Despite such demands, a standardized test to enforce minimal intellectual capacities was never introduced within the German Empire. Only abnormal "mental conditions" were classified after the early 1870s as their own pathological diagnosis, along with appropriate methods of further examination.[88] The debate over what constituted "normal" versus "abnormal" mental facilities, however, was much more intense than in other European countries. The definition of mental disabilities depended directly on how they were recorded, which created tension between the medical and administrative institutions. Although the conscription commissions had originally based their decisions concerning cases of "mental incapacity" on the reports of "district physicians [and] representatives of state, provincial, and district institutions,"[89] they increasingly turned to schools for such assessments around the turn of the century. The view that the medical examination generally provided an insufficient opportunity for the diagnosis of mental illness became accepted in the German Empire: "Much less than from the symptomatic examinations can be expected in the conscription process by the examinations conducted by the military doctor. The time available is much too short to facilitate results with any degree of certainty. At first it was believed that signs of a possible mental illness could be detected during the physical examinations. Deviations from normal cranial shape and other signs of degeneration ... are scientifically interesting but have no decisive meaning for the practical diagnosis."[90] Not least, the context of conscription itself must be considered a peculiar psychological burden for the potential recruits, which made it a problematic basis for generalization. The frequent abuse of alcohol that surrounded the conscription process made it difficult for the doctors Franz Stricker and Theodor Ziehen to tell the "numbing effects of alcohol" from more permanent limitations of the "mental state."[91]

Instead of a one-time examination, the German doctors increasingly advocated longer-term observation of potential recruits.[92] This reflects the fact that medical science was beginning to recognize mental illness as a hereditary problem that could best be understood by considering factors involving the family and milieu. Schools were compiling better lists of mental "irregularities."[93] Starting with the appendix to the regulations for the military, which went into effect in 1907, schools for pupils with disabilities were systematically required to report their pupils separately so that these could be marked accordingly in the conscription rolls and examined with especial attention.[94] Within a few weeks, plans were made public that would require normal schools in the future to report any abnormalities in the intellectual capacities of future recruits observed over the course of their school careers.[95] These plans even called for potential recruits in the future to present a school report as part of the conscription procedure.

The borderline cases of the so-called mentally inferior formed a group that was always the focus of much attention. At the same time, new methods of determination that relied less on superficial anamnesis imparted a sort of expert status to teachers, via which they could influence the "nation's military well-being."[96] In some respects, the intertwining of intellectual, physical, and psychological criteria for military fitness remained fluid for contemporaries, as well: in their examinations of candidates for a "voluntary" year of service—generally speaking, young men who had completed

Abteilung für die Staatskrankenan-
stalten,vom   Nr.
          (Name der Anstalt) . . . .

                    Vertrauliche Mitteilung.

          über eine aus der diesseitigen Anstalt entlassene Person,
          über deren Eintritt in das Heer noch nicht entschieden
          ist.

1. Name und Vorname	
2.Geburtsort und Oberamt (bei außerhalb Württembergs Geborenen Kreis u.s.w.)	
3.Tag,Monat und Jahr der Geburt.	
4.Bezeichnung der Eltern oder des Vormunds und ihres Wohnorts.	
5.Wohnort des Kranken vor seinem Eintritt in die Anstalt.	
6.Zeitpunkt des Eintritts in die Anstalt und des Austritts aus derselben.	Eintritt: Austritt:
7.Festgestellte Krankheit oder,wenn eine solche nicht festgestellt ist, Ergebnis der Beobachtung.	

                              (Unterschrift) . . . .
An die K.Stadtdirektion
    das K. Oberamt
              . . . .

          Dem Herrn Zivilvorsitzenden der Ersatzkommission
                    des Aushebungsbezirks*
                              . . . .
          zur gefl.Kenntnisnahme und weiteren Veranlassung.
              . . . . ,den . . . . . .
                              K.Stadtdirektion
                                K.Oberamt   . . . .
     *Die Mitteilung ist an den Zivilvorsitzenden derjenigen Ersatzkom-
mission zu richten,in deren Bezirk der betreffende Kranke in der
Stammrolle zu führen ist.

Figure 4.5
Form for schools to report mental illnesses, HStA S M 11 Bü 2

secondary school—military doctors observed that "fitness for service sinks noticeably the longer young people have been in school."[97] Any correlation between intellectual capacity and physical fitness, however, could be neither analytically nor statistically proven.

Assessing potential recruits based on a more or less statistical catalog of criteria meant that the results were basically static, despite efforts to include new indicators in this catalog. There were repeated calls that fitness for service should be judged based not on only a few isolated physiological statistics but rather on tests of fitness that incorporated active physical exertion.

In this case as well, Switzerland was the only country to actually implement such a physical fitness test. In 1900, the Swiss Gymnastics Commission suggested that the problematic criterion of chest circumference could be complemented by a gymnastics test. After all, they claimed, it was not chest circumference per se that was the deciding factor, but rather the "effectiveness of the respiratory organs (including the function of the lungs and heart)." Appropriate training and preparation in the schools was to facilitate the healthy development of these organs. In addition to members of the military who were trained to lead these exercises, a military doctor was to be present during the test to measure the candidate's pulse and chest circumference before and after the exertion and use these in a more dynamic assessment.[98]

At first, the Department of the Military and the surgeon general had considerable reservations due to the resources and personnel necessary for the implementation of such a system, but, in the end, a simplified form of the physical fitness test was introduced in 1905. Countless gymnastic clubs, officers' associations, and gymnastics teachers had openly supported the commission's suggestion.[99] The Department of the Interior favored expanding such tests as a method to focus public attention on physical aptitude, meaning that knowledge accumulated within the military also benefited the civil school system. In 1904, the first trials of such tests were conducted in all the local districts: "This test includes long jump, lifting a dumbbell, and sprinting. In addition, those required to appear are to report as to whether they had physical education in school, whether they were subsequently members of an association that involved physical exercise, and whether they participated in preparatory training for military service."[100]

The introduction of this test was eminently political, like that of the pedagogical examination of recruits. From the beginning, the statistical bureau was expected to compile and analyze the results; without a doubt, this was a factor that motivated the political leadership to introduce it.[101] Because the medical and pedagogical conscription examination of potential recruits was also retained, the bureau had to double the size of its personnel. Without this institutional interest in expanding its activities, it would hardly have been considered feasible; these extra tests represented a considerable expenditure of both time and money.

Indeed, the results of the gymnastics tests in Switzerland were not used only as an extension of the medical conscription examination of potential recruits. In his report on the practical implementation of the gymnastics tests, the head of the Swiss Gymnastics Commission, Colonel Guggisberg, observed in 1911 that the number of recruits who had prepared for the test in some way—by participating either in courses in the schools or in other external exercises—had risen significantly since the test's introduction, and that this had in turn significantly bolstered the military fitness of the population in general.[102]

Such side effects of changing the conscription procedure and practice of recruitment suggest, at least in the case of Switzerland, that the social concept of the institution of conscription was slowly evolving. The concepts of fitness for military fitness were increasingly more than just a technique for correlating the size of the population to the size of the military. Instead, new ways of defining the "population" beyond sheer numbers were reflected in the professional practices of medical experts and statisticians.

In regard to the medical conscription examination of potential recruits, it should be noted that the ministries of war, statisticians, and military doctors in various countries all sought to standardize the conscription process as an opportunity for scientific screening of the male population. They had diverse professional interests and were motivated by varying political viewpoints. They sought not only to define reliable numerical limits but also to develop workable indicators of fitness for service, which could be calculated by combining various measurements. Despite these efforts, the definition of such limits was guided to serve political rather than scientific interests; the formulation of reliable indexes of fitness proved to be a chimera. Many of the professional groups were latently disappointed with this failure. Decisions about which potential recruits should be drafted thus had a much less stable foundation than the catalog of criteria seems to suggest.

5 New Knowledge Systems: Statistical Knowledge Meets Practice in the Determination of Fitness for Military Service

Neither the professional practice of medical personnel and statisticians nor the needs of the military can adequately account for the career of the concept of "fitness for military service" around 1900 as various groups within society sought an unconditional and straightforward definition of this concept. The formulation of such terminology was seen as an opportunity to reconcile demographic abstraction involving the large-scale collection of statistical material with the concrete needs of industrial society.[1] "Fitness" was, after all, hardly limited to the military but also relevant for other types of labor, for the obstacles of daily life, and for ideological challenges, such as the challenges of colonialism. The conscription examinations to determine fitness for military service were, more than anything, an opportunity to reflect on the universality of these concepts.[2]

The concepts of fitness for military service prevalent in scholarship and practically implemented within the context of conscription were, however, far from homogenous and closed systems. As evidenced in chapter 4, the concrete circumstances under which these concepts were applied were far removed from those of a controlled experiment. In addition, they were affected by changing political and social factors. The conscription examinations yielded results that were far less objective and questionable than many contemporary scholars had hoped. Despite these problems, however, "the recruit" became an object of scientific study in the discourse of experts, and the analysis of the relevant statistics crystallized around set scientistic categories and research topoi. In the following section, *fitness* is understood as a term influenced by various social and political forces, as well as gender norms and scholarly interests. At the same time, it becomes evident that distinctly different demographic and military rules stood here in opposition to each other. It was precisely the renegotiations of the topic—for example, in the colonial context or the Turner movement (a nineteenth-century gymnastics movement in Germany and later the United States)—that revealed how closely scientific definitions of the concept were interwoven with social practice.

The Individual, Gender, and Nation: Fitness as an Interface of Discourses

The appraisal of fitness for military service encompassed young men, who thus became the reference group for general expressions of the demographic evolution of their respective national populaces. Studying the health and physical strength of a cohort of young men was intended to allow for statements over the development of a people and its ability to defend itself in case of war.

Gustav Wernher, a surgeon in Giessen, was quite optimistic in 1870 that there was a positive correlation between the two: "The reports over the medical examination of young men eligible for conscription deliver us a range of quite valuable material which can be extrapolated for the other age groups and the female gender in quite interesting calculations."[3] What exactly did Wernher have in mind when he pointed to these possibilities for extrapolation? Such calculations—which simply extended the results based on the examination of these young men to apply to the other gender or to other categories of age, social position, or geography—struck most of Wernher's contemporaries as problematic, for it was obvious that the statistical material collected in the military applied to only one segment of the population. Such calculations were arithmetically straightforward, but they could not adequately provide a nuanced representation of social realities.[4]

Especially in regard to the gender-specific construction of the concept of fitness, the attributions were initially quite clear. Fitness was increasingly viewed as an attribute characteristic of and manifest in the "nation of men."[5] It was thus less of a descriptive tool than a method for the normalization of body images. The measures of fitness were thus implicitly tailored to apply to male candidates. Within the realm of public perception, feminine physical fitness was often juxtaposed in an ironic sense as a sort of malformed counterpart to the ideal masculine type. For example, on postcards such as those shown in figure 4.3, figures representing feminine fitness were presented together with racist and anti-Semitic imagery in satirical contrast to the nationalized masculine body. This form of misrepresenting established norms and orders on picture postcards was ubiquitous in imperial Germany and was a strong component in the affirmation of the male, imperial German citizen. Many examples from the colonial visual repertoires confirm that cartoons of Jews and women were parallel to those

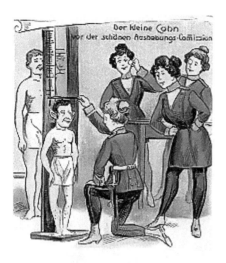

Figure 5.1a

Conscription postcard with "the Little Cohn" and women as examiners, in 1905. *Note:* "Cohn" was a common Jewish name and used in a derogatory way to refer to such caricatures of "the Jew."

Figure 5.1b

The future of our colonial troops, in 1905

of soldiers, and of the colonial "other" to the male, physically fit, white soldier. The "colonial carnival" thus was a well-established motive in the visual discourse of the Wilhelmine society.[6]

This does not mean, however, that there were no comparable conceptions of the female population. Shortly after the Franco-Prussian War, a medical captain, Eitner, described how medical examinations were conducted in Prussian orphanages. His portrayal is quite revealing of the differences in expectation for males and females. Whereas the male children were examined even during their school careers to assess their potential for military service, the blank form for girls' health assessment read as follows: "the daughter of [xy] was found in the examination conducted by me today to be completely healthy and free of any apparent physical abnormalities or weaknesses, and that, given her current physique, there is every hope that she will be sufficiently strong for her future occupation as maid, is hereby dutifully certified."[7]The "examination" for the occupation of maid, which seems surprising at first from a twenty-first century perspective, was based in gender analogies: a corresponding equivalent to the military service required of young men was sought for women, and accordingly, a set of physical criteria were laid down by which women could be assessed.[8]

Fitness for military service was thus doubly defined in gender-specific terms, both by the examination methods used and also by the national discourse over masculinity.[9] To better understand the implications of gender concepts at the societal level, many scholars had to think laterally: citing a supposedly traditional saying—"healthy women, healthy children, healthy men"—a medical captain named Lothar Bassenge, who worked in the German Ministry of War, concluded that "personal hygiene and physical training" were important for the "progenitors of future generations."[10] Contemporary understanding of heredity linked the masculine definition of fitness to a wider discourse on hygiene and health, which to some extent transcended gender but which was also specific to the female segment of the population. In debates over the degeneration of industrial society, the extent to which mothers breastfed their babies or were even able to do so at all was a frequent topic of discussion. Mothers of future soldiers were seen as the bearers of the "national military strength."[11] Within the context of the conscription examinations in the German Empire and, to a lesser extent, in France, doctors examined members of a potential recruit's family in some borderline cases involving hereditary diseases or pathological dispositions.[12] Health within the family and the social and cultural atmosphere were thus considered factors that influenced the total military strength.[13]

The term and concept of *heredity* was not a matter of routine discourse among military medical professionals. Following the teachings of Lamarck, they generally assumed that the disposition of the individual was the result of the parents' health and his social environment, in addition to proper nutrition and upbringing.[14] This philosophy was seemingly confirmed in the debate over compulsory military service in Germany around the turn of the century. Even though the metaphorical blows exchanged between the conservative followers of the theory of degeneration and more liberal economists and statisticians during this period did not result in any definitive answers, they created a space for argumentation. The military doctors, who more frequently responded to this discourse rather than initiating it themselves, attempted to prove the influence of social professional factors on the criteria of physical fitness. This in turn shaped statistical practice.[15] It also led to attempts to formulate alternative definitions in which, for example, a candidate's psychological development or paramilitarist upbringing played important roles, in addition to individual measurements and other physical factors. In the consideration of such new lists of criteria, political context often was decisive.

The Paramilitary: Training, Practice, and Play

France's defeat in 1870 cast doubts on the entire military system, including the methods of recruiting new soldiers. One of the first reactions within civil society was the alliance of veterans and pedagogues in associations (*sociétés de tir*) that aimed to improve the paramilitary training of pupils and better prepare them for a future in the army. There were repeated calls to institutionalize these initiatives within the French educational system, and some steps were taken in this direction. The parliament resolved on January 1, 1880, to make physical education obligatory for all boys; they looked thereby more to the German example set of physical exercises rather than to the sport-centric model dominant in England.[16] The focus thus was more on the training of each individual body than on competition against each other. Two years later, the French president mandated that schools should form *bataillons scolaires*, the purpose of which was to support and institutionalize the paramilitary training of their attendees. Eugen Weber has outlined the extent to which this new republican institution was seen as a threat to other established traditions, especially in rural communities. The trainings were typically scheduled on Sundays, which raised the ire of clerics.[17] Beyond these social reservations, the sometimes subversive or reactionary tendencies of Boulangism, which dominated the sociétés de tir with their hierarchies modeled on those of the military,[18] obstructed the integration of these new institutions into the state curriculum and led to the stagnation of the movement until after the turn of the century.[19]

In a programmatic treatise on the army within French democracy in 1900, French writer and pacifist Gaston Moch outlined the central ideas from a leftist perspective that were supposed to provide the foundation for a new French military system of which paramilitary training was to be a cornerstone. In addition to the physical education already obligatory for both sexes between the ages of 10 and 13, the male students between the ages of 13 and 19 were now to attend such training on Sundays. For those under sixteen, this was basically an extension of physical education classes, but older students addressed other topics: the training was to include "knowledge of rifles (how to assemble, break down, care for, and shoot them), marching on foot, orientation and field exercises, [and] map-reading." Under Moch's plan, the sociétés de tir, which had thus far not been state-sanctioned, were to be boosted and placed under the supervision of the state or even the military directly.[20] Officers were to oversee the training of the future recruits.[21] He proposed a test at the end of this training that would qualify young men for an accelerated advance through the military ranks.

Such ideas were received by the state with great interest,[22] and the Ministry of War did begin implementing some measures of this nature between 1907 and 1910,[23] until budgetary restraints meant that the government was not able to fund such costly general training on a wider scale. Instead, in the early twentieth century, the number of sociétés de tir skyrocketed, especially in regions along the border. In the département des Vosges alone, which bordered on the then German-occupied Alsace, ninety-eight such associations were privately founded in 1909.[24] Although the state provided significant support for such clubs—the ammunition for target practice, for example, was provided by the military—they remained independent organizations.

It was not only the institutionalization of this physical training for military service that faced obstacles, however. The prominent Italian physiologist Angelo Mosso vehemently advocated that school children should not be raised to the obedience and discipline required in the military, but that their bodies could be best strengthened by a "free and natural" education: "We should not forget that many of those hardships which characterize the lifestyle of primitive peoples are essential for the physical education of their youth. We should not fail to pay attention to the rural population, for there we can see the effects of those external forces and their work out of doors in the sunshine which make them physically able to withstand the privations and strain of a soldier's life."[25] As to what actually constituted an ideal education, Mosso was uncertain: "There are two parties in France and Italy. While one of these works to lend education a military touch by training the young people to shoot, the other strives for an education with a civilian character and is of the opinion that it is harmful to put weapons into the hands of the youth before they are more or less ready to use these in war."[26]

The practice of paramilitary training, which despite such differences in Italy and France was increasingly significant, was also well received on the other side of the Rhine. In the German Empire, however, civilian education and fitness for the military had a somewhat complicated relationship. Training for the military was not limited by any means to simple physical fitness. Ute Frevert has pointed out that the concepts of paramilitary training reflected precisely those values esteemed by the ambitious middle classes of Wilhelmine society, values that played a central role in their idealized conceptions of education within the family.[27] This meant that not only did the military become the much cited "school of the nation," but also that militaristic values were transposed onto pedagogical discourse. In expert circles, there was little doubt "that the structure and curriculum of advanced schools should be adjusted for the needs of the military."[28]

Compared to the institutionalized paramilitary training in France, however, German pedagogues were still far removed from a physical training narrowly targeted at preparing the youth for military service. In 1895, for the celebration of the hundredth anniversary of the Medizinisch-chirurgischen Friedrich-Wilhelms-Institut, which was to become the Kaiser Wilhelms-Akademie für militärärztliches Bildungswesen directly afterward, a well-known bacteriologist from Prague, Ferdinand Hueppe, addressed the question of to what extent school training exercises were sufficient to prepare the male body for the military. Hueppe, who himself had studied at the Friedrich-Wilhelms-Institut, reported on the correlations he saw between the national culture of the body and the capabilities of the military:

Was not our gymnastics [program] tested by fire in the great struggle of 1870/71? Was it not evident in the statistics that fewer of the gymnasts became ill than of their counterparts, and that the number of iron crosses [i.e., war medals] awarded to the gymnasts was almost twice [the average]. It would seem that the German gymnastics [program] makes an extraordinary contribution to the national military training. On the other hand, those familiar with the English circumstances know that for the most part the English owe their indestructible tough energy in all climates of the

globe—that which has thus far ensured their preeminence over their competitors—
to the sports which make them tough, in which the discipline of the voluntary sub-
mission of the individual for the benefit of the whole represents a great achievement
of nationalist instruction.[29]

Hueppe juxtaposed the ideal of individual capability—as encouraged in
the German Turner movement—with the competition of English sports,
which demanded control of the individual body in service of a greater
whole. This was not the only point on which he outlined clear differences
between the two nations' approaches. He interpreted the signs of degeneration among the soldiers, especially the growing number of short-sighted
soldiers, as characteristic for the suppression of a childish freedom of movement and of a supposedly "proto-Germanic instinct to play."[30] Individual
gymnastics, team sports, and competitive games encompassed different
expectations for the body in the different countries and thus different conceptions of fitness, which competed for recognition as universal.[31] Was not
the success of the British colonial empire sufficient evidence of the universal superiority of a body image other than that of *Turnvater* Jahn? Hueppe,
who five years later was elected the first president of the German soccer
association, was at the time of the address an active member of the Olym-
pic movement and thus refrained from answering this question clearly.[32]
In the end, the masculine body under the influence of Jahn's ideology was
too politically charged. It also served a function in compensating for social
differences, which were supposed to be obliterated by the Turner movement.[33] Hueppe was interested in expanding such a concept because "all
truly human issues are also international, even if they take on their own
national nuances."[34]

A debate had been sparked and, in the years to come, it grew increasingly
significant. In June 1899, the Zentralausschuss zur Förderung der Volks-
und Jugendspiele in Deutschland hosted a large convention in Königsberg
to address the following question: What are the demands of modern military service on youths' bodies and manners, and how can our education of
youth create circumstances to promote our national military strength? The
founder and chairman of the committee "for the encouragement of games
for the populace and youth" was Emil von Schenkendorff, a former lieutenant colonel and national liberal representative in the Prussian parliament.
He was interested in promoting a new form of premilitary and military
sport, which was to serve as" a compromise between gymnastics in a limited sense and [competitive] sports, in other words all physical exercises out
of doors, which ... foster both alertness and wit."[35] Games as a method for
strengthening the nation were not limited to one sex: the convention also

addressed the "strengthening of the female youth via active games"[36] and related this implicitly to the issue of military strength as well.

The negotiations that the association had to conduct with the various ministries of war within the German Empire point toward the lack of communication between the public, academia, and the governmental administration. Despite Schenkendorff's constant lobbying and the subcommittee he founded in Königsberg "to encourage national military strength via education,"[37] the topic garnered little political attention. The Ministry of War in the Kingdom of Württemberg responded more than sparingly to the numerous invitations of the association, claiming methodically that it was not responsible for questions of pedagogy.[38] At the same time, however, the ministry also discreetly sought information about how these questions were being addressed in other German countries. Only the Bavarian ministry was open to the invitation and sent representatives to the conventions. In Bavaria, especially, the association had broad support within the population and was backed by local elites, both civilians and military personnel.[39] High-ranking military personnel in the other German countries generally rejected attempts to influence the questions of recruitment and training and to incorporate the more recent scientific concepts of fitness.

The committee for the encouragement of games, however, pursued its goals with determination. Each year, it organized a playful competitive march with full military equipment. The first of these took place in Württemberg in 1910. The next year, it was moved to Dresden—which, in the same year, was host to the hygiene exhibition. Together with the exhibition, the movement for the physical training for military service had finally reached the necessary audience, and in the four years thereafter, the topic was addressed by school officials and the ministries of war.[40] Even before the actual opening of the exhibition, the "defense committee," as the committee had taken to calling itself, released a memorandum outlining the importance of such training for reinforcing military strength. In principle, military strength was synonymous with strength of the populace at large, for "the acquisition of those physical, mental, and moral characteristics essential for military strength are also the prerequisite for success in scholarship, occupations, or business. Moreover, [the committee] regards the physical exercises not only as a means of increasing military strength, but also as a significant means of improving social welfare."[41] The threat presented by a shrinking population during the Third Reich prompted the committee to continue supporting physical education of youth; it claimed that all the major European nations had responded to the demographic trends by taking similar measures: "In Germany it is evident as well that the physical and moral preparation of the manpower necessary for military service is in decline. ... The disadvantageous influence of these circumstances is intensified by the fact that the youth of today flee from the discipline of their parents' homes and the masters' [workshops] as quickly and often as possible, and strong intellectual currents are working to erode respect for authority, morals, and faith."[42]

At the same time, the committee was deliberately careful to respect the autonomy of the state military training. In the preliminary negotiations—for example, with the Prussian Ministry of War—it had quickly become clear that the committee's plans would be doomed to fail if they did not respect these structures of governmental autonomy.[43] Instead of practicing military drills, the first aim was simply to encourage discipline and other "secondary virtues" as a by-product of competitive sports. In addition to defining physical and sport exercises, the committee imposed a language of command that was to play a role in the physical education. A continuous principle was that "the female gender is to be trained in a similar vein to ensure the strength of future generations."

Countless skiing, hiking, and soccer clubs petitioned the ministries to deem their sport decisive for the question of fitness for military service and military strength and thus to add it to the standard curriculum. This seemed even more pressing after Prussia and Württemberg adopted a plan in May 1914 that planned to closely coordinate "school and military gymnastics."[44] The question of which form of physical activity and exercise best matched the conception of a body well-prepared for military service thus seemed likely to play an important role for years to come.

The paramilitary training of youth was increasingly viewed throughout Europe as an extension of the time served in the army. The British example of the Boy Scouts as a reaction to the shock of the Boer War is especially notable.[45] In Germany and France, this question was the subject of prominent discussion because the term of obligatory military service was successively reduced after 1870, thus reducing the potential time for training recruits. Many of those involved thought it advisable to complete parts of the training prior to the term of service. Even if a changing image of a physically fit collective body capable of defense only infiltrated some segments of the civil society after World War I,[46] the beginnings of this social evolution stem from the changes made at the school level. Popular conceptions of fitness for military service thus began to have effects far beyond the military itself.

Patterns of Geographic and Social Differentiation

The correlation between fitness for military service and education, which is highlighted by the role of clubs, schools, and paramilitary programs, suggests that interpretations of these concepts must pay attention to social contexts. There was no equal access to school education or paramilitary training; these factors stemmed instead from an individual's social and professional milieu. Could fitness for military service thus be applied as a homogenous, universal concept to the populace as a whole? The military leadership also had to ask itself whether all the social and professional groups should be equally represented in the army. In other words, was there even a global concept of fitness? And if so, was it in the army's interest to apply this concept?

The differentiation of fitness examinations according to occupation was introduced even before the debates over industrialization.[47] Throughout the entire nineteenth century, there were repeated attempts to differentiate the numbers of new conscripts according to social, geographic, and professional criteria. In 1849, Boudin was already analyzing the composition of the French army—if quite superficially—according to various social and professional categories. He concluded that the rural population was underrepresented.[48] In their conscription campaign in 1885, the Swiss military leadership also analyzed the results according to occupational groups and found, surprisingly, that among wagoners 24 percent of the candidates were rejected, whereas 52 percent of factory workers were deemed unsuitable for military service. In other words, wagoners were more than twice as likely to be deemed fit for military service than factory workers. Although craftsman were deemed fit for service at a higher than average rate,[49] those employed in agriculture were, like factory workers, less likely to pass the examination.[50]

In fact, these results, though seemingly quite decisive, appear to have unsettled the statistical bureau that compiled them. In their commentary, statisticians warned against jumping to rash conclusions based on these numbers: "There is no doubt that one's occupation, the type of activity and especially the financial circumstances which are closely related to occupation, namely one's diet and nutrition, have an influence on one's physical development and health, and thus also on one's fitness for military service. It would be a mistake, however, to view the significant differences evident in the numbers cited above as being exclusively, or perhaps even predominantly, the result of the occupations."[51] A precise analysis of the physical statistics and reasons for being judged unfit, argued the statisticians, suggested that "while many of the physical deficiencies and weaknesses which had resulted in the candidates' being unfit were already evident when they chose their respective occupations and had played a role in these choices. ... More generally speaking, this means: the individual occupations are drawn from groups with quite varied levels of strength and health, and thus in part display such varying levels of fitness for military service."[52]

The statisticians could find no explanation for the fact that students and teachers in Switzerland were also deemed fit at a much higher rate than average, especially considering the fact that this group in most European countries tested quite poorly.[53] Another occupational group that was of significance for the military presented the leadership with an especial challenge: tailors. As in all other European countries, Swiss tailors were, without a doubt, the least likely to be deemed fit—and, in fact, they were far less likely to qualify for service than even factory workers or farmers.[54] The army, however, needed tailors for the production and maintenance of uniforms, leading some countries to introduce laxer criteria for appraising their level of fitness.[55]

The Italian military doctor Ridolfo Livi compiled statistical results according to occupational groups for the Italian government based on conscription examinations conducted between 1880 and 1885, and these paint a much different picture.[56] Using the statistics that had been collected, Livi calculated the controversial measurement of chest circumference in relation to height and compared it with the regional averages of those candidates judged to be fit. With this statistically more nuanced method, Livi also concluded that coachmen and wagoners were collectively the fittest of these groups. His other conclusions, however, were quite different than those reached by the Swiss statisticians: according to his findings, students were taller than average, although their chest circumference was often lacking. This was a result of a sufficient, nutritious diet—students generally came from at least a middle-class background—and a lack of physical activity. The opposite was true of those males employed in the agricultural sector; they tended to be more fit despite being shorter than average. In Livi's opinion, these results were somewhat problematic, because having more soldiers from privileged, bourgeois backgrounds would be a decisive step in improving the quality of the army. To this aim, he suggested that "muscle-building exercises [should be] encouraged within these classes, and a love of nature and outdoor games [should be] promoted."[57] In other words, this was another call for increasing the national capacity for defense via paramilitary training, which in Italy, as in other European countries, experienced a sharp rise. In Livi's eyes, fitness for military service was an absolute figure. He did not acknowledge or reflect upon the fact that both the regional averages and the limits adopted by the military changed over time. For him, an increase in average chest circumference meant an absolute increase in the number of qualified candidates.

The German debate over the discrepancy in fitness levels between the agrarian and industrial populations (outlined in chapter one) seized upon such studies that had been conducted abroad. Most of those involved in this debate, however, were less interested in a precise breakdown along social or occupational lines than in a more general dichotomy between rural and urban societies. The studies that the agrarian lobby groups carried out in an attempt to provide more insight into the social and occupational backgrounds of the German candidates for conscription after the fact were politically charged from the very beginning. Whereas candidates in Switzerland and Italy had been asked simply to list their occupations, the German survey divided occupations into "rural" and "urban" groups, which meant that the results were embedded from the outset in these fixed categories. Furthermore, they offered an opportunity to promote various measures like agricultural training, which were intended to level out differences between the two groups while also promoting the fitness of the individuals.[58]

In other countries, such generalizations were similarly instrumentalized for political purposes. In northern France, for example, the delegate Edouard Lachaud argued that the reason industrial workers were generally significantly less fit than their rural counterparts was that many of the mothers living in urban locations no longer had time to breastfeed their babies.[59] Social differentiation was here understood to be complementary to categories of gender; they could reinforce or even replace each other in the arguments.

The search for patterns within these statistics and the politicization of these numbers becomes more obvious the more clearly the focus shifts from social to geographical differences. In a variety of ways, it was not only the difference between urban and rural areas but also purely geographic or geologic differences between various regions that seemed to determine the military strength of the populace. In 1870, Fröhlich speculated that differences in sun exposure, air pressure, latitude, air currents, and geomagnetic fields were responsible for the regional variance in the fitness of these populations.[60] In principle, then, military strength could be extrapolated from the geographical characteristics of a region, even though it was influenced at the individual level by other factors, like age and occupation. Fröhlich suggested dividing the German Empire into three fitness zones delimited by latitude: these were between the forty-seventh and fiftieth parallels, the fiftieth and fifty-third parallels, and the fifty-third and fifty-sixth parallels.[61] He did not base these distinctions on the statistical results of the conscription examinations, however, but viewed them as pragmatic, prescriptive divisions that would help to achieve a more nuanced analysis in the future. Even before the results were collected along these lines, some of those involved were already taking issue with the a priori strategy of this "geognostic" classification. They were of the opinion that, in this case, the working hypotheses and research methods formed a circular argument.

Several years previously in France, Gustave Lagneau had set out to establish a similar relationship. His study "Du récrutement de l'armée sous le rapport anthropologique" was the first in a series analyzing the results of conscription examinations in the different regions of France. Lagneau divided France according to its various ethnic groups—namely, the Aquitanians, the Gauls, the Celts, the Belgians, and so on. In other words, he adopted Caesar's divisions from *Bellum Gallicum*. He added categories to accommodate later ethnic migrations—for example, the settlement of the Bretons in Brittany and the expansion and integration of Burgundy. The grid that Lagneau used in his analysis of France was not only geographical but implicitly drew upon the chief pillars of contemporary national historiography. In a number of individual studies, he addressed those groups that he held to be most problematic and significant in light of the statistics collected in the conscription process.[62] Unlike Fröhlich, Lagneau was not attempting to explain the differences in military strength, but he used these differences to argue for his initial anthropological hypothesis. This combination of statistical research methods and established assumptions was typical of anthropological research in other countries around the turn of the century as well. For example, the president of the military doctors' association in Berlin, Heinrich Schwiening, formulated it thus in his statistical study of German volunteers: "The high rate of fitness of those born in the Thuringian states and the Reichsland[63] is remarkable. Bavaria is consistently below the average for the empire as a whole. The Silesians perform unfavorably; and it comes ... as little wonder that Berlin displays the lowest rate of fitness of all."[64]

Some statisticians endeavored to formulate this conjunction of political and statistical discourse in more precise terms. They aimed to calculate fitness quotients for clearly defined areas, via which a qualitative appraisal of the population in regard to its collective level of fitness for military service could be undertaken. In this context, for example, the previously discussed method of the Pignet index, which combined chest circumference and height, was once again relevant. Even if this did not seem precise enough to provide a medical basis for decisions about candidates' fitness for military service, it at least presented an opportunity for establishing geographical patterns after the fact—for example, "for the examination of large groups for survey reports over the general stature of those examined within a given area, for comparative study of members of a particular region or trade, and for reviewing the standards for their own demands on fitness in those districts in which the first round of examinations has already taken place."[65]

Within the federal German Empire, however, such geographical differentiation of the conscription numbers was potentially controversial. In the years leading up to the war, the Ministry of War entertained thoughts of basing the number of conscripts to be provided by the individual German states on the averages for the years 1903 to 1907—to set a benchmark, so to speak. This method had been suggested by the French statistician Taillepied de Bondy nearly seventy years earlier.[66] Those states and regions with low or even negative population growth rates—for example, the Kingdom of Württemberg—viewed such a procedure as putting them at a disadvantage compared to industrial regions, which would be required to provide proportionally fewer conscripts given their population growth.[67] The Ministry of the Interior in Württemberg nevertheless agreed to the imperial ministry's proposal, because in the end, future predictability was more important for the ministry's administration.

The decentralized structure of the German Empire effected the differentiation of the concept of fitness in a further way: the correlation between candidates' origins and the assignment to particular branches of the military. Within the German Empire, as in the other European nations, soldiers were not stationed directly in their home territories, but there was in principle a geographic connection by which certain brigades were drawn from particular regions. Place of residence could thus determine the assignment to certain units. The individual German states provided set army corps—like, for example, Württemberg provided the XIII army corps, Saxony the XII and XIX, and Bavaria the three royal Bavarian army corps. Although this strategy worked for the army, it could not be enforced for the marines. The rapid expansion of the marines around the turn of the century made drafting the necessary manpower from the coastal population alone unfeasible. Paragraph 23 of the *Wehrordnung* (military regulations) stipulated that, in addition to those present residents of coastal regions, all those born in proximity to the coast should be considered part of the "sailor and half-sailor" population and accordingly be assigned to service in the marines. Citizens of Württemberg who had been born on the coast were processed separately by the civilian chairman of the conscription commission and then sent to serve in the imperial marines. No weight was given to how long they had actually lived near the coast or to whether they had any other occupational skills that made them suited to such service.[68] From the perspective of the army administration, the qualification of the marines seemed to be based on the family's background and thus on a sort of hereditary occupational qualification. Although the number of those sent to the marines from Württemberg was small, the procedure highlights the internal weaknesses in the supposedly universal concept of fitness for military service.

Even if no blanket criteria for fitness could be formulated across the board, many of the actors involved still believed they could formulate set criteria for service within a more limited geographical area. These attempts, however, proved to be illusory whenever they were closely scrutinized. All that could be proven with the statistical material available was a social differentiation of fitness. Like so many other systems of selection, fitness seemed basically to be linked to the stratification of society as a whole.

Colonial Fitness: Generalizations about Military Strength Put to the Test

The pathological reality in European colonies forced demographers, medical professionals, statisticians, and military officials to reexamine the universality of their categories, their definitions of fitness, and the ways that science constructed notions of European superiority.[69] Recent studies have suggested that the challenges of colonialism exerted significant influence over the development of social policies, both in the colonies themselves and on the European continent.[70] The army was no exception: in fact, the pattern of a coproduction of colonial experiences and new anthropological knowledge applied even more in a coercive system such as the military hierarchy, in which colonial and European social realities overlapped directly in soldiers who moved from one place to another.

In various European countries, the marines formed the division of the army in which the supposed universality of the concepts of fitness for military service and national military strength were put to the hardest test. Within the context of European imperialism, naval forces had generally been responsible for the occupation of the colonies and for carrying out complicated campaigns in distant corners of the globe. Beginning with the very first overseas colonies and continuing into the nineteenth century, European colonial powers had experienced dramatic mortality rates.[71] A large percentage of those soldiers who participated in such military expeditions either perished or suffered significant damage to their health due to infectious diseases like typhoid fever, cholera, pox, and, most especially, forms of malaria that had previously been unknown in Europe. In some areas—for example, the seventeenth-century Dutch settlement of Batavia (modern Jakarta)—the mortality rate of soldiers and settlers was so high that the colony was nicknamed the Dutch Cemetery, and doubts were raised about the sustainability of military rule, to say nothing of a functioning governmental administration.[72] In the first African colonies, the mortality of the European residents also reached 90 percent over the first seven years.[73] Soldiers and settlers only slowly learned to adapt to the climate and prevent such illnesses.[74]

The Europeans who extensively explored Africa in the early nineteenth century in search of the source of its rivers and raw materials had similar experiences. Johannes Fabian has shown how deeply this pathological experience of tropical Africa shaped the scholarship produced by European researchers.[75] The sometimes overly simplified understandings of illness with which they set out on their journeys made Africa into a place where fever was a constant fact of life and continuous metaphor; dealing with mortal threats was a daily occurrence, which meant that, at least partially, these researchers relied on the knowledge of the local populations for answers to medical questions.[76] This "pathologizing" of the African continent in the minds of the European colonizers was intensified in the 1880s with the colonization of sub-Saharan Africa.[77] It also led to clear attempts by European doctors to develop methods for dealing specifically and successfully with the challenges of practicing medicine in tropical regions.[78] One of the goals in this field was to develop universal criteria to appraise Europeans in regards to their "fitness for tropical climates."

No European country introduced a system by which state institutions examined potential settlers to determine their level of fitness for tropical climates. In most cases, there was a dearth of those interested in settling in such colonies anyway.[79] The situation was different for members of the armed forces, however.[80] The efforts to formulate a workable definition of fitness for service in the colonies appeared to be a key element for the foundation of military power in these areas. Here, too, the medical personnel availed themselves of the extant statistical knowledge. For a time, the statistical studies seemed to affirm the doctors' expectations that European soldiers and colonists should differ most of all from the colonized populations in regards to pathology. In their analysis, doctors who studied the tropics extrapolated "racial" patterns of disease.[81] The statistical report on disease within the Dutch Army in present-day Indonesia completed in 1894 assumed distinct patterns of infection and disease among soldiers from the colonies and those from Europe; based on this, they spoke of two different races.[82]

Such hypotheses were a subject of some dispute,[83] for it quickly became clear that the state of knowledge about Europeans' reactions to these foreign diseases was quite limited. From the perspective of the military, there was a dearth of statistical material because the "European population" in the colonies was quite low and the compilation of statistics was difficult. Many of the doctors working in the tropics thus incorporated statistics collected by their colleagues from neighboring European countries into their studies.[84] In the eyes of German experts, such transnational cooperation to deepen understanding of the available statistical material was essential because—in the words of the highest ranking German medical officer stationed in Cameroon, Hans Ziemann—"the statistics for Africa still leave us very much in the lurch."[85] Even more so than in the field of statistics on the general populace, the study of colonial statistics was characterized by intense transnational traffic of knowledge, not only at the methodological level but also in regard to the results of statistical evaluations. This had the implicit effect that the European populations in tropical regions melted into one "race" in statistical research. Any differentiation along lines of national military strengths lost any relevance in the colonial context. The goal of better understanding the pathological nature of European soldiers in the colonies evolved into a sort of pan-European project because "it is only possible to do justice to the challenging task of maintaining the health of European soldiers in tropical battles if the results of theoretical research and practical experiences are shared [for everyone's] use."[86] The scientific methods and the hopes placed in social physics seemed to offer some safety in regions that had proven extremely dangerous for Europeans. In a broader sense, they were seen as instruments that would make the presence of Europeans in tropical regions feasible.

The International Congress for Hygiene and Demography in Berlin in 1907[87] became the location in which the question of fitness for tropical climates could be addressed and the groundwork could be laid for the transnational ambitions of unified criteria for fitness and set categories for international conscription statistics. In a section convened precisely to appraise the fitness for tropical climates of European soldiers, a German speaker, Major Doctor Steudel,[88] the French military doctor Reynaud,[89] and the British representative Davies[90] agreed that cooperation between the military medical personnel in the colonies was necessary to ensure that the limited statistical material available was consistent enough to allow for comparative study. In the end, they suggested that an "international colonial society" should formulate an internationally binding system for the recording of fitness criteria.[91]

The researchers tried for a long time to correlate pathologies with their concept of race in an effort to geographically limit these illnesses. During his deployment in the Philippines, for example, the American medical officer Charles Woodruff conducted a long-term statistical study in which he traced the morbidity rate by hair and skin color.[92] His research led him to conclude that it was hardly possible for those of European and North American descent to survive in the tropics over the long term. The German military doctor Th. zur Verth analyzed these results and argued furthermore for the "superiority of brunettes in the tropics," suggesting that this be introduced as a criterion for consideration in the conscription examinations of potential soldiers.[93] Such suggestions for a racial concept of fitness for tropical climates were made repeatedly,[94] but practical (often budgetary) restrictions in part precluded a more detailed, additional examination of those destined for service in tropical climates. The available knowledge was also rudimentary and uncertain to serve as the foundation for set categories. Some scientists also resisted the idea of treating the tropics—and thus usually the colonial regions—as so extremely different or more dangerous than temperate zones. In regards to diseases of the nervous system, the Brazilian doctors Juliano Moreira and Afraino Peixoto used the available statistical material to make the case to their European colleagues that these illnesses did not develop remarkably differently in the tropics than in the European context. Such health problems were not at all different in Rio de Janeiro than in Vienna or Paris: "The climate has no influence at all on the symptoms of diverse psychoses. ... The influence of the tropics on the nervous system of normal individuals hailing from colder countries varies greatly from person to person. Generally speaking, it is related to the individual's lifestyle and the organization of the nervous system."[95]

Lacking an adequate universal biological concept from which the superiority of the European soldiers could be demonstrated, those medical personnel working in the field of tropical medicine increasingly focused on cultural and social models of explanation.[96] Within the context of growing colonial ambitions, especially those of the German Empire after 1884, it was necessary for the German military to find means and methods with

which they could establish control over colonial regions. Purely anthropological explanations often were differentiated with the help of cultural
argumentation.

One year after the beginning of the German Empire's colonial campaign,
the geographer and journalist Hugo Zöller was certain that the settlement
in the tropics had taken the worst shape possible, geographically speaking. Settlements had been established not in those areas which were most
livable but rather where it was thought they would be most advantageous
for trade, in the unhealthy regions at the mouths of rivers.[97] Such circumstances, in the eyes of the ethnologist Reinhold Pallmann, also distorted
the evidence supporting a clear theory of "racial" capacity for adaptation;
under these conditions, the migration of diverse ethnic groups was bound
to fail.[98] Certain illnesses typically accompanied settlement in a different
climatic zone than one's native environment, as could be seen in the example of the Indian soldiers of the British Army who were stationed in Egypt.[99]
It was in his eyes "a fable" that the tropical climate was inhospitable; a
variety of hygienic, cultural, and social measures could enable settlers of the
"European race" to survive there. This required a new definition of fitness
for tropical climates and consideration of new questions of psychological
resilience and stress resistance. The guidebooks for the appraisal of fitness
for tropical climates after 1900 viewed these criteria as central in assessing
the viability of Europeans in the tropics. The recognition of the physiological interaction between psychological stress and a higher risk of infectious
disease was one of the primary insights of medical research around the turn
of the century and was incorporated into the catalog of criteria for fitness
for tropical climates.

The discussion focused on the acquisition of cultural skills, but also
on familial tendencies and psychological illnesses. The list of criteria for
the examination of potential soldiers that Steudel presented at the International Congress for Hygiene and Demography included the following:
"The nervous system should be examined closely during the examination
because it suffers the most often in the tropics. Individuals with a proclivity
to neuralgia, headaches, hypochondria, and those who, even at home, have
become stressed out under conditions of increased demands in the service
and required vacation, are, like those with hereditary tendencies or mental
deficiencies, not at all fit for service in tropical regions."[100]

This was also zur Verth's view. He suggested "consideration of [a candidate's] life to date and the mental condition of his near relatives in addition to objective signs" to adequately assess his mental resilience.[101] The

doctors' central argument was that the circumstances and challenges with which soldiers would be confronted demanded strong nerves and a healthy lifestyle. The consumption of drugs and alcohol by many European soldiers aggravated psychological maladies. In the year 1894, at the International Congress for Hygiene and Demography in Budapest, the highest ranking British military doctor, Charles Richard Francis, condemned the use of nicotine and alcohol in tropical regions.[102] In subsequent years, many of the most well-known experts on social medicine and hygiene issued similar warnings about the use of such substances, which could precipitate, or at least exacerbate,[103] psychological difficulties—most especially the feared "tropical madness" of the soldiers. The proclivity to consume alcohol thus became a reason for disqualification from service in the tropics.[104]

These standards also applied to the question of "tropical hygiene" in a more general sense.[105] Doctors called for a hygienization of private life in the tropical colonies, similar to that which had deeply affected the social structures of many European societies in the age of industrialization. Not only doctors but also hygienists should be sent to "open up" these countries[106]: "The question of how to deploy European troops is primarily one of practical military hygiene in the tropics in the broadest sense."[107] Individual hygiene and the internalization of a catalog of related rules were considered vital.[108] Discipline was considered an essential aspect of fitness for tropical climates. Technical aids like pith helmets or medicines like quinine (as the primary treatment for the dreaded malaria) became indispensable instruments that made survival in the tropics possible at all. At the same time, such aids and instruments also shaped the individual abilities required of soldiers deployed in tropical regions.[109]

Around 1900, European colonists and soldiers encountered new challenges due to changing colonial politics; these were not of a medical but of a military nature. The effectiveness of European troops in combat was brought into question by the colonial conflicts. The Franco-Hova War in Madagascar (1894–1895), the German expedition in China (1897), the South African War (1899–1902), and the Russo-Japanese War (1904–1905) all raised questions about the validity of the concepts of fitness.[110] In military operations and combat situations, the superiority of the European soldiers compared to those from other regions was by no means as evident as European theorists would have expected.[111]

Except in the case of the British Empire, the number of soldiers deployed in the colonies was never particularly high. In this case, then, it is not due to statistically significant numbers that the question is relevant but rather due to the way in which the "sounding room" of the tropical colonies challenged Europeans' sentiments of scientific and statistical superiority. The use of the "colonial argument" in the debates over the concept of fitness for military service shows how clearly these European conceptions were reacting to these changes. In 1911, for example, the German Society for the Encouragement of National Military Strength via Education viewed the experiences in the colonial conflicts and wars as the main reason for rethinking the prevailing concepts of education to foster fitness for military service:

Changes are necessary in regards to the demands of war, which have evolved in various ways due to the experiences and observations [in the colonies]. The demands of war shaped the specific goals of the training for which the physical exercises must aim.

The observations of the changes in the demands of combat cannot be limited to the national wars of the nineteenth century but must consider the global position of the German Empire to account for warfare with all peoples and eras, which can give us important points of reference for other regions and zones of the world.[112]

Despite the lack of a definitive social, cultural, or pathological definition of fitness for tropical climates, many scholars reached a clear fundamental conclusion: the military strength of the European troops was no longer defined in the colonial context by the number of troops deployed alone but also by their "pathological behavior" and the ability of the soldiers to adapt to the varied geographic, climatic, and sanitary surroundings of their station. The criteria of military fitness known in Europe proved not to be universal but was shown to be specific to the European realm.

The dynamic evolution of the concepts of fitness for tropical climates from biological to cultural explanations did not mean that racial stereotypes and paradigms of study were called into doubt.[113] The colonial dichotomization of the world and implicit racism remained an integral part of the atmosphere in which debates over fitness for tropical climates was waged, in the German Empire as well as in other European countries. The attempt to express this specific colonial racism[114] in clear biological categories failed, however. Instead of casting doubts on its existence, this only led to a scientific overdetermination of the understandings of difference. Culturalist arguments reinforced the biologistic ones on those points for which the latter were not convincing enough on their own.

The many faults in the scientific argumentation were not discussed further but were rather accepted as established knowledge of differences despite the internal heterogeneity of the arguments. This system of knowledge imposed a set order on diverse bodies of knowledge, most of which had been compiled by military doctors. Out of the statistical material—as deficient as it was—a "knowledge narrative" had emerged to which statisticians, military doctors, and the military in general did not necessarily have access. Such a knowledge system was not limited only to the perception of differences of gender, culture, biological disposition, or social background, however. New anthropological frames were increasingly important to understanding the correlation between debates over fitness and racial explanations.

6 Beyond the Army: Biologistic Frameworks of Interpretation

The military situation of colonization led contemporaries to differentiate between European and "colonial" populations based on European concepts of physical fitness. In this context, an especially obvious dichotomy evolved between new racial perceptions emerging in European societies and conceptions of cultural and biological otherness in the colonies.[1] This was the case both in regard to the fitness of European soldiers for service in the colonies and in the "appraisal" of potential soldiers from the colonies for service in Europe.[2] To this end, the high command of the German imperial colonial troops conducted experiments to determine the fitness of various African peoples in 1894. Eighty-nine Sudanese soldiers were stationed in Cameroon with the aim of comparing their fitness for service with that of the West-African "natives": "It could and should be only an experiment, for in both our own and in the English colonies there is insufficient experience to predict whether the Sudanese soldiers who have proven successful in East Africa are just as effective in West Africa."[3] The experiment, however, was prematurely ended; after only a short period, it became clear that the Sudanese soldiers suffered similar or even higher rates of morbidity and mortality compared to their German counterparts. The high command concluded that soldiers from Sierra Leone or Lagos—with their "quick-footedness" and lower morbidity rate—were by far preferable for deployment in Cameroon.[4] By the turn of the century, the term and concept of fitness had become an integral part of the established canon for the tendentious description of racial and anthropological differences.

Historians have argued forcefully that these intertwined cultural ideologies and scientific theories were essential elements of a worldview that favored colonial expansion and the subordination of foreign parts of the world as European colonies.[5] While there is certainly some truth to this claim, it must be noted that the vital role of the sciences in colonialism was not more than a rhetorical claim if this is understood as social and statistical knowledge about the respective populations. Indeed, a general lack of knowledge seemed to be much more characteristic than a merely functional understanding of "colonial science." In the colonies, scientists not only created new knowledge but also circulated their findings easily across imperial borders, returning to their cosmopolitan scientific institutions with a wealth of new experiences. These experiences in turn sparked changes in their academic identity and changed the foundations for the interpretations of their scientific findings. It is generally accepted that colonialism had a deep epistemic influence on the natural sciences, but less consideration has been given to the fact that this is also true for social statistics and the construction of their categories. Racial categories and phenotypology, however, were produced in and by the colonial situation, and such a correlation is more evident in the development of the field of military statistics and demography than in practically any other of these fields.

The history of these European constructions of difference reaches far into the twentieth century; for the era during and after World War I, especially, it can be seen as reciprocal with the colonies abroad.[6] Of the 485,000 colonial soldiers France deployed between 1914 and 1918, 134,004 were drawn, and often openly coerced into service, from the colonies in the tropics of West Africa.[7] With the increasing military successes of the other nations, these deployments—which were initially somewhat condescendingly seen in Germany as a "show of the nations"—eventually began undermining Europeans' anthropological self-perception and felled the popular expectation of Europeans' absolute physical superiority. German intellectuals at first painted culturally charged pictures of the prewar era to denounce the "wild Africans" as incapable of waging a civilized war,[8] but members of the military leadership, and at least some of the German public, soon recognized that this had little basis in reality. Instead of resorting to loaded stereotypes, efforts were made to develop a biologistic, racial description of the otherness of the soldiers recruited from the colonies.[9] In individual cases, the war even offered possibilities for testing new racial research methods on enemy soldiers from the colonies—for example, by conducting studies of anthropometric statistics with measurements collected in prisoner-of-war camps.[10] Basically speaking, however, the state of anthropological knowledge on the colonial populations was too rudimentary in the period leading up to and during World War I to see it as making a general dichotomy between a "white" and a "black" race. To the extent that medical personnel and anthropologists in the colonies were able to distinguish differences, they often lacked the means to describe or record these adequately.[11] Despite—or perhaps due to—this lack of knowledge and appropriate scientific methods, these firsthand experiences of differences coalesced into the racially charged stereotypes of colonialism.

This chapter addresses the interplay between Europeans' new biologistic conceptions of their own nations and the statistical research conducted within the military. In addition to positioning this question within the more general history of knowledge, it addresses concrete cases and examines the fragility of their scientific practices.

Inherited Pathologies: The Representation of Social Anxieties and Conscription Statistics

In the colonial regions, there were only limited, vague statistics available, if any at all, for the demographics of various groups within the population. At the same time, scientists increasingly aspired to develop anthropometric definitions of European ethnic groups with corresponding advances in the instruments for their research and their systems of classification. Most European nations moved in the mid-nineteenth century to more comprehensively and methodically collect statistical information and use the methods of "social physics" to study even the most intimate spheres of life in detail. Given the increasingly dense network of available information, many scholars expected that the biological and racial origins of the population could be definitively determined, just as Adolphe Quetelet had suggested in 1870 in his *Anthropométrie*.[12]

For these purposes, too, scientists were quite eager to avail themselves of the statistics collected in the military and in the conscription examinations. It was German doctor and public health official Rudolf Virchow who advocated an anthropometric report on the potential recruits at the International Congress of Statistics in 1863. He saw this as the only possibility, aside from measuring school children, to systematically compile statistics on the corporal measurements of the populace, even if this method was necessarily limited to the male population. While Virchow himself worked to compile measurements of school children,[13] as did colleagues in other European nations in the following years,[14] the Prussian Ministry of War rejected the systematic anthropometric measurement of potential soldiers. From their perspective, the collection of more detailed information in categories like circumference of the head, hair and eye color, and so on, was too expensive. School children as a group thus soon held an important place in the discussion of new scientific approaches to supposed biological differences, while the potential anthropometric contribution of the conscription examinations to the field of anthropology went largely unrealized.[15]

The racial assessment of the conscription statistics was at first colored by other patterns of argumentation. Given the deficiency or absolute lack of information on the physical stature of the potential recruits, arguments were more frequently based on statistics related to illness or discharge from the military.[16] For a long time, race was a vaguely defined category frequently used in an attempt to explain anomalies in the statistics, like a higher frequency of certain illnesses or "degenerative" characteristics.

The rampant fears of degeneration in the latter half of the nineteenth century, which transcended national borders and social classes, were directly correlated to the antagonisms within the modernizing industrial society. Processes of social upheaval generated social uncertainties and often led to a search for cultural references.[17] In light of pathological discussions, changing lifestyles became "explicable," as can be seen in the plethora of new "civilized diseases" like neurasthenia and drug and alcohol abuse.[18] Although the eroding social structures and the resulting threats to the individual and "collective" body were at first dismissed as the geographically distant phenomena of English industrialization or "modern" America,[19] Western Europeans in the late nineteenth century became increasingly conscious of this "threat" as well.[20] Proletarianization and pathological degeneration were seen as two intertwined processes within the wider social evolution.[21]

In cases in which large segments of the populace were affected by certain syndromes, many representatives of militarized nationalism perceived a threat to the national military strength. Here, too, German scholars saw the extensive statistical studies on Great Britain[22] as a cautionary commentary on how the deficiencies of modern living and working conditions negatively influenced the "racial fitness" and military fitness of potential recruits.[23] This was no longer a discussion concerning fitness at an individual level, but rather a discussion about the fitness of the group at the collective level, generalized to include entire segments of the populace. Such social angst culminated in the morally charged issue of sexually transmitted diseases, in which the realities of modern society collided with the traditional conservative norms of the elite. Conscription statistics were an ideal body of information for studying such diseases because they were collected from young men in a seemingly critical age group.[24]

One of the conflicts visible quite early within the debates on degeneration centered on the competing concepts of heredity; in the late nineteenth and early twentieth centuries, debates were still raging over biological models of heredity, both within popular discourse and scientific circles.[25] Biological and cultural arguments and definitions of race not only often coincided but were, in fact, often mutually dependent on each other.[26] Although science had made significant progress in understanding human heredity since the 1880s with the contributions of Charles Darwin and Francis Galton and the field of cell research,[27] this did not mean that the concept had found acceptance as a homogenous or general explanation. Instead, the popular expectations of heredity were characterized by the coexistence of recent theories and the more or less traditional concepts formulated by Jean-Baptiste Lamarck; both of these shaped the discourse on heredity. This was even more the case when the topic was not individual but instead supposed social or collective processes of heredity. The discourse over social degeneration rested upon a cultural thought framework that was, strictly speaking, no longer in accordance with the contemporary state of biological research. These eclectic references to various scientific schools can perhaps explain the growing social relevance of research on heredity, which was reflected in the social ambitions of the supporting classes.[28] They were prepared with a variety of answers and, depending on the problem at hand, to argue for the significance of environmental or genetic factors. The laws of Mendelian inheritance only gradually found acceptance. Not until the introduction of appropriate visual discourse and new media—for example, at the International Hygiene Exhibition in Dresden in 1911—did a more nuanced understanding of genetic heredity develop beyond specialist circles.[29]

The question of visual evidence had long been important in theories of heredity. Biological processes that were complicated and difficult to explain in lay terms became even more abstract and incomprehensible the more scientists framed their hypotheses at the collective level of social evolution rather than outlining how they concerned individuals. Such biologistic extrapolations owed their very existence and persuasive power to the range of forms of expression within visual discourse.[30] This was also why the compilation of adequate statistical material was crucial. Tracking and portraying such social evolution necessitated a quantitatively significant test group. In his influential book on the causes of "urban degeneration," published in 1889, Georg Hansen attempted to use demographic statistics on urban migrations and differences in the rates of mortality and morbidity within cities to demonstrate the negative influence of urban life on the collective populace. He envisioned this study as a sort of indicator similar to the dye tracing used to determine the sources of rivers; with its help, he expected to be able to track migrations within the population and signs of

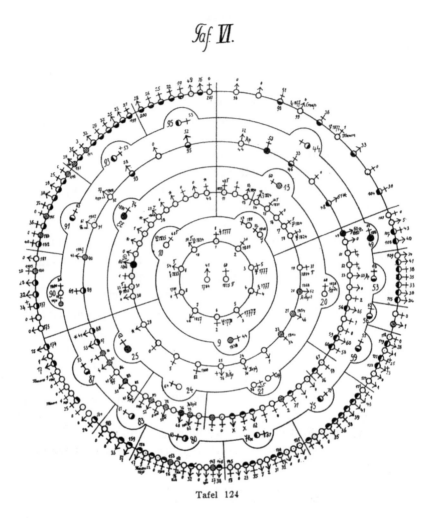

Figure 6.1
Hereditary tuberculosis, as shown in a table from the Dresden exhibition on public hygiene in 1911

this degeneration throughout time and space. Like a red and black river, one could differentiate between the various types of people who settled in the cities in the process of urbanization. After a time, the degenerative effects could then also be seen in and calculated from the anthropometric measurements.[31] Although Hansen himself used this metaphor more as a literary device, other scholars increasingly devised graphic representations. The dynamic diagrams that resulted referred to an implicitly regressive movement; the larger the number of individuals in the study, the more it seemed to provide evidence of these movements. The diagrams in question had to be straightforward and readily understandable, especially in regard to the degeneration hypothesis, as can be seen in the portrayal of the city of Mannheim's demographic development at the hygiene exhibition in Dresden.

The most significant compilation of information that provided the basis for these graphics for the Dresden exhibition was the conscription examinations—and especially Heinrich Schwiening's recently published study of candidates for a voluntary year of service. They shared a common hypothesis of a variance in military strength between urban and rural areas and served as empirical evidence to explain the topos of degeneration.[32] The supposedly neutral statistical study of the military doctor thus provided the

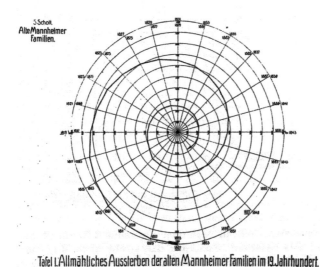

Tafel I. Allmähliches Aussterben der alten Mannheimer Familien im 19. Jahrhundert.

Tafel 161

Figure 6.2
"The dying out of the old Mannheim families," Mannheim, 1911

foundation for the much broader scientific context of the biological evolution of the society. Conscription statistics thereby began to develop into an initially descriptive but also implicitly highly normative instrument for the analysis of the society, which seemed to depict biological dispositions and the future fate of entire segments of the population.

Anthropometrics: Different Measurements of the Recruits

The correlation between degeneration and the urban population in Mannheim was, in the end, no less surprising than the fact that Mannheim had been chosen as an example of the degeneration itself. Within the German Empire, one scientist had dominated the debate over biological evidence of the decline of the species: the anthropologist and journalist Otto Ammon. Around 1890, Ammon had responded to Hansen's call and begun analyzing the varying social groups and their degenerative tendencies in urban contexts. In the interest of backing up his claims, Ammon sought to reach a critical statistical mass by using measuring tapes and calipers to develop a number of data sets.

Assisted by Dr. Ludwig Wilser, Ammon answered the call of the Anthropological Commission in Karlsruhe in 1886 to study the anthropological characteristics of the population. The commission no doubt sought thereby to replicate a recent trend of studies, based on Virchow's complex study designs.[33] However, Ammon convinced the commission to accept a slightly more simplistic set.[34] He emphasized a combination of body height and craniometrical measures more than eye color and skin pigment, which were the characteristics Virchow considered important. From the very beginning, Ammon interpreted anthropometric data as a reflection of distinct races. Although he tried to pay Virchow his respect and took up some of the established paradigms,[35] Ammon's primary interest was in proving his racist hypotheses: first, that the territory under investigation was inhabited mainly by two separate races ("doliocephalic and brachycephalic"); and second, that the process of industrialization and urbanization led to an unavoidable decline in the population—and especially in the brachycephalic population, which was unable to cope with the stress of new urban environments. He later broke down his radical conclusions based on this simplified model:

Those young people who migrate to the cities from rural areas whose heads are more than 18.5 cm long and less than 15.3 cm wide can take pleasure in the high probability that their family will prevail in the city for two generations; those, however, whose heads are shorter and wider than the limits specified will, in all probability, disappear after the first generation. In order to assure the survival of his descendants through three generations, one must possess a head at least 18.6–18.7 cm long and not wider than 15.1–15.3 cm. In such a case, the probability of success is high; in the other case it is smaller than that of the opposite outcome. Whoever wishes to have as many generations of descendants as possible must remain on his native soil, and his descendants must do so, as well.[36]

The assumption that the impoverishment of certain segments of urban populations was fundamentally epigenetic was in no way specific to Germany; there were countless parallels in the discourse of other European countries. In England, for example, the low rate of fitness for service among members of the emerging hooligan scene seemed to confirm the fears of biological degeneration; this fear was closely related to the apprehension of increasing criminal activity within the society.[37] In the United States, even before the turn of the century, anthropologists were already considering anthropometric or physiognomic techniques—like those Alphonse Bertillon had supposedly used—as a method of social selection to avoid recruiting the "dishonorable."[38]

In a radical and drastically simplified form, this meant that anthropologists questioned a "horizontal" concept of social class and suggested replacing it with a "vertical" or biologically determined, racial explanation of the differences in fitness levels.[39] The process of national selection had been interrupted by the intervention of the modern welfare state; as a result, the "bad" segments of the population were theoretically continually growing, according to this argument.[40] Due to such fears, the question of race also became a question of whether it was necessary in a modern society for the authorities to intervene to compensate for the lack of biological mechanisms of selection.[41] Ammon himself attempted, within the framework of his understanding of political economy, to find a correlation between racial classification and the individual patterns of choice that had been developed by Vilfredo Pareto and other renowned economists in Italy and France.[42] He aimed to interpret urban degeneration as the aggregate of rational, individual reproductive decisions.

The wider repercussions and assumptions that Ammon reached based on his measuring practices warrant a closer look at the way he constructed his evidence. With the support of the Anthropological Commission, Ammon and Wilser followed the recruiting commissions over several years, but instead of relying on the statistical material collected by military physicians, they were allowed to examine the young recruits separately after the official examinations. Ammon measured not only the body height of the young men standing and sitting, but also the length of their legs. However,

Ammon was most interested in the skull measurements—that is, the circumference of the head and the distance between forehead and chin. These measures, in Ammon's eyes, were the only reliable anthropometric data, as their proportions were constant over time and especially during puberty. The measurement of the skull size on which he relied was not an arbitrary choice, but incorporated the modern techniques of craniology, which had been developed within the fields of anthropology and archeology since the 1860s—though initially on the basis of only a few individual cases.[43]

On the other hand, Ammon's rich personal papers and correspondence shed light on his own practices and reveal a series of open questions, mostly with regard to the instruments he used. The caliper used not only differed in its quality from one place to another, but also had to be used in the same way and to be fixed at exactly the same spot on each recruit's face.[44]

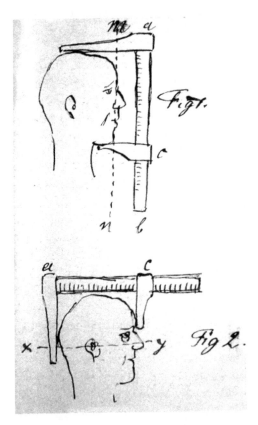

Figure 6.3
Ammon's caliper, taken from a letter to René Collignon, March 11, 1892

The body measurements, especially the length of the legs, also seemed to raise a series of different issues for scientists with regard to taking the measurements at the correct place. This led to exchanges with fellow anthropologists about their best practices. As a result of these challenges, Ammon and Wilser concluded that whereas it was the military physician's task to quickly separate the fit from the unfit,[45] it was important for their work that they develop the ability to recognize each recruit's racial profile immediately.[46]

Phenotyping across Nations

By the turn of the century, there was already a precedent for racial paradigms. Long before they had been the subject of research based on the conscription statistics, they had been an established topic of scientific discourse.[47] The parallel emergence of biologistic thought patterns and the rise of nation-states across Europe led to a process in which both concepts gained meaning and evidence from one another.[48] Some European nations integrated racial and biological narratives into their national identities from rather early on, as was the case for the alpine nations and especially for Switzerland: natural scientists of the early modern era had been struck by the unique biological and cultural traits of those native to mountainous regions within Europe.[49] Under the Enlightenment thought of Jean Jacques Rousseau, this early modern concept of *homo alpinus* developed into an idealized example of human development under the condition of natural freedom. At the same time, it should be noted that many of the anthropometric research projects, especially in Switzerland, did not necessarily follow a nationalist paradigm or ascribe to popular stereotypes of national races.[50]

In the second half of the nineteenth century, anthropological methods and researches led to a quite homogenous schema of racial subdivisions across the entire European continent. Of especial note were the French race scholar Georges Vacher de Lapouge, who outlined three main races within the peoples of Europe between the Mediterranean and the Arctic Circle: *homo mediterraneus, homo alpinus,* and *homo europaeus.* They attributed a variety of physiological, anthropometric, and physiognomic characteristics to these respective groups.[51] This meant that, in addition to the research on degeneration, there was a parallel normative understanding of racial classification within Europe.[52] Reflecting on the *homo alpinus* now was more than a mere quest for a prehistoric human who might have survived in the Alps and fed romantic ideas in the European enlightenment. Instead, in the view of some scholars, it was a question of biological realities that could determine the fate of nations.[53] The idea that ethnic maps of Europe could be drawn using not only cultural[54] but also biological "data" appealed to many anthropologists.

However, the success of scientific racism based on anthropometric methods depended upon more than the general appeal of maps, clear-cut racial boundaries, and a general taste for bipolarisms, widespread among European scholars at this time. The history of anthropometric methods is not particularly linear, and the early research practices rooted in methods of archeology and prehistory were in crisis in the 1880s.[55] Discovering the anthropometric potential of the serial conscription data was a pivotal factor in the revitalization of this strand of scientific racism.

In addition, the attempts at phenotyping European populations was unthinkable without transnational communities of scientists who eagerly accepted their colleagues' findings. The aforementioned Otto Ammon was one of the nodes of this story—and particularly interesting, as he engaged in bringing together anthropologists from throughout Europe who shared an interest in measuring young recruits.[56] Ammon's most important correspondent in this respect was the French military physician René Collignon. Born close to the German border,[57] Collignon deepened his anthropological interests and tested anthropometric measuring on the local populations while stationed with the French army in Tunisia.[58] After he returned to the French metropole, Collignon applied these experiences to his methods of measuring the recruits; in addition to the standard conscription examinations that he conducted at the *conseils de revision*, Collignon collected further anthropometric data meant to confirm the existence of two distinct races living in France.[59]

In the midst of these studies, Collignon received a letter from Ammon proposing an exchange of anthropometric measurements. The resulting correspondence and scholarly exchange between the two lasted approximately five years and was quite intense at times. Not only did it provide them with a larger collective body of data for their respective studies and developing their methods, but even more importantly it fostered discussion of their baseline assumptions: both Ammon and Collignon assumed that they had come across traces of a distinct, racially inferior population supplanted by a superior race. Hilly regions, relatively difficult to access, seemed to offer the only observatory for the original racial groups.[60] Conscription was the first time this population had been approached in any official, systematic way and thus presented a perfect opportunity for closer study.

Ammon and others repeatedly failed to find empirically sound evidence to back up their theories, and the exchange of ideas with his colleagues across borders was important to convince him that his theories were scientifically exact. Ammon's list of correspondents includes the scientists Ridolfo Livi, Georges Vacher-Lapouge, Francis Galton, and William Ripley, an American colleague. The correspondence with Ripley is particularly revealing: Ripley compiled evidence from many scholars across Europe in a monograph that was no longer intended to present open questions to the anthropologic community but rather to define the "races of Europe."[61] For this publication, Ripley asked his correspondents to send him representative examples of their findings. When Ripley asked Ammon for a photograph of the brachycephalic population typical of the Black Forest, Ammon had to admit that he did not possess one. Indeed, even after extensive consultation with several military commanders, Ammon was unable to supply a suitable photograph.[62] However, this picture was so essential for Ripley's argument that Ammon ended up sending a photograph of a recruit who was not from the Black Forest. Likewise, the picture's counterpart for the doliocephalic type did not come from Baden itself but from the barracks in the city of Mainz in the province of Palatinate.[63]

It is important to note that none of the agents involved in this network, with the exception of Ridolfo Livi, were established academic scholars but rather military employees or independent researchers. They fought for academic recognition and the attention of their fellow anthropologists at the universities. As a result, the transnational exchange was all the more important for them as an avenue to gain access to a wider audience for their idea of a racial mapping of Europe.

Despite having been initially marginalized in academic discourse, the racial paradigm was well-established by the turn of the twentieth century. Many contemporaries, however, still refused to adopt Ammon and his colleagues' deterministic view of hereditary patterns, instead calling for new, more comprehensive, long-term, and large-scale studies.[64] The interest in such a procedure was initially widespread and even transcended differences in scholars' political positions: both forerunners of national conservative thought, most prominently those in the school of the eugenicist Alfred Ploetz, and liberals like Lujo Brentano favored a systematic study of racial origins.[65] Brentano suggested that such "exacting assessments of this nature" were much easier to pursue in Germany than in England because "the governmental agencies in Germany have access to the population during the vaccination process, in the schools, and, later, when they perform their compulsory military service. It requires thus only an organization for the compilation and development of these studies to produce definite, clear results concerning the physical value of individuals."[66]

Following the precedent set by Virchow, many statisticians did not couple their anthropological interests with political or ideological viewpoints. Up until the turn of the century, the discourse on the biology of race was associated neither with the "nation" as a point of reference nor with a selective program of eugenics.[67] Virchow's large serial studies aimed to portray a plurality of races on the European continent without positioning these within a hierarchy. Anthropological research around 1900 explicitly adopted this goal as well, but in the period between Virchow's research proposals and publications in the 1860s and 1870s and the turn of the century, important factors had changed. These changes were not entirely, but nevertheless largely, related to the emergence of the recruit as an object of anthropological study. Brentano's statements in 1897 already suggest the extent to which the racial research had become linked to questions of the "value of a person" for the collective military strength and, at the same time, how the nation became the predominant frame of reference, a frame defined by exclusively masculine parameters. This was true despite the fact that many scholars continued to explicitly argue against the connection between the discourses on race and nation.[68]

However, the nation and scientific racism were linked in many different ways: national ambitions and competition between national scientific communities driven by institutional agendas played an increasing role in the construction of biologistic evidence.[69] This often meant that researchers observed their colleagues in other countries and jealously tried to replicate their results in order to glorify their own national sciences. Borderlands, and especially the newly defined Franco-German border, played an important and "productive" role in this respect.[70]

The extent to which political developments and anthropological statistical research were intertwined is most evident in the anthropological classification of Alsace-Lorraine. With the founding of the Kaiser-Wilhelm-Universität in Strassbourg in 1871, anthropological research was established as a prominent discipline.[71] In 1872, Wilhelm Waldeyer, one of the most important German anthropologists, assumed the professorship for anatomy. When Waldeyer moved to the Friedrich-Wilhelms-Universität in Berlin, he was succeeded in Strasbourg by Gustav Albert Schwalbe. Both scholars, together with their students, were especially interested in the question of how to classify Alsace in anthropological terms—more specifically, whether the political inclusion of the region in the German Empire could be biologically justified. It was Schwalbe, in fact, who produced large-scale anthropometric studies on this topic and published a series on the anthropology of Alsace-Lorraine. One of his students, Gustav Adolf Brandt, addressed the topic of the "height of those liable for compulsory service in the Reichsland of Alsace-Lorraine."[72] His results seemed quite definitive: he found a reduction in height the nearer one came to the French border. Brandt created visual material illustrating his conclusions, which included a map showing the distribution of the tallest potential soldiers. The color variation between a rich green and pale pink stressed the statistically legitimate delineation of the border. The saturated colors became paler as one approached the border, suggesting a reduction in vitality. The map with the sum average heights, however, reveals the fragility of these clearly defined differences: the difference between the various military cantons was one to two centimeters at the most.

These attempts to develop an anthropological typology were mirrored in scholarship on the other side of the border. In France, the formulation of such classifications had a long tradition. In addition to the aforementioned Gustave Lagneau and René Collignon,[73] other scholars began reacting to German anthropological studies. Georges Hervé investigated body height in the Alsace and tried to disprove Brandt's theses.[74]

Statisticians and anthropologists across Europe accepted the "racial realities" described by their foreign colleagues[75] even though the theory of racial distribution on the European continent was never scientifically proven. For example, the chairman of the Anthropological Institute of Great Britain, John Beddoe, spoke of a "general confirmation of long-standing assumptions."[76] This hodgepodge of speculative confirmation of nearly transcendental presuppositions was quite characteristic of the "data-based" research on scientific racial categorization.

It was Italian studies, however, rather than those of France, that were widely adopted as a reference point for many anthropometric surveys. Impressed by the anthropological studies conducted during the American Civil War, which were limited more or less to a pathological classification,[77] the Italian Ministry of War followed the advice of the military doctor Guida in 1879[78] and began a comprehensive study of potential conscripts. Starting with the cohort born in 1859 and drafted in 1880, and for the next five years, a *foglio di sanità* recorded eye and hair color, nose shape, hair type (curly or straight), and circumference of the head according to two measurements, in addition to the established standards of height, weight, and chest circumference; the measurements were repeated after the first three months of service and recorded on the same form. After a soldier was discharged, this record was sent to Rome. By 1885, 299,355 soldiers had been thus appraised, and Ridolfo Livi, an Italian military doctor, along with a large number of assistants, was assigned the task of analyzing the statistics.[79] In 1896 and 1905, respectively, after years of number crunching, they released two volumes of an atlas containing these statistics, the *Antropometria militare*, a work that catapulted Livi into prominence as one of Europe's most influential anthropometrists.[80] Livi did not limit his analysis to simply depicting how these physical traits were distributed throughout the Italian kingdom, but devised formulas for correlating these characteristics to each other and drew maps illustrating these correlations, which included height/hair color, hair color/skull circumference, eye color/hair color, and others.

Originally, Livi had planned to extend his analysis to include statistics on social and geographic factors. In the end, however, the effort involved proved too extensive and he capitulated to the methodological difficulties, limiting himself to a few statements on the difference of height between students who had been drafted and the general populace.[81]

The anthropological studies around the turn of the century in the individual European states thus did not develop independently of each other. Scientists like Livi were members of multiple national anthropological societies. In formulating his research questions and methods, Livi drew directly on the examples set by his colleagues, Virchow and Kollmann. He corresponded with all the important European scholars of race and actively influenced the conception of new anthropological research within the military.

Such international influences were especially influential in the case of the German Anthropological Society, which, in 1903, recommended the project of measuring potential conscripts, a project their recently deceased cofounder Rudolf Virchow had formulated four years earlier. The measurements of pupils according to Virchow's methods had become increasingly problematic for technical and methodological reasons.[82] In November 1903, the new officers—Gustav Schwalbe, Eugen Fischer, and Wilhelm Waldeyer—approached the Ministry of War with a related petition. The text of the application reveals the primary motivations of the society:

Whereas there are sweeping studies for Sweden, France, and Italy—indeed, even for Spain—northern and central Germany [are] relatively unknown in anthropological terms.

Because knowledge of the physical constitution of the residents of the German Empire is not only of particular anthropological interest but also makes a valuable contribution to appraising many questions of social and intellectual life, it could be

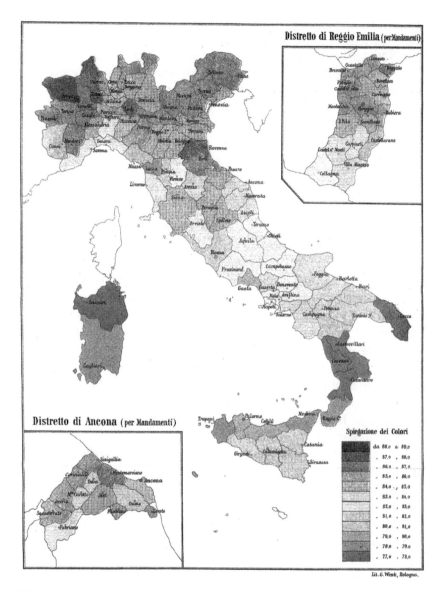

Figure 6.4
Map from Ridolfo Livi, *Antropometria militare*, 1896

considered to be in the interest of the state to support the efforts to compile information concerning the physical constitution.

It will likely prove difficult in the near future to conduct a general survey of
important anthropological characteristics (height, head shape, hair and eye color) as
part of the census. The only alternative, in order to collect as many observations as
possible, thus temporarily remains to consider those eligible for the draft and to record their anthropological characteristics on the occasion of their appearance before
the conscription commission.[83]

The necessity of intensifying efforts in the area of anthropological
research was evident for the Anthropological Society in the comparison to
other countries that were actively pursuing such projects. German anthropologists were concerned that they would miss the opportunity to develop
the "racial" classification of their native population before scholars in other
countries had already done so.

Examining the records of the relevant international conventions reveals
the extent of this imbalance: at the twelfth International Congress of
Medicine in Moscow, for example, there was a meeting of the section for
anatomy and anthropology. While the German representatives were basically limited to making some anatomical claims, representatives of other
countries, especially the Norwegian military doctor Carl Arbo, were able to
present significant statistical compilations. Arbo had been measuring the
circumference of potential recruits' heads for twenty years and now outlined the topographical distribution of these statistics across Norway and
in relation to height. It is telling that Arbo referred to Ammon again and
again in his research.[84]

Apparently, those responsible for such projects in the German Ministry
of War were so aware of the urgency of a similar German anthropometric
project that they sent the request directly to Imperial Chancellor Bülow.
The undersecretary of state, Arthur von Posadowsky-Wehner, was mostly
responsible for dealing with it. He had also been responsible for raising the
toll on grain imports and thus had strengthened the position of the agricultural lobby in the debate over the transformation of the German Empire
into an industrial state;[85] he had thus already been a key player years earlier
in the conflict between Sering and Brentano. In direct conversations with
the three representatives of the anthropological society—especially with
the president, Waldeyer, who had worked for some years as the rector of
the university in Berlin—Posadowsky-Wehner asked the society to develop
a practical concept for the realization of such a statistical survey. In March
of 1904, the society answered by outlining a plan suggesting that measurements be made in a procedure parallel to the conscription examinations in

a separate room or area partitioned off for this purpose. The anthropometric examination was not to be the task of the official administrative or military representative responsible for the conscription examination; instead,
"doctors were preferably to be trained to make these observations, followed
by teachers with a scientific background; only as a last resort can private
individuals be considered." The results, which were to be processed by the
Swiss ethnologist Rudolf Martin,[86] were noted on cards that included space
to record

aside from the name, age, and birth place of the eligible candidate, the following
details ...:

Anthropological: color of the skin, hair, and eyes: shape of the face and the nose;
form and volume of the cranium; height; physical proportions.

Sociological: religion; native language; occupation; wage bracket; degree of fitness
for military service; parents' birth places and occupations.[87]

They noted that the intended aim was not only to define geographically
"both races (the Nordic and the Alpine)" of which the population of the
German Empire is composed, where these could be "localized neither by
linguistic or dialectic boundaries nor along political borders."[88] In addition,
it was hoped that the results would shed additional light on more exact
factors in the determination of fitness for military service—in other words,
on the question of whether culture, the "physical environment," or biological disposition was the deciding factor in determining the abilities of male
soldiers. The final concept was signed not only by Waldeyer, Fischer, and
Schwalbe, but also by the ethnologist Felix von Lauschan from Berlin and
by Rudolf Martin himself from Zurich.

The society had even loftier goals, however: not only was the list of the
physical characteristics to be recorded expanded considerably in the internal negotiations—for example, to include the distance from the "tip of the
middle finger to the floor"—but the society also considered linking the conscription examination to the completion of potential recruits' schooling so
that those who were generally released from the requirement to appear
before the conscription commissions would be included and the survey
would thus yield a more comprehensive body of information on the populace at large.[89] Only the question of biological sex remained untouched, as
the anthropological measurement would continue to be limited to men.
Schwalbe, the president of the society, also proposed that a set catalog
of questions should be created that could later be used in other countries as well. Contacts were established for this purpose between professional anthropological associations in Austria, Hungary, Belgium, England,

Denmark, Norway, and Ireland. In March 1904, the Austrian scholar Carl Toldt invited representatives to Vienna to develop an international form for recording anthropometric measurements. The German representatives were the very same men who had just approached the imperial ministry, and, with their project, they were prominent participants in the meeting.[90]

Despite the initial progress, however, the negotiations to institute an extra examination broke down in the end: Minister of War Einem once again proved reluctant to adopt the society's suggestions. His primary interest was in keeping the conscription process from becoming the subject of further scientific study. The costs involved with and difficulties of practical implementation during conscription examinations presented further difficulties. In other countries, the suggestion had already been made that it would make more sense to measure recruits who had already entered the military.[91] Starting in 1904, these proposals were realized in the reports "on the physical constitution of potential conscripts." The anthropometric information gathered in the conscription examinations was to be compiled in lists to be published every ten years starting in 1906.[92] With a certain sense of resignation, the German Anthropological Society sought to acquire the necessary resources and to keep their proposal on the list of political priorities. Waldeyer at least admitted that measuring the required "human material" to "come closer to a solution of this highly important question" would require "not insignificant resources."[93]

Anthropological research around 1900 was somewhat meandering between ill-defined anthropometric methods and unclear hypotheses. However, wars acted as a catalyst by catapulting anthropological questions into the center of nationalist public discourse. This had already been the case for the Franco-Prussian war of 1870, when the doyen of physical anthropology, Henri de Quatrefages, publicly interpreted this conflict as a "racial war" and suggested a biologistic explanation for the French defeat.[94] This was even more the case for the South African War, the Russian-Japanese War, and, of course, World War I.[95] While this study does not address post-1914 developments, it should be observed that the war context represented a certain vanishing point for defining the anthropometric methods applied. Once these nations were at war, more attention was given to the anthropologists' definitions of anthropological characteristics of the peoples waging war on one another and appraisals of the military fitness of foreign soldiers.[96] Still, many prominent anthropologists had reservations about defining nations in racial terms. A rather liberal anthropology that stressed individual psychological factors in the notion of race remained

present during the war years.[97] The German anthropologists' anthropometric measurement of prisoners of war—many of whom were natives of
the French and British colonies—redirected anthropological research away
from the question of European races into the question of a racial map of the
world and shaped the professional experiences and careers of anthropometric scientists in the decades that followed.[98]

Analyzing the Omissions

The combination of nationalist points of reference in the measurement
of potential recruits and transnational attempts to develop a workable
methodology for typology had surprising repercussions: common anti-
Semitic stereotypes generally played a subordinate role in the debates over
the anthropometry of the recruits. Liberal anthropologists around Virchow
were not the only ones who rejected a popular, simplistic racist model
based upon sentiments of racial superiority and anti-Semitism;[99] even
anthropometric scholars who were much more radical in their conclusions
had difficulties integrating concepts of anti-Semitism into their scientific
thinking, as it did not really match the schematic idea of a racial map of
Europe. Only occasionally did scholars analyze their measurements along
confessional lines and thereby attempt to identify "specifically Jewish"
characteristics. The most prominent claim in this vein was Otto Ammon's
assertion in his *Anthropologie der Badener* (*Anthropology of Those from Baden*)
that the negative tendency of degeneration was exacerbated by the influence of the "Jewish race." Georg Nicolai, a physiology professor in Berlin,
on the other hand, pointed to his predecessor Martin Kirchner's studies
which claimed that one "need think less of a racial distinction [here]; it is
only ... that the Jews, due to their early physical and intellectual maturity,
are especially prone to near-sightedness to higher degrees of the same."[100]
Unlike Ammon, however, Nicolai and Kirchner assumed there was a social
explanation for this and rejected a clear racial or anti-Semitic definition.
Their reticence to adopt a populist and simultaneously highly political
anti-Semitism was in accordance with a certain tradition that had pervaded
German anthropology since Virchow's examinations of school children,
but was also common in foreign anthropological associations.[101] Virchow
had not wanted to include questions about a subject's confession on his
original questionnaire, but his colleagues in the anthropological society
convinced him to do so in 1873. Nevertheless, his study led him to reject
the idea of a biological Jewish race.[102] It was presumably the crumbling
relationship between racial classification and national frameworks that was

responsible: the definition of "national military strength" presupposed a homogenous populace. Additional differentiation of the approaches along social lines was counterproductive to the militarized themes of nationalist rhetoric.

Possibly the growing nationalization of an initially transnational knowledge discourse was one reason that the efforts to standardize methods and categories for anthropometric study leading up to World War I failed. These attempts did not end completely, however.[103] In 1912, a committee was formed under the leadership of the Oxford ethnologist and anthropologist Robert Marett, with the goal of formulating a standardized anthropometric questionnaire. The anthropologists hoped this questionnaire would—as had happened in the case of Italy—help effect a comprehensive statistical compilation on European recruits.[104] The same year, the First International Eugenics Congress met in London. On such occasions, it became clear how little of Virchow's liberal anthropology was left; instead, the field was now dominated by an openly racist hierarchy of peoples and nations.[105]

Although the transnational exchange of conscription statistics had been taken for granted—for the purposes of addressing both their significance for the welfare state and possible biological implications for the understanding of race—until shortly before the First World War, these statistics were increasingly placed under the shroud of military confidentiality as tensions grew. Regular statistical compilations like the German "Bericht zur Körperbeschaffenheit der Rekruten" (report on the physical constitution of the recruits) were still published, even during the war, but these publications served an entirely different purpose and made no pretense of conforming to international standards.[106] The question of potential recruits' biological "race" was similarly nationalized.

The body of information on military statistics thus became increasingly symbolic. The conscription statistics had contributed to establishing a racial map of the European continent, or at least to a fundamental differentiation of the population into clearly delineated races for the purposes of anchoring these in political discourse. At the same time, this racial framework for interpretation was not the only option or indeed even the predominant method for analyzing military statistics prior to World War I. It was the consequence of the pathological and endemic studies and their differentiation between national populations; it can be read as the result of the politicization of the military. It was by no means inevitable; many experts did not resort to such racial interpretations in their scholarship. The statistical material gathered in the armies by 1914 was used in the treatment of a plethora of questions on the evolving welfare state and social sensitivities. The topic of a scientifically quantifiable racism remained a register employed by various actors at various moments to highlight the significance of their own interests. This was true for liberal statisticians and economists like Brentano and Kuczynski as well; the racist arguments themselves were of little interest to them but were useful in underlining the importance of their social and economic arguments.

Racial classifications were thus neither the core nor the vanishing point of all academic discussion of conscription and military statistics. The combination of the specific power of the military topos and the nationalist, stylized "military strength" were one more element granting the combination of racist and military statistical studies a certain credibility in public discourse.

Conclusion

Science and the military: two segments of society that were intertwined prior to 1914. Historians have said that the military was a motor of knowledge transfer.[1] This study contributes more evidence in support of this idea. Above all, colonial situations can be understood as a particular transnational sphere—albeit deeply anchored in highly national politics. The scope of this book, however, was broader than depicting another transnational epistemic community. In many regards, it showed how the military—or rather, agents who were part of the military hierarchy—succeeded in establishing new fields of expertise. They made a case for the urgency of this expertise by suggesting that the assessment of the quantity *and* the quality of a military population would be crucial in the case of a conflict—an important point in this age of increasing European nationalism. Paradoxically, this encouraged a new form of cooperation across national borders, of mutual exchange, and methodological transfer, even as the competition between these nations that was a foundational element of these scientists' working environments was increasing.

This basic pattern of constructing new anthropologic evidence alone is very telling about the working mode of these new epistemics and how the rather precarious data derived from military recruiting could become the basis of new anthropologic 'certainties': in the history of science, "objectivity"—one of the foundational myths of modern society—has to be understood as embedded in respective socioeconomic and political discourses. Elements of the discourse on the "strength of the nation," "national military strength," or "racial disposition" of the soldiers seem disconcerting and hardly scientific from today's perspective. They seem to draw on a repertoire of dull stereotypes and national prejudices, chauvinistic defamation and racist self-glorification, which our contemporary age hardly regards as characteristics of modern scientific thought. Indeed, "military strength" or the "strength of the nation" were not scientific concepts per se, but rather should be understood as largely ideological generalizations. Despite the fact that there are no "objective truths" at the heart of these scientific practices, however, they reveal a lot about the place of knowledge in European societies around 1900. In a period when the integration and differentiation of these disciplines within the academic system was incipient, the definition of valid social knowledge could, at times, bypass the academic system. The army served not only as an important object of study but also as an institutional platform that enabled new research practices. This was especially true for the field of demographic knowledge, which, up until the turn of the century, was not yet an academic discipline. For this emerging field, the military offered a sort of laboratory to develop new insights. In return, many within the military leadership viewed demographic hypotheses as an instrument with which they could transpose their daily experiences within the military onto broader political and social contexts.

Focusing on the object of study itself rather than thinking in terms of academic disciplines when reflecting on scientific discourse and practice leads to a different understanding of the construction of scientific methods on the one hand and of the activities of the scientists involved and their understanding of their own roles on the other. In this regard, consideration of the military recruitment process, which brought together experts from various disciplines and institutional backgrounds, can contribute to the discussion on the construction of objectivity. In all the countries studied here, military physicians and statisticians were motivated by their social ambitions within the context of the increasing institutionalization of their fields of expertise over the course of the nineteenth century. They formed alliances among themselves that did not conform to fixed academic structures. This is especially clear in the tension between the transnational and national levels, which, rather than being mutually exclusive, benefited each other. It was only via the transnational circulation of knowledge that the new discourse over military statistics gained such significant persuasive power. Experts in numerous European countries produced studies in this field, which in turn resulted in increased attention and funding for their colleagues' projects in other countries—as is evident, for instance, in the emergence of the field of military statistics and anthropometric and eugenicist projects of the later nineteenth century.

The tension between the transnational methods of scholarship and the nationalization of knowledge cannot be so easily dismissed, however: as Pascal Grosse shows for the German Empire, it was not easy for the civil society of the empire to transpose the transnational biological interpretations into their narrow understanding of their own nation and its place in history.[2]

It was not only nationalism that left its mark on the statistical material: the composition and organization of the army in various European countries, the position of the military medical personnel, and the international network of these expert circles fundamentally influenced the function and scope of these military statistics, especially in regard to who was considered authorized to interpret them. From the very beginning, military statistics were closely related to reforms within the armed services and with the transformation of the mercenary army into a standing army based on the principle of general conscription. Around the middle of the nineteenth century, modern European armies relied on statisticians and the precision of their methods. Statistical offices were given responsibility for calculating the number of future soldiers, and the census was used for the compilation of conscription rolls—that is, lists of potential recruits.

It was no coincidence that parallel processes of institutionalization occurred in many European countries during this period: since the Napoleonic wars, nearly all European countries—or, more precisely, their respective military leadership—had looked to developments in the neighboring countries for inspiration. After the Franco-Prussian War in 1870, for example, the French military leadership closely observed developments in Germany. Similarly, in the military reforms of 1874 and the changes in military training around 1900, the Swiss military paid close attention to the situation in Prussia. This was even more the case for military medical personnel, who in many cases had completed their education at Prussian institutions like the Kaiser Wilhelms-Akademie für militärärztliches Bildungswesen. The military system in Germany—as in other European countries—was in turn modeled foremost on the French example. Although in many respects Great Britain pursued its own strategies, other European militaries did look to the British example in regard to the organization of colonial troops.

The strength of the international attention paid to the military statistics insured that they remained politically charged. This politicization of military numbers, however, was not always about the military itself: proponents of social reforms, for example, employed medical statistics collected within the armed forces in their argumentation. Military settings like the barracks became centers for the struggle to implement modern hygienic standards and the source of remarkably detailed statistical material. In France, this dimension seems to have been the most significant: fears of the newly unified German Empire led to the military's becoming a center of accelerated modernization. In regard to the comparison of relevant statistical material across national borders, however, both French and German authorities were noticeably reticent. It was the smaller countries that advocated a more intense exchange, whereas the larger European powers hesitated to cooperate by making such statistics public.

It was precisely this decidedly political dimension that sparked repeated conflicts between experts and members of their respective governments. In most European nations, military doctors vehemently opposed statistical analysis of the information by anyone other than themselves. These conflicts ended in some cases with mutual blockades, as has been shown for the example of Switzerland. This case confirms that, in the long term, the bureaus of statistics, with their greater proximity to state authorities, had more pull. Conflicts over statistical material resulted in part from the fact that the medical examination of recruits was highly dubious by scientific standards. Problems with the equipment used for the exams led to great discrepancies in the measurements collected. Regardless of the country or region, the materials used in the doctors' examination of potential recruits were often faulty and lacking. The results thus could not be interpreted in any meaningful way. Furthermore, soldiers were not passive objects of study: they became drunk prior to the examination, showed signs of nervosity, misinterpreted the instructions given to them, and faked or hid illnesses or handicaps to their own advantage. Doctors were occupied with limiting the damage of these factors. This social interaction meant that the conscription process was the setting for gaining knowledge and for the transformation of scientific discourse in everyday contexts. For many of these young men, the measurements taken by military doctors were the first medical examinations of their lives. These were thus moments in which their bodies were seen for the first time as quantifiable objects—and perhaps also the first instance in which they were confronted with the question of their own fitness and how they compared to a standardized physical norm.

Even if scientific objectivity during the conscription process remained an illusion, the various parties involved were clearly invested in their own evaluations and interpretations of the statistical material thus obtained. Especially in those scientific circles that were not directly related, "fitness for military service" was often treated as though it was a set scientific concept. Alternatives to this pathological concept of fitness for conscription were proposed by various social groups around the end of the nineteenth century. This was true for the various gymnastics and sports movements around the turn of the century, as well as for the new tests of achievement and education in schools, which developed parallel to the military medical exams of physical condition. Psychological and cultural concepts of fitness became increasingly important in the colonial debates, which shaped these concepts in turn.

In the last third of the nineteenth century, and even more so in the first decade of the twentieth century, biological and racial interpretations became more common in the social contexts in which conscription and military medical statistics were employed. The introduction of anthropometric methods of examination made it possible to create an ethnic map of Europe; the conscription statistics provided the first concrete numbers for such an endeavor. The subsequent failure of these efforts to create such a biologistic classification speaks volumes: the bodies of information that were thereby created quickly became so expansive that scientists were overwhelmed. In the cases of the Italian *foglii sanitari*, of Otto Ammon's and René Collignon's studies in Baden and France, and so many other cases, such collections of anthropometric data became a sort of "information cemetery" from which information could only be unearthed with great effort and in which meaningful analysis remained an only partially obtainable goal. It proved impossible to establish clear categories, and the comparison of the statistical material, given the absolute lack of consistency in the methods of collection and the quality of the information obtained, was an endless task worthy of Sisyphus. Nevertheless, the racial interpretation of these statistics became an established element of the demographic discourse of scholars on conscription. In the end, these biologistic racial hypotheses seemed credible even without unambiguous scholarship to back them.

This new level of anthropometric research on conscription, however, was just one variety of the scientific discourse on military statistics. It was the most radical and far-reaching of the interpretations, but other parallel interpretations persisted that fit into alternative knowledge systems. The probabilistic calculations of governmental institutions relied on the conscription statistics, as did the hygienic measures taken to benefit public health and welfare.

The outbreak of World War I in 1914 abruptly ended many of these scientific practices and statistical approaches. Some of the lines of discourse, however, remained surprisingly lively and shaped not only the understanding of the "soldier" but also the militarist dimensions of the concept of "population" in lasting ways, which helped to transform these into new forms of common knowledge.

In modern South America, the judgment "No te da el piné" is spoken when a person is pronounced to be fundamentally incapable of a task. The word *piné*, however, is not originally Spanish; it is, instead, derived from the name of Maurice Pignet, who proposed the fitness index for conscription examinations in France in 1901 based on height, weight, and chest circumference. His methods of calculating fitness were soon adopted in South America, where the army used his index a criterion for conscription. A large segment of the male population was appraised using this method, so it is no surprise that the *piné* became established as a thought category.

Even beyond the limits of this etymological archeology, however, the impact of these debates prior to World War I is evident. In the postwar period, the separation of "humanities" from the "natural sciences" was completed. Virchow's methods, which had drawn on physical anthropology and incorporated findings of primitive and early history and ethnology, were replaced by more clearly defined disciplines. The seeming abundance of statistical sequences combined with the recent paradigms of biological heredity became a standard pattern of argumentation which increasingly neglected historical accuracy.[3] The anthropometric measurements of the potential recruits, which stretched back fifty years, now developed into a new field of research in countries like Switzerland, which initially had been somewhat reticent in this respect.[4] The final step in making the concept of "national military strength" more credible was the proliferation of the racial paradigm under the National Socialists.[5] Even if this had become engrained within demographic scholarship, however, World War I destroyed any optimistic faith of scientists that they could extrapolate military statistics to systematically analyze the populace at large. In effect, the tide had turned: after 1914, demographers felt it was their task to explain the military capabilities of these societies. The earlier expectation that social problems could be analyzed and addressed using the military's statistical material was increasingly regarded as an illusion.

The end of the war and rise of National Socialism relegated the conversation over the militarist demography of European countries to history. Along with large subfields of demographic research, it had become a dead-end street of statistical study. The military and the populace—this alliance of a state-sanctioned institution and a scientific concept—is much less obvious than it was one hundred years ago. Both elements seem to have evolved in their own directions, and their correlation is no longer—or at least much less frequently—the center of political debates. The military of today thrives on specialization and technology; its operational efficiency relies more on state-of-the-art equipment and skilled leadership than on the corporal strength of soldiers. Meanwhile, the study of the "populace" has become a key concept in the intervention of the welfare state. The concept is less tinged with a nationalist pathos than it was a century ago. Even though the direct coalition between these two concepts is no longer as central as it once was, both display lasting effects as a result of this historical alliance, the resonance of which can still be perceived today.

Notes

Introduction

1. Rainer Maria Rilke, *Diaries of a Young Poet*, trans. Edward Snow and Michael Winkler (New York: W. W. Norton & Company, 1998).

2. Rainer Maria Rilke, *Sämtliche Werke*, vol. 4, *Frühe Erzählungen und Dramen* (Frankfurt: Insel-Verlag, 1961), 601–609.

3. These bandages were made to close small wounds. They consisted of a woven fabric coated on one side with a glue made of isinglass (fish bladder). This glue could be moistened easily to apply or remove the bandages, which made them useful for administering first aid.

4. In this text, we have elected to translate the German term *Volkskörper* with the English phrase *collective body*. The German term makes a sort of analogy between the state of the nation (*das Volk*) as a collective and the bodies (*die Körper*) of its individual members.

5. Philipp Sarasin and Jakob Tanner, "Physiologie und industrielle Gesellschaft," in *Physiologie und industrielle Gesellschaft: Studien zur Verwissenschaftlichung des Körpers im 19. und 20. Jahrhundert*, ed. Sarasin and Tanner (Frankfurt: Suhrkamp, 1998), 16ff.

6. Wolfgang Kaschuba, "Die Nation als Körper: Zur symbolischen Konstruktion 'nationaler' Alltagswelt," in *Nation und Emotion: Deutschland und Frankreich im Vergleich 19. und 20. Jahrhundert*, ed. Etienne François, Hannes Siegrist, and Jakob Vogel (Göttingen: Vandenhoeck & Ruprecht, 1995), 291–299; Ute Planert, "Der dreifache Körper des Volkes: Sexualität, Biopolitik und die Wissenschaft vom Leben," *Geschichte und Gesellschaft* 26, no. 4 (2000): 543.

7. A classic in this regard is Jean-Paul Aron, Paul Dumont, and Emmanuel Le Roy Ladurie, *Anthropologie du conscrit français: D'après les comptes numériques et sommaires du recrutement de l'armée (1819–1826)* (Paris: Mouton de Gruyter, 1972). This was followed up by Guy Soudjian, *Anthropologie du conscrit parisien sous le second Empire* (Paris: Lauvauzelle, 1978). For the Habsburg Monarchy, economic historian John

Komlos made a comparable effort in the 1980s to a violent dispute about the methods applied in historical anthropology: John Komlos, "Stature and Nutrition in the Habsburg Monarchy: The Standard of Living and Economic Development," *American Historical Review* 90 (1985): 1149–1161. French historians have begun to actively reconsider this method: see Laurent Heyberger, *La révolution des corps: Décroissance et croissance staturale des habitants des villes et des campagnes en France, 1780–1940* (Strasbourg: Presses Universitaires de Strasbourg, 2005); Laurent Heyberger, *L'histoire anthropométrique* (Bern: Peter Lang, 2011); and Jean-Michel Selig, *Malnutrition et développement écnomique dans l'Alsace du XIXe siècle* (Strasbourg: Presses Universitaires de Strasbourg, 1996).

8. See the response to John Komlos and the following debate in the early 1990s: Hermann Rebel, "Massensterben und die Frage nach der Biologie in der Geschichte: Eine Antwort an John Komlos," *Österreichische Zeitschrift für Geschichtswissenschaft* 5 (1994): 279–286.

9. Staffan Müller-Wille and Hans-Jörg Rheinberger, *A Cultural History of Heredity* (Chicago: Chicago University Press, 2012).

10. The foundational study here was Eugen Weber, *Peasants into Frenchmen: The Modernization of Rural France, 1870–1914* (Stanford, CA: Stanford University Press, 1976), 292ff.; for Germany and France, see Jakob Vogel, *Nationen im Gleichschritt: Der Kult der "Nation in Waffen" in Deutschland und Frankreich, 1871–1914* (Göttingen: Vandenhoeck & Ruprecht, 1997).

11. Hans-Ulrich Wehler, "Der Aufbruch in die Moderne 1860 bis 1890: Armee, Marine und Politik in Europa, den USA und Japan," in *Das Militär und der Aufbruch in die Moderne 1860 bis 1890: Armeen, Marinen und der Wandel von Politik, Gesellschaft und Wirtschaft in Europa, den USA sowie Japan*, ed. Michael Epkenhans and Gerhard P. Groß (Munich: Oldenbourg Verlag, 2003), xxi–xxix; Jörn Leonhard, *Bellizismus und Nation: Kriegsdeutung und Nationsbestimmung in Europa und den Vereinigten Staaten 1750–1914* (Munich: R. Oldenbourg, 2008), 775ff. and 797ff.; Frank Becker, "Synthetischer Militarismus: Die Einigungskriege und der Stellenwert des Militärischen in der deutschen Gesellschaft," in *Aufbruch*, ed. Epkenhans and Groß, 125–142. For France, see especially Jean-François Chanet, *Vers l'armée nouvelle: République conservatrice et réforme militaire, 1871–1879* (Rennes: Presses universitaires de Rennes, 2006); more generally, see Jutta Nowosadtko, *Krieg, Gewalt und Ordnung: Einführung in die Militärgeschichte: Historische Einführungen* (Tübingen: Edition Diskord, 2002), 156ff.

12. Ute Frevert, *A Nation in Barracks: Modern Germany, Military Conscription and Civil Society* (Oxford: Berg Publishers, 2004). On this topic, see also Heinz Stübig, *Militär und Gesellschaft in Deutschland: Studien zur Entwicklung im 19. Jahrhundert* (Cologne: Böhlau, 1994), 142–143. On the topic of the military as a cache of radical sentiments in middle-class society in the German Empire, see Isabel V. Hull, *Absolute Destruction: Military Culture and the Practices of War in Imperial Germany* (Ithaca,

NY: Cornell University Press, 2005); and Bernd Ulrich, Jakob Vogel, and Benjamin Ziemann, *Untertan in Uniform: Militär und Militarismus im Kaiserreich 1871–1914: Quellen und Dokumente* (Frankfurt: Fischer, 2001). For Great Britain, see Hew Strachan, "Militär, Empire und Civil Society: Großbritannien im 19. Jahrhundert," in *Militär und Gesellschaft im 19. und 20. Jahrhundert*, ed. Ute Frevert (Stuttgart: Klett-Cotta, 1997), 78–94.

13. Markus Ingenlath, *Mentale Aufrüstung: Militarisierungstendenzen in Frankreich und Deutschland vor dem Ersten Weltkrieg* (Frankfurt: Campus, 1998); Christa Hämmerle, "Ein gescheitertes Experiment? Die Allgemeine Wehrpflicht in der multiethnischen Armee der Habsburgermonarchie," *Journal of Modern European History* 5 (2008): 222–243; Stig Förster, "Militär und staatsbürgerliche Partizipation: Die allgemeine Wehrpflicht im Deutschen Kaiserreich 1871–1914," in *Die Wehrpflicht. Entstehung, Erscheinungsformen und politisch-militärische Wirkung*, ed. Roland G. Foerster (Munich: R. Oldenbourg, 1994), 55–70.

14. The situation is somewhat different for the East European region, especially due to the work of Dietrich Beyrau and Werner Benecke: Dietrich Beyrau, *Militär und Gesellschaft im vorrevolutionären Russland* (Cologne: Böhlau, 1984); and Werner Benecke, *Militär, Reform und Gesellschaft im Zarenreich: Die Wehrpflicht in Russland 1874–1914* (Paderborn: Schöningh, 2006). On this topic, see also Jörn Happel, *Nomadische Lebenswelten und zarische Politik: Der Aufstand in Zentralasien 1916* (Stuttgart: Franz Steiner Verlag, 2010), 111ff.

15. Frevert, *Nation in Barracks*; Odile Roynette, *"Bons pour le service": L'expérience de la caserne en France à la fin du XIXe siècle* (Paris: Belin, 2000); Marianne Rychner, "Frau Doktorin besichtigt die Männerwelt—ein Experiment aus dem Jahr 1883 zur Konstruktion von Männlichkeit im Militär," in *Soziale Konstruktionen: Militär und Geschlechterverhältnis*, ed. Christine Eifler and Ruth Seifert (Münster: Dampfboot, 1999), 94–109; and Marianne Rychner and Kathrin Däniker, "Unter 'Männern': Geschlechtliche Zuschreibungen in der Schweizerarmee zwischen 1870 und 1914," in *Weiblich-Männlich. Geschlechterverhältnisse in der Schweiz: Rechtsprechung, Diskurs, Praktiken*, ed. Rudolf Jaun and Brigitte Studer (Zurich: Chronos, 1995), 159–170.

16. Among many others, Kate Fisher and Sarah Toulalan, eds., *The Routledge History of Sex and the Body: 1500 to the Present* (London: Routledge, 2013); and Ina Zweiniger-Bargielowska, *Managing the Body: Beauty, Health and Fitness in Britain, 1880–1939* (Oxford: Oxford University Press, 2010).

17. Eneia Dragomir, "Programmierte Instruktion—gesteuertes Verhalten? Die Auseinandersetzung um die Ausbildung der Schweizer Armee und die Anthropologie des Soldaten nach 1945," in *Pulverdampf und Kreidestaub: Beiträge zum Verhältnis zwischen Militär und Schule im 19. und 20. Jahrhundert*, ed. Lukas Boser, Patrick Bühler, Michèle Hofmann, and Philippe Müller (Bern: Bibliothek am Guisanplatz, 2016), 365–387.

18. This holds particularly for historiographies of World War I, like Sabine Kienitz, *Beschädigte Helden: Kriegsinvalidität und Körperbilder, 1914–1923* (Paderborn: Schöningh, 2008); and Elisabeth Bronfen, *Specters of War: Hollywood's Engagement with Military Conflict* (New Brunswick, NJ: Rutgers University Press, 2012).

19. Although there are hints in the scholarship, these attempts to integrate social structures of the military into the wider society have not yet made significant inroads into the broader scholarship; see Ralf Pröve, *Militär, Staat und Gesellschaft im 19. Jahrhundert* (Munich: R. Oldenbourg, 2006), 77–78.

20. So far, scholars have begun to formulate new approaches resulting from this alternative perspective, but their systematic implementation is still lacking. See Marcus Funck, "Militär, Krieg und Gesellschaft. Soldaten und militärische Eliten in der Sozialgeschichte," in *Was ist Militärgeschichte?*, ed. Thomas Kühne and Benjamin Ziemann (Paderborn: Schöningh, 2000), 157–174; and Anne Lipp, "Diskurs und Praxis: Militärgeschichte als Kulturgeschichte," in *Militärgeschichte?*, ed. Kühne and Ziemann, 211–228.

21. A significant exception here is the question of military psychology, which has repeatedly been the subject of attention—primarily, but not only, in regard to the question of trauma related to war. For example, see Martin Lengwiler, *Zwischen Klinik und Kaserne: Die Geschichte der Militärpsychiatrie in Deutschland und der Schweiz 1870–1914* (Zurich: Chronos, 2000); Paul Lerner, *Hysterical Men: War, Psychiatry, and the Politics of Trauma in Germany, 1890–1930* (Ithaca, NY: Cornell University Press, 2003); and Babette Quinkert, Philipp Rauh, and Ulrike Winkler, eds., *Krieg und Psychiatrie, 1914–1950* (Göttingen: Wallstein, 2010).

22. There are numerous examples, such as Theodore M. Porter, *Trust in Numbers: The Pursuit of Objectivity in Science and Public Life* (Princeton, NJ: Princeton University Press, 1995); and Libby Schweber, *Disciplining Statistics: Demography and Vital Statistics in France and England, 1830–1885* (Durham, NC: Duke University Press, 2006).

23. Jakob Vogel, "Von der Wissenschafts—zur Wissensgeschichte: Für eine Historisierung der 'Wissensgesellschaft,'" *Geschichte und Gesellschaft* 30, no. 4 (2004): 639–660.

24. François Caradec, *Alphonse Allais* (Paris: Belfond, 1994), 57ff.

25. This is most obvious in a story that Marianne Rychner tells about an examination in 1883 in the Swiss canton of Appenzell, where the presence of a woman caused not only local furor but also unrest within the army's administration. See Rychner, "Frau Doktorin."

26. This is true, for example, of the series of lectures and publications by the Countess of Streitberg: Gisela von Streitberg, *Die Bevölkerungsfrage in weiblicher Beurteilung*, vols. 1–6 (Leipzig: Dietrich, 1908–1909). On this topic, see also Ursula Ferdinand, *Das malthusische Erbe: Entwicklungsstränge der Bevölkerungstheorie im 19. Jahrhundert*

und deren Einflüsse auf die radikale Frauenbewegung in Deutschland (Münster: LIT, 1999).

27. Ian Hacking, *The Taming of Chance* (Cambridge: Cambridge University Press, 1990), 7.

28. Bénédict Augustin Morel, *Traité des dégénérances* (Paris: J.-B. Baillière et fils, 1857); and Rae Beth Gordon, *Dances with Darwin, 1875–1910: Vernacular Modernity in France* (Surrey: Ashgate, 2009), 81–82.

29. David G. Horn, *The Criminal Body: Lombroso and the Anatomy of Deviance* (London: Routledge, 2003). On the reception in Germany, see Jonas Menne, *"Lombroso redivivus?" Biowissenschaften, Kriminologie und Kriminalpolitik von 1876 bis in die Gegenwart* (Tübingen: Mohr, 2017). For an internationally comparative perspective, see articles in Peter Becker and Richard Wetzell, eds., *Criminals and their Scientists: The History of Criminology in International Perspective* (Cambridge: Cambridge University Press, 2006); and Mary Gibson, *Born to Crime: Cesare Lombrose and the Origins of Biological Criminology* (London: Praeger, 2002).

30. This has been argued for the Italian case by David G. Horn, *Social Bodies: Science, Reproduction and Italian Modernity* (Princeton, NJ: Princeton University Press, 2001), 18ff. For a more biographical account, see Theodore M. Porter, *Karl Pearson: The Scientific Life in a Statistical Age* (Princeton, NJ: Princeton University Press, 2004), 278ff.

31. Arthur Herman, *The Idea of Decline in Western History* (New York: Free Press, 1997), 46ff.

32. Douglas Lorimer, *Science, Race Relations and Resistance: Britain, 1870–1914* (Manchester: Manchester University Press, 2013), 108ff.; Gibson, *Born to Crime*, 97ff.; and Michael Hau, *The Cult of Health and Beauty in Germany: A Social History 1890–1930* (Chicago: University of Chicago Press, 2003), 82ff.

33. Herman, *Idea of Decline*, 109ff.

34. Daniel Pick, *Faces of Degeneration: A European Disorder, c. 1848–1918* (Cambridge: Cambridge University Press, 1989), 155ff. For the British case, see Kelly Hurley, *The Gothic Body: Sexuality, Materialism, and Degeneration at the Fin de Siècle* (Cambridge: Cambridge University Press, 1996), 59ff. For France, see Gordon, *Dances with Darwin*; Anne Seitz, *Wimmeln und Wabern: Ansteckung und Gesellschaft im französischen Roman des Naturalismus und Fin-de-siècle* (Bielefeld: Aisthesis, 2015); and Matt T. Reed, "From Aliéné to Dégénéré: Moral Agency and Psychiatric Imagination in Nineteenth-Century France," in *Confronting Modernity in Fin-de-Siècle France: Bodies, Minds and Gender*, ed. Christopher E. Forth and Elinor Accampo (Hampshire: Palgrave Macmillan, 2010), 67–89.

35. Robert Nye, "Degeneration, Neurasthenia and the Culture of Sport in Belle Epoque France," *Journal of Contemporary History* 17 (1982): 51–68; and Eugen Weber,

"Gymnastics and Sports in Fin-de-Siècle France: Opium of the Classes?," *The American Historical Review* 76, no. 1 (1971): 70–98.

36. This has been most pointedly illustrated by Bruno Latour, Steve Woolgar, and Michel Callon, among others: Bruno Latour and Steve Woolgar, *Laboratory Life: The Social Construction of Scientific Facts* (Beverly Hills: Sage Publications, 1979); and Michel Callon, ed., *La Science et ses réseaux: Genèse et circulation des faits scientifiques* (Paris: Éditions La Découverte, 1989).

37. Stefan Beck and Jörg Niewöhner, "Somatographic Investigations across Levels of Complexity," *Biosocieties* 1, no. 2 (June 2006): 219–227; and Ian Hacking, *The Social Construction of What?* (Cambridge, MA: Harvard University Press, 1999).

38. Vogel, "Von der Wissenschaft."

39. Mitchell G. Ash, "Wissenschaft und Politik als Ressourcen füreinander," in *Wissenschaften und Wissenschaftspolitik: Bestandsaufnahmen zu Formationen, Brüchen und Kontinuitäten im Deutschland des 20. Jahrhunderts*, ed. Rüdiger vom Bruch and Brigitte Kaderas (Stuttgart: Steiner, 2002), 32–51.

40. Arne Schirrmacher, "Nach der Popularisierung: Zur Relation von Wissenschaft und Öffentlichkeit im 20. Jahrhundert," *Geschichte und Gesellschaft* 34, no. 1 (2008): 79ff. See also Sybilla Nikolow and Christina Wessely, "Öffentlichkeit als epistemologische und politische Ressource für die Genese umstrittener Wissenschaftskonzepte," in *Wissenschaft und Öffentlichkeit als Ressource füreinander: Studien zur Wissenschaftsgeschichte im 20. Jahrhundert*, ed. Sybilla Nikolow and Arne Schirrmacher (Frankfurt: Campus, 2007), 273–289.

41. Hans-Jörg Rheinberger, "Objekt und Repräsentation," in *Mit dem Auge denken: Strategien der Sichtbarmachung in wissenschaftlichen und virtuellen Welten*, ed. Bettina Heintz and Jörg Huber (Zurich: Springer, 2001), 55–61.

42. Many contemporaries, in fact, understood this appraisal to reflect the entire population and seemed hardly to realize that this included the female population only very indirectly.

43. Paul-André Rosental, "Pour une histoire politique des populations," *Annales* 61 (2006): 18ff.

44. Eva Barlösius, "Bilder des demografischen Wandels," in *Zukunftswissen: Prognosen in Wirtschaft, Politik und Gesellschaft seit 1900*, ed. Heinrich Hartmann and Jakob Vogel (Frankfurt: Campus, 2010), 231–248.

45. Georg Mayr, "Statistik und Gesellschaftslehre," in *VIIIe congrès international d'hygiène et de démographie tenu à Budapest du 1er au 9 septembre, Comptes rendu et mémoires* (Budapest, 1895), 299.

46. Jean Dermoor, Jean Massart, and Emile Vandervelde, *L'évolution régressive en biologie et en sociologie* (Paris: Alcan, 1897). On the ability to apply academic research

methods to the "collective body" as a predecessor of eugenics, see Petra Gehring, "Biologische Politik um 1900: Reform, Therapie, Experiment?," in *Kulturgeschichte des Menschenversuches im 20. Jahrhundert*, ed. Birgit Griesecke (Frankfurt: Suhrkamp, 2009), 48–77.

47. Emile Cheysson, "Les méthodes de la statistique: Conférence faite le 30 Novembre 1889 à la réunion des Officiers," in *Œuvres choisies* (Paris: A. Rousseau, 1911), 169.

48. This analogy and the placement of statistics in a "set" of nearly self-evident "modern" techniques of governments are often, in my opinion, premature. See, for example, Jörn Leonhard and Ulrike von Hirschhauen, *Empires und Nationalstaaten im 19. Jahrhundert*, 2nd ed. (Göttingen: Vandenhoeck & Ruprecht, 2011).

49. Dietrich Beyrau, "Aus der Subalternität in die Sphären der Macht: Die Juden im Zarenreich und in Sowjetrussland (1860–1930)," in *Moderne Zeiten? Krieg, Revolution und Gewalt im 20. Jahrhundert*, ed. Jörg Baberowski (Göttingen: Vandenhoeck & Ruprecht, 2006), 67ff.

50. Paul Weindling, *Health, Race and German Politics between National Unification and Nazism, 1870–1945* (Cambridge: Cambridge University Press, 1989), 146.

51. On the question of transnationalism and the importance of such an independent sphere, which began with the international conferences, see Madeleine Herren, "'Die Erweiterung des Wissens beruht vorzugsweise auf dem Kontakt mit der Aussenwelt': Wissenschaftliche Netzwerke aus historischer Perspektive," *Zeitschrift für Geschichtswissenschaft* 49 (2001): 197–207; and Martin H. Geyer and Johannes Paulmann, "Einleitung," in *The Mechanics of Internationalism, Culture, Society and Politics from the 1840s to the First World War*, ed. Geyer and Paulmann (Oxford: Oxford University Press, 2001), 1–26.

52. Alison Bashford, "Nation, Empire, Globe: The Spaces of Population Debate in the Interwar Years," *Comparative Studies in Society and History* 49, no. 1 (2007): 186ff.; and Petra Overath, "Bevölkerungsforschung transnational: Eine Skizze zu Interaktionen zwischen Wissenschaft und Politik am Beispiel der International Union for the Scientific Study of Population," in *Die vergangene Zukunft Europas: Bevölkerungsforschung und -prognosen im 20. und 21. Jahrhundert*, ed. Petra Overath (Cologne: Böhlau, 2011), 57–83. For the case of the anthropologists, see Penny H. Glenn, "Wissenschaft in einer polyzentrischen Nation: Der Fall der deutschen Ethnologie," in *Wissenschaft und Nation in der Europäischen Geschichte*, ed. Ralph Jessen and Jakob Vogel (Frankfurt: Campus, 2002), 84ff.

53. Following the usage in Sebastian Conrad and Jürgen Osterhammel, "Einleitung," in *Das Kaiserreich transnational: Deutschland und die Welt 1871–1914*, ed. Conrad and Osterhammel (Göttingen: Vandenhoeck & Ruprecht, 2004), 12–13.

54. Rudolf Jaun, *Preussen vor Augen: Das schweizerische Offizierskorps im militärischen und gesellschaftlichen Wandel des Fin de siècle* (Zurich: Chronos, 1999), 161ff.; Niklaus Meienberg, *Die Welt als Wille und Wahn: Elemente zur Naturgeschichte eines Clans* (Zurich: Limmat Verlag, 1987), 63ff.

55. After the war's outbreak, for example, the minimum height restriction in the German military was abolished. A similar claim can be made for the extra examination for sexually transmitted diseases: "Anleitung für die militärische Beurteilung der Kriegsbrauchbarkeit beim Kriegsmusterungsgeschäft, bei den Bezirkskommandos und bei der Truppe, 1916," Bundesarchiv—Militärarchiv Freiburg i.Br., Druckschriften Preussisches Heer, PHD 6/115.

1   Computing Military Strength

1. Johann Peter Süßmilch, *Die göttliche Ordnung in den Veränderungen des menschlichen Geschlechts aus der Geburt, dem Tode und der Fortpflanzung desselben* (Berlin: Verlag der Realschule, 1761), 401. *Populace*, as used in Süßmilch's sense, refers to the settlement of a particular territory. Only in the course of the nineteenth century did the abstract, analytical concept with which we are familiar in modern language develop.

2. The equation of some concept of population with military strength was a foundational premise that Plato had already formulated and that was reproduced by diverse writers in the early modern age.

3. Johann Heinrich Gottlob von Justi, *Staatswirtschaft oder systematische Abhandlung aller ökonomischen u. Cameralwissenschaften*, vol. 1, 2nd ed. (Leipzig, 1758), 160; Jacqueline Hecht, "L'idée de dénombrement jusqu'à la révolution," in *Pour une histoire de la statistique*, ed. Institut national de la statistique et des études économiques, vol. 1 (Paris: INSEE, 1977), 21–81; Harald Michel, *Der Bevölkerungsgedanke im Zeitalter des Merkantilismus* (Berlin: Institut für Angewandte Demographie, 1994), 12–13; and Paul Mombert, "Die Anschauungen des 17. und 18. Jahrhunderts über die Abnahme der Bevölkerung," *Jahrbücher für Nationalökonomie und Statistik* 135, no. 4 (1931): 481–503.

4. Hans-Ulrich Wehler, *Deutsche Gesellschaftsgeschichte*, vol. 1, *Vom Feudalismus des Alten Reiches bis zur Defensiven Modernisierung der Reformära 1700–1815*, 3rd ed. (Munich: C. H. Beck, 1996), 246–247.

5. Antoine-Audet Hargenvilliers, *Recherches et considérations sur la formation et le recrutement de l'Armée en France* (Paris: Didot, 1817).

6. Annie Crépin, *La conscription en débat ou le triple apprentissage de la nation, de la citoyenneté, de la République: 1789–1889* (Arras: Artois presses université, 1998); Crépin, *Défendre la France: Les Français, la guerre et le service militaire, de la guerre de Sept Ans à Verdun* (Rennes: Presses universitaires de Rennes, 2005).

7. For a detailed narrative of the social practices that accompanied these recruitment procedures, see Selig, *Malnutrition et développement*, 32ff.; and Heyberger, *Révolution des corps*, 124ff.

8. Gerd Krumeich, "Zur Entwicklung der 'nation armée' in Frankreich bis zum Ersten Weltkrieg," in *Die Wehrpflicht, Entstehung, Erscheinungsformen und politisch-militärische Wirkung*, ed. Roland G. Foerster (Munich: R. Oldenbourg, 1994), 139.

9. Receuil de pièces, "Tirage au sort du service militaire," BNF 4-WZ-13318. If we turn to a later topos, brochures advertising such insurance policies suggest that bodily characteristics played no role, with the exception of the oldest recruitment criterion: height.

10. Crépin, *Défendre*, 173ff.

11. This concept appears with more or less force around the turn of the century in French sources and is evident in the military reforms of 1905, which abolished the majority of those privileges attached to social status and rank. A short time later, Frocard described the previous social consequences as *"profondment illogiques"* because the "burden of the military system [had rested] entirely on the shoulders of the nation's least wealthy classes." Frocard, *Aptitude militaire des contingents français* (Paris, 1911), 14; see also Krumeich, "Entwicklung," 141ff.

12. François-Marie Taillepied de Bondy, *Recrutement de l'armée. Observations pratiques sur les inégalités du mode actuel de répartition des contingents entre les départements et les cantons, et proposition d'un nouveau mode* (Auxerre: E. Perriquet, 1841).

13. Frank Becker, "'Bewaffnetes Volk' oder 'Volk in Waffen'? Militärpolitik und Militarismus in Deutschland und Frankreich 1870–1914," in *Der Bürger als Soldat: Die Militarisierung europäischer Gesellschaften im langen 19. Jahrhundert: Ein internationaler Vergleich*, ed. Christian Jansen (Essen: Klartext, 2004), 158–174; Jakob Vogel, "Lernen vom Feind: Das Militär als Träger des deutsch-französischen Kulturtransfers im 19. Jahrhundert," in *Vom Gegner lernen: Feindschaften und Kulturtransfers im Europa des 19. und 20. Jahrhunderts*, ed. Martin Aust and Daniel Schönpflug (Frankfurt: Campus, 2007), 95–113; and Jean-François Chanet, *Vers l'armée nouvelle: République conservatrice et réforme militaire, 1871–1879* (Rennes: Presses universitaires de Rennes, 2006), 43.

14. The different possibilities to shirk service, but also budgetary restrictions, led the delegate Ballue to claim bluntly before the *Assemblée nationale* in 1883 that "the soldier who serves a five-year term is a myth." The difficulties of implementing the five-year term resulted in a shortening of service to a period of three years in the new law of 1889. Crépin, *Défendre*, 331ff.

15. David French, *Military Identities: The Regimental System, the British Army, and the British People, c. 1870–2000* (Oxford: Oxford University Press, 2005), 31ff.

16. Ingenlath, *Aufrüstung*; Hans Rudolf Fuhrer, "Das Schweizer System: Friedenssicherung und Selbstverteidigung im 19. und 20. Jahrhundert," in *Die Wehrpflicht*, ed. Foerster, 193–206; Ute Frevert, "Das jakobinische Modell: Allgemeine Wehrpflicht und Nationsbildung in Preußen-Deutschland," in *Militär und Gesellschaft*, ed. Frevert, 27ff.; and Crépin, *Défendre*, 342ff.

17. Ingenlath, *Aufrüstung*, 61ff.

18. Christa Hämmerle, "Ein gescheitertes Experiment? Die Allgemeine Wehrpflicht in der multiethnischen Armee der Habsburgermonarchie," *Journal of Modern European History* 5 (2007): 233ff.; and Werner Benecke, "Die allgemeine Wehrpflicht in Russland: Zwischen militärischem Anspruch und zivilen Interessen," *Journal of Modern European History* 5, no. 2 (2007): 244–263.

19. Benecke, "Allgemeine Wehrpflicht," 258ff.; and Adam Marcinkowski and Andrzej Rzepniewski, "Die Wehrdienst- und Wehrpflichtformen in Polen zwischen der Verfassung von 1791 und der Gegenwart," in *Die Wehrpflicht*, ed. Foerster, 156ff.

20. Leonhard and Hirschhausen, *Empires*, 84–85.

21. Auguste Charles Joseph Vitu, *Histoire civile de l'armée; ou, Des conditions du service militaire en France depuis les temps les plus reculés jusqu'à la formation de l'armée permanente* (Paris: Didier, 1868), 555ff. German authors argued especially vehemently for the position that every citizen should perform military service as a duty to his fatherland, ascribing nationalistic characteristics to it. See Eduard Otto, *Zur Geschichte der Theorie der allgemeinen Wehrpflicht in Deutschland* (Hamburg: J. F. Richter, 1900), 4ff.; Ingenlath, *Aufrüstung*, 32ff.; Stig Förster, "Militär und staatsbürgerliche Partizipation: Die allgemeine Wehrpflicht im Deutschen Kaiserreich 1871–1914," in *Wehrpflicht*, ed. Foerster, 60f; and Wiegand Schmidt-Richberg, "Die Regierungszeit Wilhelms II," in *Handbuch zur deutschen Militärgeschichte, 1648.1939, VI. 5 Von der Entlassung Bismarcks bis zum Ende des Ersten Weltkriegs (1890–1918)*, ed. Hans Meier-Welcker and Wolfgang von Grothe (Frankfurt: Bernard und Graefe Verlag, 1968), 51–52.

22. Frevert, "Das jakobinische Modell," 39ff.

23. Ingenlath, *Aufrüstung*, 433ff.

24. Thomas Hippler, *Citizens, Soldiers and National Armies: Military Service in France and Germany, 1789–1830* (London: Routledge, 2008), 24ff. and 166ff.

25. On a side note, it is remarkable how long the myth of equal representation of the total population in the military was perpetuated in German historiography, even if the social selection processes through the recruiting were open to the very same authors; see Schmidt-Richberg, *Die Regierungszeit*, 100.

26. Around the end of the nineteenth century, these privileges were extended to members of certain other traditional crafts. In addition, a general test of fitness for

military service was introduced for those drafted, which had to be taken by all recruits. The criteria for this examination were adapted over time to accommodate a quite detailed profile of abilities. Frevert, *Nation in Barracks*.

27. Ibid., 157ff.

28. In the kingdom of Württemberg after 1894, there were decrees aiming to prevent such groups from entering the military. The decree from 1907, however, stipulated with some force that this exclusion applied only to leaders of these movements, not to the entire group or to those who were only nominal members. Royal ministry of the interior, Württemberg, to the city administration of Stuttgart (marked as confidential registered mail), dated May 1, 1907, HStA Stuttgart S M 11 Bü 11; see also Förster, "Militär," 58ff.; and Ulrich, Vogel, and Ziemann, *Untertan in Uniform*, 173ff.

29. "Analyse sur nos effectifs" of the *premier bureau*, dated August 6, 1900, SHAT 7 N 130. In addition, see also "Note relative à la comparaison du nombre des naissances masculines et du nombre des incorporations annuelles," January 1902, État major—Bureau de l'organization et de la mobilisation générale SHAT 7 N 100; and Heinrich Hartmann, "Normieren und Errechnen: Zur Korrelation von Bevölkerungsprognosen und Musterung vor 1914," in *Zukunftswissen*, ed. Hartmann and Vogel, 137–152.

30. Francis Ronsin, *La grève des ventres: Propagande néo-malthusienne et baisse de la natalité en France, XIXe–XXe siècles* (Paris: Aubier Montaigne, 1980).

31. "Loi modifiant la loi du 15 juillet 1889 sur le recrutement de l'armée et réduisant à deux ans la durée du service dans l'armée," *Journal officiel*, March 23, 1905. The law did not mean that the French army was reduced by a third; instead, articles 21 and 23 abolished numerous privileges related to exemptions from service. This served to minimize the effective reduction. These measures were based in large part on the calculations and suggestions of the general staff.

32. "Calcul de l'effectif probable de l'armée en 1912, dans l'hypothèse du service de deux ans," État major—Bureau de l'organization et de la mobilisation générale SHAT 7 N 100. In this case, military officials calculated an average decrease in overall size of the military of fifty thousand soldiers.

33. De Bondy, *Recrutement*, 5ff.

34. Jean-Christian Boudin, *Hygiène militaire comparée, et statistique médicale des armées de terre et de mer* (Paris: J.-B. Baillière et fils, 1848), 3.

35. *Neueste Mittheilungen*, vol. 4, no. 66 (June 30, 1885).

36. Diterici compiled such reports in 1831, 1837, 1840, 1843, 1846, 1849, and 1852–1854; his successor, Engel, produced them on an annual basis between 1855

and 1862. *Mittheilungen des statistischen Bureaus in Berlin*, no. 4 (1855), 325, and *Zeitschrift des Königlich preussischen statistischen Bureaus*, no. 4 (1864), 65ff. and 173ff.

37. Thomas L. W. Bischoff, *Über die Brauchbarkeit der in verschiedenen europäischen Staaten veröffentlichten Resultate des Recrutirungs- Geschäftes zur Beurthielung des Entwicklungs- und Gesundheitszustandes ihrer Bevölkerung* (Munich: Verlag der königlichen Akademie, 1867), 61.

38. Ibid., 62.

39. This term will play a role in debates outlined later in this book: *stock figures* are concrete numbers collected for a specific point in time or an appointed date, whereas *flow figures* describe movement over time. For example, a national census aims to determine total population (a stock figure) and to calculate birth and death rates over time (flow figures), which can in turn be used to make projections about how the size of the total population is likely to evolve.

40. *Annuario estadistico de Espana correspondiendo á 1839 y 1860* (Madrid: Imprenta Nacional, 1860).

41. Fröhlich, "Zur Musterungsstatistik," *Allgemeine militäräztliche Zeitung*, no. 14 (April 3, 1870).

42. Hans-Rudolf Fuhrer, "Wehrpflicht in der Schweiz—ein historischer Überblick," in *Wehrpflicht und Miliz—Ende einer Epoche? Der europäische Streitkräftewandel und die Schweizer Miliz*, ed. Karl W. Haltiner and Andreas Kühner (Baden-Baden: Nomos, 1999), 73–74; and Lengwiler, *Zwischen Klinik und Kaserne*, 279ff. To this point, the system of conscription and the criteria employed therein were left up to the administration of the respective cantons. Beginning in 1850, there was a sole central regulation concerning subsequent discharge. It stipulated the exact "psychological and physical shortcomings" that would result in discharge from service. Letter of the Swiss surgeon general to the Swiss Department of the Military, commenting on the decree, October 2, 1850, BAR E 27 Tit 5804.

43. BAR E 27 Tit 5848.

44. Nele Bracke, "For State and Society: The Production of Official Statistics in 19th-Century Belgium," in *Jenseits von Humboldt: Wissenschaft im Staat 1850–1990*, ed. Axel C. Hüntelmann and Michael C. Schneider (Frankfurt: Peter Lang, 2010), 259ff.; and Morgane Labbé, "Le Séminaire de statistique du Bureau prussien de statistique (1862–1900): Former les administrateurs à la statistique," *Journal Electronique d'Histoire des Probabilités et de la Statistique* 2, no. 2 (2006), https://eudml.org/doc/117567.

45. Ernst Engel, ed., *Compte-rendu général des travaux du "Congrès international de statistique" dans ses sénaces tenues à Bruxelles 1853, Paris 1855, Vienne 1857, et Londres 1860* (Berlin: Imprimerie Royale, 1863), 183–184. On Engel's activity as leader of the Prussian statistical office and in regard to international scholarship, see Ian Hacking,

"Prussian Numbers 1860–1882," in *The Probabilistic Revolution*, vol. 1, ed. Lorraine Daston et al. (Cambridge, MA: MIT Press, 1987), 377–394.

46. Hacking, "Prussian Numbers," 381ff.

47. Ezekiel B. Elliott, *On the Military Statistics of the United States of America* (Berlin: Congrès international de statistique, 1863). The relevant information concerning the context in which it was produced refers to the author's explanations in the introduction.

48. Rudolf Virchow at the Statistical Congress in 1863, cited from Fröhlich, "Musterungsstatistik." See chapter 6 for more information; see also Constantin Goschler, *Rudolf Virchow: Mediziner, Anthropologe, Politiker* (Cologne: Böhlau, 2002), 170ff.

49. "I believe that whoever is responsible for writing the history of military medical statistics and whenever he does so, he will not be able to do so without mention of this important phase." Adolph Zemanek, *Werth und Bedeutung der Militär-Sanitäts-Statistik* (Vienna, 1884), 13.

50. Geyer and Paulmann, "Einleitung"; and Herren, "Erweiterung."

51. Otto von Schjerning, "Ansprache Seiner Exzellenz des Generalstabsarztes des Armee Professors Dr. Schjerning bei Eröffnung des XIV. internationalen Kongresses für Hygiene und Demographie am 23. September 1907," in *Bericht über den XIV. Internationalen Kongress für Hygiene und Demographie, Berlin 23.–29. September 1907*, vol. 1 (Berlin, 1908), 817.

52. Relevant here is topic 6 of section 8 for demography.

53. Esp. Heinrich Schwiening, *Beiträge zur Kenntnis der Verbreitung der venerischen Krankheiten in den europäischen Heeren sowie in der militärpflichtigen Jugend Deutschlands* (Berlin: A. Hirschwald, 1907); and Heinrich Schwiening and Wilhelm Nicolai, *Über die Körperbeschaffenheit der zum einjährig-freiwilligen Dienst berechtigten Wehrpflichtigen Deutschlands: Auf Grundlage amtlichen Materials* (Berlin: A. Hirschwald, 1909).

54. This discussion is documented in *Bericht über den XIV. Internationalen Kongress für Hygiene und Demographie, Berlin, 23.–29. September 1907*, vol. 4 (Berlin: A. Hirschwald, 1908), 767–773.

55. Albert Maitrot de La Motte-Capron, *Nos frontières de l'est et du nord: Le service de deux ans et sa répercussion sur leur défense* (Paris: H. Charles-Lavauzelle, 1913), esp. p. 87.

56. This is contrary to the picture painted by Christiane Dienel. At the same time, it is fitting that it was not until the 1880s that this fear of depopulation had a significant political impact. Christiane Dienel, *Kinderzahl und Staatsräson: Empfängnisverhütung und Bevölkerungspolitik in Deutschland und Frankreich bis 1918* (Münster: Westfälisches Dampfboot, 1995), 153ff.

57. Jean-Charles Chenu, *Recrutement de l'armée et population de la France* (Paris: Masson et fils, 1867), 23.

58. This is especially the case of the classic study by Jacques Bertillon, "La colonisation de l'Europe par les Allemands," *La réforme économique: Revue des question sociales, politiques, fiscales, scientifiques, industrielles, agricoles et commerciales* 1 (1875), 154–169.

59. Georges Morache, *Considérations sur le recrutement de l'armée et sur l'aptitude militaires dans la presse française* (Paris: J. Dumaine, 1873), 60ff.

60. Ibid., 62–63.

61. Frocard, *Aptitude*, 19.

62. Ibid., 24.

63. This slogan literally means "priests put your backpacks on."

64. J.-B. Duvergier, ed., *Collection complète des lois, décrets, ordonnances et règlements, Nouvelle série*, vol. 13 (Paris: A. Guyot et Scribe, 1913), 549–570. See also Krumeich, "Entwicklung."

65. "Présentation d'un projet de loi, modifiant la loi du 21 mars 1905 sur le récrutement de l'armée, par M. Eugène Etienne, ministre de la guerre, au nom du président de la république," Conseil supérieur de la guerre, in SHAT 1 N 12, Séances 1889–1913. The minister viewed this as the most important argument, however. A general change in the development of population was in his opinion an illusion: "Despite the indisputable improvement to the race via hygienic practice and the sports program for youth, considering the low birth rate, we can no longer expect the number of suitable recruits for military service to grow."

66. Michael Jeismann, *Das Vaterland der Feinde: Studien zum nationalen Feindbegriff und Selbstverständnis in Deutschland und Frankreich 1792–1918* (Stuttgart: Klett-Cotta, 1992), 280ff.

67. État major de l'armée, "Note pour M. le Ministre concernant l'Incorporation en France du contingent algérien," January 18, 1899, SHAT 7 N 132. Such a regular draft remained the exception, however. In 1895, it was also introduced on the island of Réunion in the Indian Ocean. See Fernand Théron, "Le récrutement à la Réunion," *Archives de la médecine navale et coloniale* 68 (July 1897): 5–18.

68. Commentary of the Ministry of War, "Organisations des réseaux indigènes—du récrutement des indigènes," February 1, 1906, SHAT 7 N 132; and Adolphe Messimy, *Le statut des indigènes algériens* (Paris: H. Charles-Lavauzelle, 1913), 16.

69. This is the conclusion reached in "Analyse sur nos effectifs" from the premier bureau in the Ministry of War, dated August 6, 1900, SHAT 7 N 130.

70. "Analyse Incorporation en France d'une partie du contingent algérien," État major, premier bureau—effectifs, March 1911; and Rapport au Ministre, note Annexe no. 1 au sujet des moyens pour relever les effectifs de paix, May 31, 1912; both SHAT 7 N 134.

71. Answer of the Ministry of War to the premier bureau organisation/mobilisation, dated August 12, 1911, SHAT 7 N 108. The pedagogical dimension of compulsory military service, so to speak, in a quasi-colonial context can be seen in the case of Tunisia, where a systematic draft along the lines used in France was also introduced: "The only difference is ... that the Tunisian must serve for three years because this is the time required to turn an Arab into a good soldier." Messimy, *Statut*, 13.

72. von Schmidt, "Vergleiche zischen der Deutschen und französischen Armee: Vortrag gehalten im Deutschen Wehrverein, Ortsgruppe Stuttgart am 29 Mar. 1912 und ergänzt nach dem Stand Ende 1912" (Stuttgart: Grüninger, 1912). On this topic, see also Christian Koller, *"Von Wilden aller Rassen niedergemetzelt": Die Diskussion um die Verwendung von Kolonialtruppen in Europa zwischen Rassismus, Kolonial- und Militärpolitik (1914–1930)* (Stuttgart: Steiner, 2001); Pascal Grosse, *Kolonialismus, Eugenik und bürgerliche Gesellschaft in Deutschland 1850–1918* (Frankfurt: Campus, 2000), 31–32; and Stefanie Michels, *Schwarze deutsche Kolonialsoldaten: Mehrdeutige Repräsentationsräume und früher Kosmopolitismus in Afrika* (Bielefeld: Transcript, 2009), 78ff.

73. On the history of the association: Virginie de Luca Barrusse, *Les familles nombreuses: Une question démographique, un enjeu politique: France, 1880–1940* (Rennes: Presses universitaires de Rennes, 2008), 24ff.; Petra Overath, "Transfer als Verengung? Zur internationalen Diskussion über den Geburtenrückgang in Frankreich in Texten von Fernand Boverat, Roderich von Ungern-Sternberg sowie Joseph John Spengler in den späten 30er Jahren des 20. Jahrhunderts," in *Les figures de l'État en Allemagne et en France/Figuren des Staates in Deutschland und Frankreich (1870–1945)*, ed. Alain Chatriot and Dieter Gosewinkel (Munich: Oldenbourg Verlag, 2006), 187ff.; Dienel, *Kinderzahl*, 158ff.; and Ronsin, *Grève*, 121ff.

74. *La Patrie est en danger* (Paris: Alliance nationale pour l'accroissement de la population française, 1913).

75. De Luca Barrusse, *Les familles*, 161ff.

76. Jacques Bertillon, *La dépopulation de la France: Ses conséquences, ses causes: Mesures à prendre pour la combattre* (Paris: Alcan, 1911), 20.

77. Ibid., 15.

78. Julius Wolf, *Geburtenrückgang: Die Rationalisierung des Sexuallebens in unserer Zeit* (Jena: Fischer, 1912); Reinhold Seeberg, *Der Geburtenrückgang in Deutschland* (Leipzig: Deichert, 1913); and Max von Gruber, *Ursachen und Bekämpfung des Geburtenrückgangs im Deutschen Reich: Bericht erstattet an die 38. Versammlung des Deutschen Vereins für öffentliche Gesundheitspflege am 19. September 1913 in Aachen* (Munich: J. F.

Lehmann, 1914). See also Ursula Ferdinand, "Geburtenrückgangstheorien und 'Geburtenrückgangs-Gespenster' 1900–1930," in *Herausforderung Bevölkerung: Zu Entwicklungen des modernen Denkens über die Bevölkerung vor, im und nach dem "Dritten Reich"*, ed. Josef Ehmer, Ursula Ferdinand, and Jürgen Reulecke (Wiesbaden: VS Verlag für Sozialwissenschaften, 2007), esp. p. 86ff.

79. Georg Hansen, *Die drei Bevölkerungsstufen: Ein Versuch, die Ursachen für das Blühen und das Altern der Bevölkerungen nachzuweisen* (Munich: Lindauer, 1889).

80. Max Sering, "Rede vor dem Deutschen Landwirtschaftsrat," *Archiv des Deutschen Landwirthschaftsraths* 20 (1892).

81. In this context, see George Vascik, "Agrarian Conservatism in Wilhelmine Germany: Diederich Hahn and the Agrarian League," in *Between Reform, Reaction, and Resistance: Studies in the History of German Conservatism from 1789 to 1945*, ed. Larry Eugene Jones and James N. Retallack (Providence: Berg, 1993), 229–260; Geoff Eley, "Anti-Semitism, Agrarian Mobilization, and the Conservative Party: Radicalism and the Containment in the Founding of the Agrarian League 1890–93," in *Between Reform*, ed. Jones and Retallack, 187–228; and Rita Aldenhoff-Hübinger, "'Les nations anciennes, écrasées …': Agrarprotektionismus in Deutschland und Frankreich, 1880–1914," *Geschichte und Gesellschaft* 26 (2000): 439–470.

82. On Sering's wider ideological background and the lasting repercussions of his concept of colonization of the "empty" rural areas on the later political atmosphere in Germany, see Robert L. Nelson, "The Archive for Inner Colonization, the German East, and World War," in *Germans, Poland, and Colonial Expansion to the East: 1850 through the Present*, ed. Nelson (New York: Palgrave Macmillan, 2009), 65–94.

83. *Ein Vermächtnis Moltke's: Stärkung der sinkenden Wehrkraft* (Berlin: Eisenschmidt, 1892), 11.

84. Ursula Ferdinand, "Die Debatte 'Agrar- vs. Industriestaat' und die Bevölkerungsfrage," in *Das Konstrukt Bevölkerung vor, in und nach dem "Dritten Reich"*, ed. Rainer Mackensen and Jürgen Reulecke (Wiesbaden: VS Verlag für Sozialwissenschaften, 2005), 112; Ingenlath, *Aufrüstung*, 145ff.; and Hans-Ulrich Wehler, *Von der "deutschen Doppelrevolution" bis zum Beginn des Ersten Weltkrieges 1849–1914* (Munich: C. H. Beck, 1995), 646ff.

85. Outlined, for example, in Brentano's description of a "crisis of economic studies." Lujo Brentano, "Die Krisis der deutschen Wirtschaftswissenschaften," *Die Nation*, no. 48 (August 28, 1897) and no. 49 (September 4, 1897).

86. For a more detailed description, see also Dieter Lindenlaub, *Richtungskämpfe im Verein für Sozialpolitik: Wissenschaft und Sozialpolitik im Kaiserreich vornehmlich vom Beginn des "Neuen Kursus" bis zum Ausbruch des 1. Weltkriegs* (Wiesbaden: F. Steiner, 1967); and Dieter Krüger, *Nationalökonomen im wilhelminischen Deutschland* (Göttingen: Vandenhoeck & Ruprecht, 1983), 18ff.

87. An examination of well-known publications in 1896 and 1897—for example, the liberal *Nation*—confirms this impression. Brentano used this journal over a longer period to defend the agrarian reforms in Prussia and articulate his criticism of Sering's concept and aim at an "internal colonization." Lujo Brentano, "Die Agrarreform in Preußen," *Die Nation*, no. 24 (March 13, 1897), no. 25 (March 20, 1897), no. 26 (March 27, 1897) and no. 27 (April 3,1897). See also Brentano, "Wollen oder Erkennen? Ein ernstes Wort an Herrn Prof. Dr. Max Sering," *Die Nation*, no. 43 (July 24, 1897).

88. ZLB Sammlung Kuczynski, KUC 7-3-3-59 and KUC 7-3-3-63.

89. Instead, the *Volkszeitung* described Brentano's impressive performance at the lecture and his effect on the young audience: "Whoever lays eyes on him for the first time would assume that this fiery, chiseled head belongs to an artist and not a scholar. And the spirit with which he delivers the lecture would strengthen this impression. The speaker speaks not only with his entire spirit, but also with his entire body. His voice makes it possible for him to reach the farthest corners of the expansive room with no great effort." The content of Sering's lecture, however, was appraised quite negatively. In *Volkszeitung. Organ für Jedermann aus dem Volke*, October 12, 1895.

90. Ammon based his ideas on a series of data of body measurements that he gathered in the southwest of Germany. These projects of racial classification will be analyzed at length in chapter 6.

91. Kuczynski's research for his dissertation, ZLB KUC 7-1-2-371/1.

92. Robert René Kuczynski, *Der Zug nach der Stadt, Statistische Studien über die Bevölkerungsbewegungen im Deutschen Reich* (Stuttgart: Cotta, 1897).

93. The *Allgemeinen Zeitung* published the following polemical account of the activities of the farmers lobby and their statistical endeavors in the parliament: "The most worn-out melodies were played once again. These included a greater consideration of agriculture. The minister of war could prove, however, once again that no justified and feasible wish had been denied. The lamentations continued nevertheless. In the previous session it was demanded that the conscription statistics be outlined. Now they are available, but the results are not those for which the majority wish. So at present attempts are being made in a delightful manner to present these numbers as fully meaningless and to find other reasons to justify the greater burden placed on agriculture." *Allgemeine Zeitung*, October 29, 1897.

94. A report of this lecture was promptly published in various German newspapers, including the *Münchener Neueste Nachrichten*, October 30, 1897; and *Frankfurter Zeitung und Handelsblatt*, November 2, 1897.

95. Brentano himself published a synopsis of his lecture in the *Nation* in an effort to make his objections, at least in an abbreviated form, available to a wider audience:

Lujo Brentano, "Die heutige Grundlage der deutschen Wehrkraft," *Die Nation* 5 (October 30, 1897): 67–71. On these social political styles of argumentation, see also Eckhart Reidegeld, *Staatliche Sozialpolitik in Deutschland*, vol. 1, *Von den Ursprüngen bis zum Untergang des Kaiserreiches 1918*, 2nd ed. (Wiesbaden: VS Verlag für Sozialwissenschaften, 2006), 270ff.

96. Just a couple of examples of these debates in German newspapers: "Wirthschaftliche und soziale Verschiebungen in Deutschland," *Berliner Tageblatt*, November 3, 1897; and *Norddeutsche Allgemeine Zeitung*, November 2, 1897.

97. "Stadt und Land," *Neue Preußische Zeitung*, November 3, 1897. A short time later, Karl Hoffmann wrote in *Die Grenzboten* of the "well-nourished Jews in Berlin, who have avoided agricultural work where possible for almost two millennia": Karl Hoffmann, "Wieviel Rekruten stellt die Landwirtschaft," *Die Grenzboten: Zeitschrift für Politik, Literatur und Kunst* 57 (January 27, 1898), 202.

98. "Unsere Rekruten," *Neue Preußische Zeitung*, February 13, 1897.

99. Lujo Brentano, "Die Wehrfähigkeit der deutschen Nation," *Münchener Neueste Nachrichten*, November 6, 1897; Brentano, "Ein agrarisches Zugeständnis," *Die Nation*, no. 7 (November 20, 1897): 97; Brentano, "Die Grundlage der Deutschen Wehrkraft noch einmal," *Die Nation*, no. 8 (November 27, 1897): 111–113.

100. "Der Schutzverband gegen agrarische Übergriffe," *Neue Preußische Zeitung*, November 9, 1897.

101. "Die heutige Grundlage der deutschen Wehrkraft," *Beilage zur Neuen Preußischen Zeitung*, no. 39 (January 25, 1898).

102. Hoffmann, *Wieviel Rekruten*, 203ff.

103. Otto Ammon, *Die Bedeutung des Bauernstandes für den Staat und die Gesellschaft* (Berlin: Trowitsch, 1894). The theme of rural life as a fountain of youth for the strength of the nation and the military became entrenched as a recurrent theme. See Heinrich Sohnrey, "Wie kann der Landentfremdung der Mannschaften während der Militärdienstzeit entgegengewirkt werden?" *Tägliche Rundschau/Unterhaltungs-Beilage*, March 9, 1898, March 10, 1898, and March 11, 1898; "Gegen die Landbevölkerung," *Tägliche Rundschau*, March 10, 1898; "Die Wurzeln der Volkskraft," *Neue Preußische Zeitung*, October 6, 1898, and October 7, 1898; and "Noch einmal die Wehrkraft im Agrarstaat und Industriestaat," *Neue Preußische Zeitung*, January 13, 1899. The broader body of literature on these subjects refers repeatedly to this formulation; see, for example, Georg Bindewald, *Die Wehrfähigkeit der ländlichen und städtischen Bevölkerung* (Halle: Pierer, 1901), 46 and 62.

104. Heinz Starkenburg, "Volkswirthschaftliche Fabeln in wissenschaftlicher Beleuchtung," *Neuland: Monatsschrift* (February 1898): 299–300.

105. It is quite obvious that the newspaper launched new articles on this topic whenever interest in it seemed to be waning. In fact, the editorial staff initiated a small series—partly to celebrate the first anniversary of the debate's beginning—which was an opportunity for Kuczynski's renewed involvement.

106. Lujo Brentano and Robert René Kuczynski, *Die heutige Grundlage der deutschen Wehrkraft* (Stuttgart: Cotta, 1900).

107. Wehler, *Gesellschaftsgeschichte*, 650ff.; and Hubert Kiesewetter, *Industrielle Revolution in Deutschland: 1815–1914* (Frankfurt: Suhrkamp, 1989), 109.

108. Ministry of War, division for general matters of the army and personnel—Agricultural instruction in the army, HStA M 1/4 Bü 595. It was quite easy to combine these projects intended to protect the farming class with ambitions of an "internal colonization"—for example, in Dade's report in 1914 to the Ecclesiastical Social Congress in Wiesbaden: Dade, *Die Notwendigkeit der Erhaltung und Vermehrung des Deutschen Bauern- und Landarbeiterstandes für die Volks- und Wehrkraft* (Leipzig: Deichert, 1914).

109. Ministry of War, division for general matters of the army and personnel—Results of the conscription proceedings: Copy of the petition from January 23, 1911, to the German Reichstag sent to the royal Ministry of War in Württemberg, HStA S M 1/4 Bü 610.

110. Brentano had written his *Habilitationschrift* (a second dissertation required of academics aspiring to professor status in Germany) in the 1870s on the connection between labor output and social policy.

111. Brentano, "Grundlage," alluded to in Brentano and Kuczynski, *Grundlage*, 13ff.

112. Angelo Mosso, *Una Ascensione d'inverno al Monte Rosa* (Milan: Fratelli Treves, 1885); and Mosso, *Die Ermüdung* (Leipzig: Hirzel, 1892). On Mosso's study of fatigue, see Philipp Felsch, *Laborlandschaften: Physiologische Alpenreisen im 19. Jahrhundert* (Göttingen: Wallstein, 2007), 89ff.; Anson Rabinbach, *The Human Motor: Energy, Fatigue and the Origins of Modernity* (New York: Basic Books, 1990), 133ff.; and François Vatin, "Arbeit und Scheitern: Entstehung und Scheitern der Psychophysiologie der Arbeit," in *Physiologie und industrielle Gesellschaft*, ed. Philipp Sarasin and Jakob Tanner, 356ff.

113. Arthur Dix, "Ueber Volksvermehrung und Wehrkraft in Deutschland," *Preußische Jahrbücher* 91 (January 1898): 51–68.

114. Bindewald, *Wehrfähigkeit*, 4.

115. Ibid., 50ff.

116. Walter Claaßen, "Die abnehmende Kriegstüchtigkeit im Deutschen Reiche in Stadt und Land," *Archiv für Rassen- und Gesellschaftsbiologie*, no. 1 (1909); and Ignaz

Kaup, *Ernährung und Lebenskraft der ländlichen Bevölkerung* (Berlin: Heymann, 1910), 1–51.

117. Alfons Fischer, *Militärtauglichkeit und Industriestaat* (Leipzig: Dietrich, 1912), 4ff.; Moritz Alsberg, *Erbliche Entartung bedingt durch Soziale Einflüsse* (Kassel: Th. G. Fisher, 1903), esp. p. 15ff.

118. Otto von Schjerning, *Sanitätsstatistische Betrachtungen über Volk und Heer* (Berlin: A. Hirschwald, 1910), 3–40.

119. In addition, in Bavaria, the same information, but for the parents of the conscripts, was collected. Robert René Kuczynski, *Ist die Landwirtschaft die wichtigste Grundlage der deutschen Wehrkraft?* (Berlin: Simion, 1905), 10.

120. Kaup, *Ernährung*, 5.

121. Only Carl Ballod and Josef Goldstein noticed that the arguments used in the German debates and those in the English debates that predated these by forty years were partially identical down to the word: Carl Ballod, *Die Lebensfähigkeit der städtischen und ländlichen Bevölkerung* (Leipzig: Duncker & Humblot, 1897); and Josef Goldstein, "Pseudostatistik," *Frankfurter Zeitung*, August 17, 1898. There is an abundance of scholarship on this long tradition of criticism of urbanity—most recently, for example: Ariane Leendertz, *Ordnung schaffen: Deutsche Raumplanung im 20. Jahrhundert* (Göttingen: Wallstein, 2008), 36ff.; Graeme Davison, "The City as Natural System: Theories of Urban History," in *The Pursuit of Urban History*, ed. Derek Fraser and Anthony Sutcliffe (London: E. Arnold, 1983), 349–370; and Sally Sheard and Helen J. Power, eds., *Body and City: Histories of Urban Public Health* (Aldershot: Ashgate, 2000).

122. The former general of the infantry, Wilhelm von Blume, did this in 1913 basically by refraining from complicated extrapolations and qualitative assessments. Instead, his arguments drew solely on troop numbers and an analysis of the institutions. Wilhelm von Blume, *Die Wehrkraft Deutschlands im Vergleich mit der der anderen europäischen Großmächte* (Berlin: Mittler, 1913).

123. Contract between the Carnegie Endowment for International Peace and Dr. René Kuczynski, director of the statistical office of the city of Schoneberg, signed June 26, 1912. Topic: "Influences of changes in occupations of a people upon the composition and efficiency of armies and influences of the changes in the composition of armies on the economic life, in Germany, Austria, and Switzerland" (other countries are to be included in 1914 and 1915), ZLB KUC 7-2-C 174.

124. Ibid.

125. Especially between Josef Goldstein, a statistician in Zurich, and Carl Ballod in Berlin. Compare Josef Goldstein, "Zur 'agrarischen' Beweisführung," *Schweizerische Blätter für Wirtschafts- und Socialpolitik*, no. 1 (1900): 372–375; Carl Ballod, "Zur 'agrarischen' Beweisführung," *Schweizerische Blätter für Wirtschafts- und Socialpolitik*,

no. 4 (1903): 217–222; and Josef Goldstein, "Zur 'agrarischen' Beweisführung," *Schweizerische Blätter für Wirtschafts- und Socialpolitik*, no. 4 (1903): 382–384.

126. Walter Abelsdorff, *Die Wehrfähigkeit zweier Generationen* (Berlin: G. Reimer, 1905).

127. Oswald Heer, a scholar working in Basel, dedicated himself to exploring these topics simultaneously with the emergence of the discussion in Germany. Oswald Heer, *Beitrag zur Kenntnis der Rekrutierungsverhältnisse der landwirtschaftlichen und industriellen Bevölkerung der Schweiz* (Schaffhausen, 1897). To a certain degree, this topic remained current in the scholarship of the subsequent years—for example, in Ernst Laur, *Die Wehrkraft des Schweizer Volkes und des Bauernstandes* (Zurich: Rascher, 1915).

128. Heinrich Schwiening, "Über einige Irrtümer auf dem Gebiet der Heeres-Sanitätsstatistik," *Allgemeine militärmedizinische Zeitschrift* (1910), 637–643.

129. *La Patrie est en danger* (Paris: Alliance nationale pour l'accroissement de la population française, 1913).

2 From Pathologies to Topographies

1. In the French context as well, the Crimean War is often cited as a turning point in the compilation of statistics on illness. However, the revisions the military doctor Chenu made to the French statistics ten years after the war ended adjusted the rate of morbidity and mortality significantly upward and mostly eliminated the seeming advantage of the French military. Chenu concluded that of the ninety-five thousand soldiers who died in the Crimean War, seventy-five thousand did so as the result of illness and epidemic rather than as a direct result of injuries sustained on the battlefield. Jean-Charles Chenu, *Rapport aux Conseil de Santé des armées sur les résultats du service médico-chirurgial aux Ambulances du Crimée et aux hôpitaux militaires français de Turquie pendant la campagne d'Orient en 1854–1855–1856* (Paris: Masson et fils, 1865). In subsequent years, Chenu referred to the Crimean War as a definitive moment leading to increased emphasis on the collection of military medical statistics within the French army. Chenu, "Statistique médico-chirurgiale de la campagne d'Italie en 1859–1860," *Allgemeine militärärztliche Zeitung*, no. 31 (July 31, 1870): 215–216, and no. 32–33 (August 14, 1870): 229–230.

2. Helen Rappaport, *No Place for Ladies: The Untold Story of Women in the Crimean War* (London: Aurum, 2007), 164ff.

3. Mark Bostridge, *Florence Nightingale: The Woman and Her Legend* (London: Viking, 2008), 230.

4. It was "honored" as such nearly 150 years later by the English magazine *The Economist*: "Worth a Thousand Words," *Economist*, December 22, 2007, 70–72.

5. Bostridge, *Nightingale*, 417ff.

6. "Notes on Nursing," in *Florence Nightingale: The Nightingale School, Collected Works of Florence Nightingale*, vol. 12, ed. Lynn McDonald (Waterloo, Ontario: Wilfrid Laurier University Press, 2009), 676. The reception of "Notes on Nursing" abroad testifies to the intensity with which these problems were felt there, too. The first German translation was published the same year as the English original, and a second German translation appeared the next year.

7. Adolphe Quetelet, *Sur l'homme et le développement de ses facultés* (Paris: Bachelier, 1835).

8. Ian Hacking, "Prussian Numbers 1860–1882," in *The Probabilistic Revolution*, ed. Lorenz Krüger, Lorraine J. Daston, and Michael Heidelberger (Cambridge, MA: MIT Press, 1987), 377–394; Hacking, *The Taming of Chance* (Cambridge: Cambridge University Press, 1990).

9. Theodore M. Porter, *The Rise of Statistical Thinking, 1820–1900* (Princeton, NJ: Princeton University Press, 1986), 236.

10. Schmidt reached the same conclusion for the research of the early office of statistics in the 1850s as well: Daniel Schmidt, *Statistik und Staatlichkeit* (Wiesbaden: VS Verlag für Sozialwissenschaften, 2005), 158–159. This was most impressively outlined by Arthur Schiff, a doctor from Vienna, at the International Congress for Hygiene and Demography in Berlin: Arthur Schiff, "Über die Morbiditätsstatistik der Krankenkassen," in *Bericht über den XIV. Internationalen Kongress für Hygiene und Demographie, Berlin, 23.–29. September 1907*, vol. 4 (Berlin, 1908), 802.

11. On the chronological divergence from knowledge, legislation, and politics, see also François Ewald, *Der Vorsorgestaat* (Frankfurt: Suhrkamp, 1993), 46ff.; and on the question of prevention and care versus liberal pragmatism, ibid., 92ff.

12. E. Peter Hennock, *The Origin of the Welfare State in England and Germany, 1850–1914: Social Policies Compared* (Cambridge: Cambridge University Press, 2007).

13. Peter Baldwin, *Contagion and the State in Europe, 1830–1930* (Cambridge: Cambridge University Press, 1999), 128ff.

14. Odile Roynette, "La statistique médicale de l'armée française au XIXe siècle: Un instrument de savoir et de pouvoir démographiques?," in *Bevölkerungsfragen: Prozesse des Wissenstransfers in Deutschland und Frankreich (1870–1939)*, ed. Petra Overath and Patrick Krassnitzer (Cologne: Böhlau, 2007), 68–69.

15. Louis Benoiston de Châteauneuf, "Essai sur la mortalité dans l'infanterie française," *Annales d'hygiène publique et de médecine légale* 10 (1833): 269; cited from Roynette, *Statistique*, 69.

16. Jean-Christian Boudin, "Études sur le récrutement de l'armée," *Annales d'Hygiène Publique et de médecine légale* 41 (1849).

17. Ibid., 28–29.

18. Boudin also strove to make comprehensive international comparisons, but came to the conclusion that the information available for most countries was quite insufficient. Using ancient sources in part, he compared the military health statistics of the French army to those of the Roman army, but also with statistics from Prussia, England, Saxony, and the United States; however, he could only reach partial conclusions. See Boudin, *Hygiène militaire*. Interestingly, he found that in all the countries he had compared, those troops who were stationed in rural areas had a lower morbidity rate than those in urban areas (138).

19. Ibid., 1.

20. *Statistical Report on the Sickness and Mortality in the Army of the United States* (Washington, DC: Bowman, 1840).

21. As Schmidt—somewhat generally—assumes for the early professional ambitions of the statisticians: Schmidt, *Statistik*, 104ff.

22. Ernst Engel, ed., *Der Internationale Statistische Congreß in Berlin: Ein Bericht an die Vorbereitungs-Commission der V. Sitzungsperiode des Congresses über die Gegenstände der Tagesordnung derselben* (Berlin: R. Decker, 1863), 11.

23. Ibid., 12.

24. Ibid., 14.

25. Cited from Fröhlich, "Musterungsstatistik."

26. Von Hassinger and Pundschu, "Statistischer Bericht über die Resultate der Assentirung im Stellungsjahre 1869," *Allgemeine militärärztliche Zeitung*, no. 28–29 (July 17, 1870), 187–191; and "Rekrutirungs-Resultate," *Der Militärarzt*, no. 6 (March 20, 1869). The report differentiates among occupations when detailing disease patterns. Simultaneously, the authors aimed for a systematic comparison to other European countries. The comparison to the English army was thereby especially important: "Zur Medizinalstatistik: Sanitäre Verhältnisse der englischen Armee im Jahre 1867," *Der Militärarzt*, no. 22 (November 6, 1869); Glatter, "Englische Militärstatistik," *Der Militärarzt*, no. 7 (April 16, 1870); and Glatter, "Was in England geschieht und was in Österreich geschehen sollte," *Der Militärarzt*, no. 23 (December 24, 1870).

27. Zemanek, *Werth und Bedeutung*, 12.

28. There were isolated surveys that began earlier, but these lacked analytical depth. In France, the first statistics were published in 1864. Odile Roynette describes their qualitative development: "The first volume of the series created a descriptive frame, the structure of which was not questioned until the outbreak of World War I, even though it did adapt to accommodate developments within the field of medical knowledge and new concerns related to the respective hygienic threats" (author's

translation). Roynette, "Statistique médicale," 70. The report appeared as "Statistique médicale de l'armée pendant l'année 1862" (Paris, 1864). And, in a similar vein, at the behest of the House of Parliament, *Army Medical Department Report for the Year 1878* (London, 1880).

29. Wilhelm August Roth, *Jahresbericht über die Leistungen und Fortschritte auf dem Gebiete des Militär-Sanitätswesens, Nr. 7* (Berlin: Mittler, 1881). On Roth, one of those who founded his own school of "military hygiene," see Rolf Rehe, "Wilhelm August Roth (1833–1892)," *Sächsische Biografie*, ed. Institut Für Sächsische Geschichte Und Volkskunde e.V., 2007, http://saebi.isgv.de/biografie-druck/Wilhelm_August_Roth _(1833-1892) (accessed May 11, 2018).

30. "Sanitätsbericht über die Königlich Preußische Armee" (Berlin, 1882 [and subsequent years]), cited from Zemanek, *Werth und Bedeutung*, 22.

31. This situation was only different for 1870 to 1871, when they were at war; for this period, comprehensive medical statistics were later published: *Sanitätsbericht über die Deutschen Heere im Kriege gegen Frankreich 1870/71*, ed. Medizinal-Abtheilung des Königlich-Preussischen Kriegsministeriums, 5 vols. (Berlin, 1884), Bundesarchiv—Militärarchiv Freiburg i.Br., PHD 6/161.

32. Paul von Myrdacz, "Internationale Militär-Sanitätsstatistik," *Der Militärarzt* 32, no. 11–12 (1898): 90.

33. *Atti dell'XI Congresso Medico Internazionale, Roma, 29 Marzo–5 Aprile 1894*, vol. 4 (Rome, 1895), 51–52.

34. Paul von Myrdacz, "Ergebnisse der internationalen Militärsanitätsstatistik," in *Compte rendu du XVI congrès international de médecine, Budapest août-septembre 1909. Séction XX: Services sanitaires militaire et maritime* (Budapest, 1910), 299.

35. After the major reforms in the organization of the military in 1875, the first statistical reports were compiled in 1876; BAR E 27–No. 5848.

36. The Swiss military officials and doctors were those who worked together with statisticians from the very beginning on this point, because they feared not only a misuse of the relevant statistical material but also the possibility that the work of the conscription committees might be otherwise influenced. Statement of the Swiss surgeon general, dated May 31, 1879; BAR E 27–No. 5856; see also chapter 3.

37. Myrdacz, "Ergebnisse," 318ff.

38. Correspondence between the Swiss surgeon general and the Swiss Department of the Military, March 1911; BAR E 27–19502. It should not go unmentioned that the first studies on medical discharges for illness—a summary of those figures for the years 1886–1905—had been published in 1906 in *Schweizerische Zeitschrift für Statistik*.

39. Myrdacz, *Internationale Militär-Sanitätsstatistik*.

40. "The calculation of the tables [was previously] carried out in part by office personnel within this department, and in part by external employees; the text of the first part, however, was prepared group by group by the commanding medical officers in the medical division itself. … This latter task has been assigned since the year 1898 to the leader of the laboratory for hygiene and chemistry in the Kaiser Wilhelms-Akademie, Professor Dr. Pfuhl, who at that time carried the rank of major doctor; [in addition], a captain in the medical corps was appointed to serve the academy for this purpose." Hermann Schmidt, *Die Kaiser Wilhelms-Akademie für das militärärztliche Bildungswesen. Von 1895 bis 1910. Festschrift zur Einweihung des Neubaues der Akademie* (Berlin: Mittler, 1910), 85.

41. Medical reports on the German army, 1906–1929, BArch Reichsgesundheitsamt R 86 2399; see also Heinrich Hartmann, "Die Produktion der Wehrbevölkerung: Musterungskommissionen als Begegnungsort von Demografie und medizinischem Expertenwissen, 1890–1914," in *Jenseits von Humboldt: Wissenschaft im Staat 1850–1990*, ed. Axel C. Hüntelmann and Michael C. Schneider (Frankfurt: Peter Lang, 2010), 149–164.

42. Letter from the Ministry of War to the minister of foreign affairs, dated March 2, 1907, BArch R 1501–11163.

43. Schjerning, "Ansprache." On Schjerning and his career, both as a scholar within the military and as a politician, see Robin Joppich, "Otto von Schjerning (4.10.1853–28.06.1921). Wissenschaftler, Generalstabsarzt der preußischen Armee und Chef des deutschen Feldsanitätswesens im Ersten Weltkrieg" (PhD diss., Heidelberg University, 1997).

44. Correspondence between the Ministry of the Interior and the Imperial Chancellery, including assorted texts dealing with the preparation for the congress, BArch R 1501–111164.

45. Memorandum from the government to the German embassy in Paris, dated July 31, 1907, BArch R 1501–111164.

46. Schjerning, "Ansprache," 818.

47. Myrdasz, *Ergebnisse*.

48. The question of "recruitment statistics" had definitively been separated from military medical statistics since the Berlin congress in 1907. The topic was covered in section 6 of the eighth subdivision of the congress. *Bericht über den XIV. Internationalen Kongress für Hygiene und Demographie, Berlin, 23.–29. Sept. 1907*, vol. 3, no. 2 (Berlin: A. Hirschwald, 1908), 1202–1212.

49. Letter from Minister of War Einem to the Ministry of the Interior, dated November 23, 1905, BArch R 1501, Reichsministerium des Inneren—Militaria, Militärsanitätswesen, Band 112506.

50. We will discuss this point further in chapter 3.

51. Myrdasz, *Ergebnisse*, 317.

52. The parallels in these fears is best illustrated in a report released by the British government in 1903 on "physical deterioration" among the populace. Paradoxically, a close reading of this report reveals that the relevant data collected in the course of military examinations had shown general improvement for years rather than deteriorating. Letter of the undersecretary of state, Almeric W. Fitz Roy, to the British Ministry of War, dated October 26, 1903, in *Report of the Inter-Departmental Committee on Physical Deterioration, Band 1: Report and Appendix*, ed. Houses of Parliament by Command of His Majesty (London: H. M. Stationery Office, 1904), 100.

53. Philip Curtin, *Disease and Empire: The Health of European Troops in the Conquest of Africa* (Cambridge: Cambridge University Press, 1998); Heinrich Hartmann, "Soldaten in den Tropen, Soldaten aus den Tropen: Neudefinitionen der Wehrkraft im kolonialen Kontext zwischen 1884 und 1914," in *Koloniale Politik und Praktiken Deutschlands und Frankreichs 1880–1962/Politiques et pratiques coloniales dans les empires allemands et français, 1880–1962*, ed. Alain Chatriot and Dieter Gosewinkel (Stuttgart: Steiner, 2010), 223–246.

54. "Statistische Sanitätsbericht über die Kaiserlich Deutsche Marine," ed. Medizinalabteilung des Reichsmarineamtes (Berlin, 1874–1899). Later, the report was called simply "Sanitätsbericht über die Kaiserlich Deutsche Marine."

55. Similar regular reports or reports for individual campaigns were available for all the colonial powers in Europe. For example, Robert, "Rapport médical d'inspection générale de 1899 sur le 4e régiment de tirailleurs tonkinois," *Archives de médecine navale* 73 (1900), 321–366; and "Statistique médicale de l'armée des indes Néerlandaise orientales pour 1894," *Geneeskundig Tijdschrift voor Nederlandsch Indie*, no. 2 and 3 (1895).

56. Hartmann, "Soldaten."

57. Elliott, *Military Statistics*, 25–26.

58. Armand Joseph Meyenne, *Eléments de statistiques médicales militaires* (Brussels, 1859), 1.

59. "Die Armee und ihre Erkrankungen," *Allgemeine militärärztliche Zeitschrift* 23 (June 5, 1879), 157–158.

60. Claire Fredj, "Médecins en campagne, médecines des lointains: Le service de santé des armées en campagne dans les expéditions lointaines du Second Empire (Crimée, Chine-Cochinchine, Mexique)" (unpublished PhD diss., Ecole des Hautes Études en Sciences Sociales, 2006), 36–37.

61. Chenu, *Recrutement*, 3ff.

62. Chanet, *Vers l'armée*, 227. Such efforts to improve healthcare also played an important role in the German context. At the medical congress in Berlin, the Hessian military doctor Alfred Villaret reported on reforms implemented in urban barracks: Alfred Villaret, "Militär-Sanitätswesen," in *Verhandlungen des X. Internationalen Medicinischen Congresses, Berlin 4.–9. Aug. 1890*, vol. 1 (Berlin, 1891), esp. pp. 327–328.

63. Frocard, *Aptitude*, 7.

64. Ibid., 235–236.

65. Fredj, "Médecins," 106.

66. Lachaud, *Pour la race: Notre Soldat, sa caserne* (Paris: H. Charles-Lavauzelle, 1909), 6.

67. Ibid., 17. In a similar vein, see Frocard, *Aptitude*, 7ff.

68. Such reporting requirements, especially for tuberculous patients, were instituted by the Prussian Ministry of War despite Einem's open skepticism. Copy of the instructions of the minister of war, dated March 22, 1906, Reichsministerium des Inneren/Militaria—Militärsanitätswesen, BArch 112506; and instructions on the completion of the registration form, BArch 112507. The requirement originated in the health department in the overseeing authority, the Imperial Office of the Interior. On institutionalized prevention in the field of hygiene, see Axel C. Hüntelmann, *Hygiene im Namen des Staates: Das Reichsgesundheitsamt, 1876–1933* (Göttingen: Wallstein Verlag, 2008). On attempts within the military to stem epidemics, as reflected in the statistics, see also Schjerning, "Ansprache."

69. Baldwin, *Contagion*, 525.

70. Fröhlich, "Musterungsstatistik," 94.

71. Von Hassinger and Pundschu, "Statistischer Bericht," 188.

72. Ibid.

73. Ibid., 210–213.

74. An early study of conscription statistics for mountainous regions in France found a similar increased frequency of goiter: Vincent Nivet, *Etudes sur le goitre épidémique* (Paris: J.-B. Baillière et fils, 1873).

75. Lengwiler, *Zwischen Klinik*, 279.

76. BA Bern, E 27 Tit 5856.

77. This disease had been "discovered" in Switzerland four decades before, when Doctor Guggenbühl issued his "cry for help" that went on to become famous: Johann Jakob Guggenbühl, "Hülfsruf aus den Alpen, zur Bekämpfung des schrecklichen Cretinismus," in *Maltens Bibliothek der neuesten Weltkunde*, vol. 1 (Aarau: Sauerländer, 1840).

78. Josef Hürlimann, *Ueber die Ergebnisse der Sanitarischen Rekruten-Musterung in der Schweiz während der Jahre 1875 bis 1879: Eine populäre militärärztliche Skizze (erstes Referat an die Festversammlung der schweizerischen gemeinnützigen Gesellschaft, 21.09.1880 in Zug)* (Zurich: J. Herzog, 1880), 47.

79. Jean-Pierre Colombo, *Heinrich Bircher (1850–1923): Chirurg, Demograph und Militärarzt* (Stuttgart: B. Schwabe, 1961), 15 and 59ff.

80. Heinrich Bircher, *Der endemische Kropf und seine Beziehung zur Taubstummheit und zum Cretinismus* (Basel: Schwabe, 1883).

81. "There are, however, no observable differences in the outer characteristics of the soil; in the physical geological properties; in the races and social circumstances (industrial vs. agricultural, etc)." Heinrich Bircher, *Die Rekrutierung und Ausmusterung der schweizerischen Armee* (Aarau: Sauerländer, 1886), 20.

82. Ibid.

83. Ibid., 21.

84. Records of Heinrich Bircher's preparations for his statistical study in the 1880s and 1890s, Medizinhistorisches Archiv Zürich PN 10.1 50.

85. Heinrich Bircher, *Die Armeeorganisation und Militärkreiseinteilung der schweizerischen Eidgenossenschaft auf Grundlage der Tauglichkeitsziffern* (Aarau: Sauerländer, 1886), 35. Bircher here used a scientific "stylistic device" that was frequently employed in the debate over "military strength"—namely, historical comparison. Such comparisons involved a rather indiscriminate conglomeration of supposedly confirmed historical statements—for example, from ancient sources like Tacitus's description of the Germanic peoples. Depending on whether scholars compared contemporary European nations to those in antiquity or the Middle Ages, with the Romans or with the Germanic tribes, their arguments could be trimmed in accordance with their ideological and scientific tendencies. For example, see Moritz Alsberg, *Militäruntauglichkeit und Großstadt-Einfluß: Hygienisch-volkswirtschaftliche Betrachtungen und Vorschläge* (Leipzig: Teubner, 1909); and Ferdinand Hueppe, "Ueber die Körperübungen in Schule und Volk und ihren Werth für die militaerischen Uebungen," in *Festschrift zur 100 jährigen Stiftungsfeier des medizinisch-chirurgischen Friedrich-Wilhelms-Instituts, 2. Dezember 1895* (Berlin: Mittler, 1895), 485-486. Especially revealing for the French case, for which this element had a longer tradition in the scholarship, see Vitu, *Histoire civile*; and Boudin, *Hygiène militaire*.

86. Richard A. Soloway, *Demography and Degeneration: Eugenics and the Decline of Birthrate in Twentieth-Century Britain* (Chapel Hill: University of North Carolina Press, 1990). We will discuss this point further in chapter 6.

87. Bircher, *Armeeorganisation*, 12.

88. Ibid., 16.

89. Armee Sanitätsstatistik 1895–1910—Dossier 1906; BArch Militärarchiv E 5540 no. 521, vol. 1.

90. François Naville, *Contribution à l'étude de l'aliénation mentale dans l'armée suisse et dans les armées étrangères: Etude clinique, statistique, et de prophylaxie* (Geneva: Librairie Kündig, 1910).

91. In 1889, Chassagne formulated the ambitious goal for France of "contributing to a medical geography of France and North Africa via the examination of each individual garrison for dominant and endemic illness." Chassagne, *Les cahiers de 1889 de la médecine militaire française: Officiers du corps de santé miliaire de l'armée active, réserve et armée territoriale* (Paris: H. Charles-Lavauzelle, 1889), 59.

92. This dynamic, including the development of the thematic map as a new zenith of demographic visualization, is described, for example, in Hermann Hasse, *Die Statistik als Hilfsmittel der Sozialwissenschaften: Mit besonderer Berücksichtigung des Schaubildes* (Leipzig: Dietrich, 1911), 9. On the history of the demographic map, see Sybilla Nikolow, "Die Nation als statistisches Kollektiv: Bevölkerungskonstruktion im Kaiserreich und in der Weimarer Republik," in *Wissenschaft und Nation*, ed. Ralph Jessen and Jakob Vogel (Frankfurt: Campus, 2002), 235–259; and Morgane Labbé, "Die Grenzen der deutschen Nation: Raum der Karte, Statistik, Erzählung," in *Die Grenze als Raum, Erfahrung und Konstruktion. Deutschland, Frankreich und Polen*, ed. Etienne François, Jörg Seifarth, and Bernhard Struck (Frankfurt: Campus, 2007), 293–319. On this topic, see also Helmut Walser Smith, "An Preußens Rändern, oder: Die Welt die dem Nationalismus verloren ging," in *Kaiserreich*, ed. Sebastian Conrad and Jürgen Osterhammel (Göttingen: Vandenhoeck & Ruprecht, 2004), 149–169.

3   In the Realm of the Experts

1. Gustave Lagneau, *Considérations médicales et anthropologiques sur la réorganisation de l'armée en France: Mémoire lu à l'académie de médecine le 18 juillet 1871* (Paris: Masson, 1871), 4.

2. Frocard, *Aptitude*, 24.

3. Fischer, *Militärtauglichkeit*, 7–8.

4. Wolfgang U. Eckart, *Medizin und Kolonialimperialismus: Deutschland 1884–1945* (Paderborn: Schöningh, 1997); Fredj, "Médecins en campagne," 106ff.

5. "Die allgemeine Wehrpflicht und die Aerzte: Von einem österreichischen Feldarzt," *Der Militärarzt*, no. 2 (January 22, 1868): 12; Du Cazal, *Petit guide adminsitratif du Médecin militaire* (Paris: Berger-Levrault, 1882), 5; and C. Lasalle, *Code-manuel des obligations: Manuel général du recrutement et des réserves* (Paris: Berger-Levrault, 1893), 61.

6. It should be mentioned, however, that this formal principle of scientific expertise only gradually found recognition. Paragraphs 44 and 45 of the French regulations for conscription stipulated that if there was a lack of qualified military personnel, local policemen or quartermasters could examine recruits. *Manuel du recrutement ou recueil des ordonnances, instructions approuvées par le Roi, circulaires et décisions ministérielles, auxquelles l'exécution de la loi du 10 mars 1818 a donné lieu*, ed. Ministry of War of France (Paris: Imprimerie nationale, 1820).

7. See the correspondence of the Ministry of War with the civilian chairman of the *Oberrekrutierungsrat* in Württemberg between 1876 and 1880. These letters also reveal the extent to which these structures relied on Prussia's example, because the controversy between the Ministry of War and the *Oberrekrutierungsrat* was only solved by a Prussian suggestion and the adoption of Prussian structures. Ministry of War, division for general matters of the army and personnel, HStA S M 1/4 Bü 575. See also Ingrid Mayershofer, *Bevölkerung und Militär in Bamberg 1860–1923: Eine bayerische Stadt und der preußische-deutsche Militarismus* (Paderborn: Schöningh, 2010), 161ff.

8. On this point, too, there was a great structural similarity to other European countries. The mode of operation of this conscription process was always accompanied by political, administrative, and military concerns. Therefore in France, too, where ten members made up the commission (five representatives and five substitutes), there were a number of minor reforms around the turn of the century that affected the process. Organisation und Mobilisation générale, 1907–1908, État major, SHAT 7 N 105; see especially the correspondence between the minister of war and the president of the Council of Ministers. See also the numerous modifications in *Instruction relative aux opérations du conseil de revision pour la formation des classes* (Paris, R. Chapelot, 1890 [and subsequent years]).

9. A particularly early witness is found in *Instructionen für die, zu den Rekruten-Aushebungen commandirten Militäraerzte* (Berlin, n.d. [1858]); Borowski, *Die Aushebung: Ein Ratgeber für die Ober-Ersatz und Ersatzkommissionen* (Berlin: Liebmann, 1890); *Instruction relative*; Du Cazal, *Petit guide*; and O. Kunow, *Musterung, Aushebung und Prüfungsgeschäft. Für Sanitätsoffiziere und die bei diesen Geschäften mitwirkenden Offiziere und Zivilbeamten* (Berlin: Mittler, 1907).

10. Ingenlath, *Mentale Aufrüstung*; Kunow, *Musterung*.

11. Borowski, *Aushebung*, 7.

12. Although the job titles and at times the level in the hierarchy of individual members in the countries of the German Empire could vary, after German unification the basic methods of the conscription councils were adjusted to comply in principle with the Prussian example. This was due in part to direct pressure the imperial government exerted on the army leadership in the individual countries. See correspondence between the Ministry of War of Württemberg and the *Oberrekrutier-*

ungsrat, 1876–1880, "Ober-Rekrutirungsrath." Ministry of War, division for general matters of the army and personnel, HStA S M 1876/1880 Bü 575.

13. Kunow, *Musterung*, 4ff.

14. Borowski, *Aushebung*, 24.

15. See the appendix to "Verhandlungen der XXXII. Plenarversammlung des Deutschen Landwirtschaftsraths," *Archiv des Deutschen Landwirthschaftsraths* 32 (1904): 257–260.

16. Kuczynski, *Ist die Landwirtschaft*, 12; "Gemeinsamer Antrag der Referenten," in "Verhandlungen der XXXII. Plenarversammlung," 281–282.

17. Frevert, *Jakobinische Modell*, 39.

18. Roynette, *Bon pour le service*, 182ff.

19. Letter of the Royal Ministry of the Interior to the royal *Oberrekrutierungsrat*, Royal Superior Conscription Commissions, Royal Conscription Commissions, and the Royal City Administration of Stuttgart and the Royal *Oberämter*, dated August 16, 1913; Verordnungen, Oberersatzkommission, HStA S M 11 Bü 2.

20. *Instructionen*.

21. Fröhlich, "Musterungsstatistik."

22. Emile Duponchel, *Du diagnostic de la faiblesse de constitution au point de vue du recrutement militaire* (Paris: O. Doin, 1887), 6–7.

23. Ridolfo Livi, "Über den Nutzen anthropometrischer Grenzwerte für die Assenier-ung" (article series), *Der Militärarzt* 40, no. 1–4 (1911); and "Über den Nutzen anthropometrischer Grenzwerte für die Assenierung (Kommentar und Zusammen-fassung)," *Allgemeine militärärztliche Zeitschrift* 40, no. 8 (1911).

24. Kunow, *Musterung*, 70. The Swiss doctor Hürlimann made similar claims: he described the attempts of the Swiss Federal Council to influence the criteria employed in the examination of potential recruits and the reactions of the military doctors who sought to defend their own professional independence. In a similar vein of argumentation, Bircher emphasized the importance of trusting the "expert eyes" in the final decision. Bircher, *Rekrutierung und Ausmusterung*, 4ff.; and Hürli-mann, *Ergebnisse*, 10.

25. Hahn, "Besprechung von O. Kunow: Musterung, Aushebung und Prüfungsge-schäft: Zweite und vermehrte Auflage, Berlin 1907 (Mittler)," *Allgemeine militärärztli-che Zeitschrift* 37, no. 8 (1908): 330–331.

26. Camille Billot, *Conférence: Rôle du médecin dans le régiment* (Paris, 1891).

27. Lachaud, *Pour la race*, 16–17.

28. See chapter 1.

29. Correspondence between "Premier bureau—effectifs" and the Ministry of War, March 1895. Circular to the conseils de revisions, dated March 2, 1895, Premier bureau "effectifs." 1895–1896, État major, SHAT 7 N 125.

30. Rapport au ministère de la guerre, "Réorganisation des Cadres du Corps de Santé," June 4, 1895; Premier bureau "effectifs." 1895–1896, État major, SHAT 7 N 125.

31. Alphonse Dumas, *Le conseil de révision: Ce qu'il est, ce qu'il devrait être* (Montpellier: C. Boehm, 1891), 4.

32. Selig, *Malnutrition et développement*, 50ff.

33. Emile Duponchel, *Traité de médecine légale militaire* (Paris: O. Doin, 1890), 26.

34. Alphonse Dumas, *Les étudiants en médecine: La loi de "deux ans"* (Montpellier: Delord-Boehm et Martial, 1904), 6.

35. Dumas, *Conseil*, 5.

36. Similar situations are reported time and time again: Dumas, *Conseil*, 4–5; Duponchel, *Traité*, 43; Billot, *Conférence*; and Chassagne, *Cahiers*. See also Fredj, "Médecins en campagne," 128ff.

37. Adrien Barthélemy, *L'examen de la vision devant les conseils de revision et de réforme dans la marine et dans l'armée et devant les commissions des chemins de fer* (Paris: J.-B. Baillière et fils, 1889), 12–13.

38. Copy of a report to the surgeon general, "Réorganisation des cadres du corps de santé," État major, Premier bureau—effectifs, SHAT 7 N 125, June 6, 1895.

39. Dumas, *Etudiants*. Despite these frequent vehement complaints, the situation hardly changed before the war's outbreak. In 1911, the general staff of the army urgently reported to the Ministry of War that the number of doctors available within the military was insufficient to effectively examine potential recruits and that civilian doctors were often called upon to assist in the procedure. "Note pour le Cabinet du ministre (Section d'Etudes) par l'État major," 27.12.1911, Actes diverses sur le recrutement, 1870–1914, État major, SHAT 7 N 26.

40. Duponchel, *Traité*, 47; and Duponchel, *Du diagnostic*, 6–7.

41. See also Dienel, *Staatsräson*; Ronsin, *Grève*; and DeLucca, *Famille*.

42. This was in part thanks to the radical socialist representative Lachaud, who raised the question repeatedly in publications and in the political debates of the *assemblée nationale*. Lachaud, *Pour la race*.

43. Frocard, *Aptitude*, 24–25.

44. This discussion is reproduced in *Bulletin bi-mensuel de la Société de médecine militaire française* 7 (1913) and 8 (1914): 238–247.

45. According to the Médecin-major Albouze from Paris; *Bulletin bi-mensuel* 7 and 8: 238–239.

46. Description of Doctor Rouget; *Bulletin bi-mensuel* 7 and 8: 246–247.

47. Report by the military doctor Solomon; *Bulletin bi-mensuel* 7 and 8: 414.

48. *Bulletin bi-mensuel*, no. 17 (1913): 609.

49. Compared to Germany, for example, this process was somewhat delayed in France. Susanne Michl has pointed to differences in the professional situation of doctors in general, which resulted in turn from the varied models of public insurance. Susanne Michl, *Im Dienste des "Volkskörpers": Deutsche und französische Ärzte im Ersten Weltkrieg* (Göttingen: Vandenhoeck & Ruprecht, 2007), 49ff. See also *Histoire de la médecine aux armées*, vol. 2, *De la Révolution française au conflit mondial de 1914*, ed. Comité d'Histoire du Service de Santé (Paris: C. Lavauzelle, 1984), 251ff.; and Lachaud, *Pour la race*, 114–115.

50. *Der Militärarzt; Militärärztliches Wochenblatt*; and *Bulletin bi-mensuel de la Société de médecine militaire française*. An exception regarding such foundations was found in Austria-Hungary, which founded its own bureau for military statistics in 1861. As a result, the military did not view it as necessary to form an additional institution that would lack a central program. Von Hassinger and Pundschu, "Statistischer Bericht," 188.

51. Frocard, *Aptitude*, 63–64.

52. For example, Ferdinand Hueppe, a doctor in Prague, pointed to the importance of the examination for the professional identity of military medical professionals: Ferdinand Hueppe, "Unsere Militärärzte," *Allgemeine militärärztliche Zeitschrift* (1907): 1023.

53. Clearly, for example, in Brühl, "Bedürfen grosse Militärstaaten einer eigenen Bildungsanstalt für die Ärzte ihrer Armeen oder nicht?," *Der Militärarzt*, no. 12 (June 8, 1867): 177–180, and no. 13 (June 22, 1867): 193–196.

54. For an overview, see Hans Bischoff, *Festschrift zur 50jährigen Stiftungsfeier der Berliner Militärärztlichen Gesellschaft am 20.2.1914* (Berlin: Mittler, 1914), 10; see also Hartmann, *Produktion*, 156ff.; on the association for military doctors in Berlin, see Johannes Riegler, *Das medicinische Berlin* (Berlin: Mittler, 1873), 115ff.

55. Schjerning, *Sanitätsstatistische Betrachtungen*, 7–8. Infantry General von Blume ensured that the military's position was heard and that the public debate was corrected somewhat by emphasizing the role of the political will in the formation of criteria for military fitness. Von Blume, *Wehrkraft*, 14–15.

56. Schjerning, *Sanitätsstatistische Betrachtungen*; and Joppich, *Otto von Schjerning*, 72.

57. Statutes of the Société des médecine militaire française, dated October 30, 1906, printed in *Archives de médecine navale* 11, no. 86 (1906): 390–392.

58. Forward to the first edition of the *Bulletin bi-mensuel de la Société de médecine militaire française*, published in 1907.

59. Although the military administration did attempt to codify such vague judgments by doctors in some way: paragraph 32 of the Prussian instructions for appraising suitability for military service issued in 1909 outline unquantifiable characteristics that are nevertheless recommended to the military doctors as criteria: "Outer general signs of a healthy body are firm, elastic skin, a strong neck, broad shoulders, a well-formed chest, a well-built back, properly situated shoulder blades, strong bones, firm muscles, flexible arms and hands, healthy legs and feet, and an appropriate weight." *Dienstanweisung zur Beurteilung der Militärdienstfähigkeit und zur Ausstellung von militärärztlichen Zeugnissen* (Berlin: Mittler, 1909).

60. Bischoff, *Brauchbarkeit*, 16–17.

61. F. Kratz, *Recrutirung und Invalidisierung: Eine militärärztliche Studie* (Erlangen, 1872), 1.

62. Ibid., 5ff.

63. Ibid., 3.

64. On this point, Ingenlath contributes valuable insights, especially for the situations in Bavaria and France: Ingenlath, *Mentale Aufrüstung*, 136ff. On the other hand, Ingenlath's claim that the statistical registration of members of the military represents the beginnings of a "modern registration state" (*Erfassungsstaat*) seems questionable, given the situation described later in this chapter regarding the professional interests and frequent apathy of or even rejection on the part of the state authorities.

65. "Die Armee und ihre Erkrankungen," *Allgemeine militärärztliche Zeitung*, no. 21–22 (May 29, 1870): 149.

66. On March 20, 1879, the director of the Swiss Bureau of Statistics submitted a petition to the Federal Council that was responsible for this area. Ten days later, the Swiss surgeon general noted, "The statistics can only be considered to the extent to which this does not infringe upon their main purpose." Letter of the Swiss surgeon general to the Swiss Department of the Military, dated March 31, 1879, BA Bern, E 27 5856; military regulation passed 1874; BA Bern, E 27 Tit 5826.

67. The Department of the Interior also vehemently fought for the interests of the statisticians and did not shy from confrontation with the Department of the Military. Compare the corresponding petition of the Department of the Interior from

June 18, 1879, to the surgeon general's reply, dated June 24, 1879; BA Bern, E 27 Tit 5856.

68. Heer, *Beitrag*; and Lengwiler, *Zwischen Klinik*, 281.

69. The assembly of chief medical officers filed such a petition in April 1888, while observing that the situation had changed little despite the complaints filed in the preceding years. Letter to the Swiss Department of the Military, April 14, 1888; BA Bern, E 27 Tit 5830.

70. For example, *Resultate der Recrutenmusterung im Herbste 1885*, ed. Statistisches Bureau des eidgenössischen Departements des Inneren (Bern, 1886); also in BA Bern, E 27 Tit 5856.

71. Letter of the Swiss surgeon general to the Swiss Department of the Military, March 31, 1879, BA Bern, E 27 Tit 5856.

72. Letter of the Swiss surgeon general to the Swiss Department of the Military, May 5, 1888, BA Bern, E 27 Tit 5830.

73. Letter of the Swiss surgeon general to the Swiss Department of the Military, May 31, 1888, BA Bern, E 27 Tit 5830.

74. BA Bern, E 27 Tit 5830.

75. Conferenz der Schweizerischen Erziehungs-Directoren, 10.6.1882, E 27 Tit 5862.

76. For example, the letter from the council in Graubünden, dated April 30, 1879, BA Bern E 27 Tit 5827.

77. The Department of the Military's criticism of the statistical bureau was at times so intense that the analysis of the "medical examination of potential recruits" was halted in the 1890s and only the pedagogical surveys were centrally compiled. It says something that the Swiss surgeon general suggested in 1903 that these studies should be resumed to have a better overview of the regional differences in physical characteristics: "From the perspective of these considerations, it would be advantageous if the confederate bureau of statistics would resume the statistical compilation of the conscription results which has been discontinued for a number of years. I myself cannot complete these work without the appointment of an assistant versed in statistical methods. Signed, the Swiss surgeon general of the confederate army of Switzerland." Department of the Military, Bern, June 30, 1903, in BA Bern E 27 Tit 5831.

78. Similar petitions were filed in the 1870s and 1880s by the Cantons of Uri, Solothurn, Fribourg, Nidwalden, Graubünden, and Appenzell (with multiple petitions); BA Bern, E 27 Tit 5869.

79. These complaints were made after the Department of the Military issued new regulations for the compilation of military statistics. Petition of the Canton of

Appenzell Innerrhoden, dated August 7, 1900, and Appenzell Außerrhoden, dated August 11, 1900.

80. For example, the letter from the cantonal government of Thurgau, dated September 3, 1900.

81. Werner Lustenberger, *Pädagogische Rekrutenprüfung: Ein Beitrag zur Schweizer Schulgeschichte* (Chur: Rüegger, 1996), 90ff.

82. The inspector of the examination of recruits to the federal counselor, head of the Department of the Military, March 27, 1893; BA Bern, E 27 Tit 5862.

83. Swiss Department of the Military, July 6, 1893; BA Bern, E 27 Tit 5862.

84. Decree of the Swiss Department of the Military to the senior pedagogical experts, October 21, 1905; BA Bern, E 27 Tit 5862.

85. Letter of the Swiss Department of the Military to the executive council of the Canton of Bern, dated June 20, 1907; E 27 Tit 5862.

86. "Examens de recrues," *Le Démocrate*, June 13, 1907.

87. Heer, *Beitrag*, iv–v.

88. Conscription report, recruitment results 1912–1945; BA Bern E 27 Tit 5825.

89. The doctoral student J. Schädler, who was working on the statistical material compiled in the "medical conscription statistics" during this time, for example, had the misfortune of having access to the information denied mid-project. It took intervention from the Swiss Bureau of Statistics, the Swiss surgeon general, and the Department of the Interior to regain access. Schädler, however, seems to have been so discouraged by the complicated procedure that he gave up the project; there is no finished dissertation on file. See the relevant correspondence from March 1914; BA Bern E 86 Bd. 14, Dossier 159. A similar case is documented for the kingdom of Württemberg. The general practitioner Pfleiderer petitioned the Ministry of War in 1908 for access for "statistical purposes." The Ministry of War for Württemberg replied that the relevant permission could only be granted with the approval of the imperial ministry and that the information requested was not "all available here, anyway." Pfleiderer ultimately was granted only the right to consult a few overviews within the ministry itself. Decree of the Ministry of War, dated March 5, 1908; Ministry of War, division for general matters of the army and personnel, HStA S M 1/4 Bü 610.

90. The somewhat euphoric view of things of the French military doctor Frocard was typical: "[The statistical reports] are now much more complete and richer; general conscription, which made a medical examination of all young men of a certain age group a requirement, at the same time led to a demographic precision of the reports' tables as had never been seen before in the previous system of defense." Frocard, *Aptitude*, 5–6.

91. The specific dynamic of the discussion in the German Empire deserves special mention, because the question of how to deal with conscription statistics was seen after 1906 as highly relevant to the security of the state. In this discussion, the Prussian Bureau of Statistics took the lead, such that it also managed the studies for army divisions in Bavaria, Saxony, and Württemberg, much to the amazement of economic scholars—especially Lujo Brentano. Lujo Brentano, "Unbrauchbarkeit."

92. These dimensions are manifest at the transnational level—for example, in statements made by Director Guillaume of the Swiss Bureau of Statistics, who repeatedly found reasons to send representatives of the second and third tiers of the hierarchy to the conventions at which the International Statistical Institute was founded. He quite explicitly stated his disdain for such international cooperation. BA Bern, E 86, Dossier 179. The German representatives at the foundation of the Office International d'Hygiène Publique in Paris in 1908 behaved similarly. Despite repeated requests from Paris, there was little willingness to cooperate prior to World War I. Reichsministerium des Inneren—Medizinalpolizei, "Die Errichtung eines internationalen Gesundheitsamtes in Paris," BArch R 1501, no. 111228.

93. Quetelet as quoted in Emile Cheysson, "Les méthodes de la statistique: Conférence faite le 30 Novembre 1889 à la réunion des Officiers)," in Cheysson, Œuvres choisies (Paris: A. Rousseau, 1911), 166.

94. Hasse, Statistik als Hilfsmittel, 2.

4   Measuring European Soldiers

1. In chapter 3, we discussed how Quetelet used the statistical material collected in the military to develop curves showing the probabilistic distribution of norms. Adolphe Quetelet, Anthropométrie ou mésures des différentes facultés de l'homme (Brussels: C. Muquardt, 1870), 169ff.

2. Fröhlich, "Musterungsstatistik," 93.

3. Ministry of War of France, Manuel du recrutement.

4. Granjux and Simon report that the limit for farsightedness was successively adjusted over the course of the nineteenth century from four diopters to seven. Alphonse Granjux and Simon, "De la statistique du recrutement," in Bericht über den XIV. Internationalen Kongress für Hygiene und Demographie, Berlin, 23.–29.9.1907, vol. 3/2 (Berlin: A. Hirschwald, 1908): 1204.

5. Morache, Considérations sur le recrutement, 43.

6. "One side complains about the dip in the percentage of those deemed fit for service, and the other side demands that the number of those conscripted should remain as low as possible in the interest of frugality. ... Signed, the Surgeon General of the Confederate Army of Switzerland." Militärdepartement Bern, June 30, 1903,

in BA Bern E 27 Tit 5831-01. A similar strategy had been employed twenty years prior in Switzerland: in 1876, in anticipation of a particularly large cohort of potential conscripts, the minimum height was raised by a centimeter to prevent an increase in military expenditures. Bircher, *Rekrutierung und Ausmusterung*, 4.

7. This was already the case in Chenu, *Recrutement*, 8ff.; *Instructionen*, § 1; Barthélemy, *L'examen de la vision*, 11–12; Moch, *L'Armée*, 342–343; Schjerning, *Sanitätsstatistische Betrachtungen*, 18–19; and "Bericht von der IV. Sanitätsoffiziersversammlung, Sonntag, den 23.11.1913," *Militärärztliche Beilage zum Correspondenzblatt für Schweizer Aerzte*, no. 1 (1914).

8. Dumas, *Le conseil de revision*, 5.

9. This term, coined most notably by the demographer Rudolf Goldschied, was quickly integrated into the demographic and economic discourse of the age. Concepts such as "human capital" and the like also became engrained in the vocabulary of demographers and administrative terms used within governmental institutions. Rudolf Goldscheid, *Entwicklungswerttheorie, Entwicklungsökonomie, Menschenökonomie: Eine Programmschrift* (Leipzig: Klinkhartdt, 1908).

10. Jakob Vogel, "Der Undank der Nation: Die Veteranen der Einigungskriege und die Debatte um ihren 'Ehrensold' im Kaiserreich," *Militärgeschichtliche Zeitschrift* 60, no. 2 (2001): 343–366.

11. Bircher, *Rekrutierung und Ausmusterung*, 4.

12. S. Bernstein, *Körperlänge, Brustumfang und Körpergewicht zur Beurteilung der physischen Widerstandskraft der Soldaten* (Vienna, 1865); Lane Fox, "Note on the Chest Measurement of Recruits," *Journal of the Anthropological Institute of Great Britain and Ireland* 5 (1876): 102; Roynette, *Bon pour le service*, 185ff.

13. Fröhlich, "Zur Rekrutenstatistik," *Allgemeine militärärztliche Zeitschrift*, no. 15 (April 10, 1870): 103.

14. Hertel, "Über die Methoden der Untersuchung der Brustorgane beim Ersatzgeschäft," lecture to the Berlin Society of Medical Military Personnel, delivered on December 21, 1872.

15. Hertel, "Methoden der Untersuchung," 103; Roynette, *Bon pour le service*, 186–187.

16. H. Busch, *Grösse, Gewicht und Brustumfang von Soldaten: Studien über ihre Entwicklung und ihren Einfluss auf die militairische Tauglichkeit* (Berlin: A. Hirschwald, 1878).

17. Carl Toldt, *Studien über die Anatomie der menschlichen Brustgegend mit Bezug auf die Messung derselben und auf die Verwerthung des Brust-Umfanges zur Beurtheilung der Kriegsdiensttauglichkeit* (Stuttgart: Enke, 1875), iv.

18. Marianne Rychner, "'Mit entblößtem Oberkörper'—Blicke auf den Mann im Untersuchungszimmer: Männlichkeit, Nation und Militärdiensttauglichkeit in der Schweiz um 1875" (unpublished licentiate thesis, University of Bern, 1996), 73ff.

19. Pierre-Mathieu Rigal, *De l'aptitude et de ses modifications sous linfluence des exercises militaires et des marches en pays de montagne: Etude sur le récrutement et l'examen des hommes du 12e bataillon de chasseurs* (Paris: Berger-Levrault, 1882), 15.

20. Duponchel, for example, suggested that this be combined with other criteria, especially measurements of the length of time for which candidates could continuously exhale and their pulse rates. Duponchel, *Du diagnostic*, 6–7.

21. Circular from the surgeon general to the division doctors, dated August 5, 1882; BA Bern E 27 Tit 5855.

22. Letter from the surgeon general to the Swiss Department of the Military, dated May 30, 1884; BA Bern E 27 Tit 5829.

23. BA Bern E 27 Tit 5829.

24. Adolf Zemanek, "Discussion," in *Comptes rendus du XII congrès international de médecine, Moscou 7–14 août 1897, Séction X: Médecine militaire* (Moscow, 1899), 95.

25. Ridolfo Livi, "Taille et périmètre thoracique des militaires en rapport avec les professions," in *Comptes rendus du XII congrès international de médecine*, 92–95. We will discuss this point further in chapter 6.

26. Georg Schmidt, "Militärdienst und Körpergewicht," in *Allgemeine militärärztliche Zeitschrift* (1903): 65ff.

27. Schmid-Monnard, "Über den Werth von Körpermaassen zur Beurtheilung des Körperzustandes von Kindern," *Korrespondenz-Blatt der deutschen Gesellschaft für Anthropologie, Ethnologie und Urgeschichte*, no. 11–12 (November–December 1900): 130–133.

28. "Bericht über die 83. Versammlung Deutscher Naturforscher und Ärzte, vom 24.-30.9.1911 in Karlsruhe, Sektion Militär-Sanitätswesen," *Der Militärarzt. Zeitschrift für das gesamte Sanitätswesen der Armeen* 45 no. 22 (1911): 247–251.

29. Schwiening and Nicolai, *Körperbeschaffenheit*, 191.

30. "Pignet's robustness rating does not constitute a proper measure of resilience, although it cannot be denied that there is a certain harmony between height, weight, and chest circumference. The purpose of the draft is not, as it was in bygone days, to collect a select troop of the strongest and most formidable individuals, but rather to exclude the weak [candidates]. The conscientious and experienced observer will be able to develop a detailed picture of a [potential] soldier's suitability for service based on the totality of outer appearance without the quite convenient aid of looking quite mechanically at a prescribed scale." "Über den Nutzen

anthropometrischer Grenzwerte für die Assenierung," *Allgemeine militärärztliche Zeitschrift*, no. 8 (1911): 334.

31. Friant and Champaux, "Contribution à l'étude des indices de robusticité," cited from "Besprechung," *Allgemeine militärärztliche Zeitschrift*, no. 1 (1911): 22–25.

32. Seyffarth, "Beitrag zur Verwertbarkeit des Pignetschen Verfahrens," *Allgemeine militärärztliche Zeitschrift*, no. 21 (1908): 835–841. The author, who was himself a military doctor in East Prussian Gumbinnen, argued in addition: "The use of this procedure thus seems suited only for the examination of large groups for survey reports over the general stature of those examined within a given area, for comparative study of members of a particular region or trade, and for reviewing the standards for their own demands on fitness in those districts in which the first round of examinations has already taken place."

33. Léopold Arnaud, "Sur un essai d'appréciation de la robusticité," cited according to *Allgemeine militärärztliche Zeitschrift*, no. 1 (1911) : 22–25.

34. "Circulaire modifiant le circulaire du 13 janvier 1908, relative à l'élimination des hommes physiquement impropres au service," cited from *Instruction relative*.

35. Duponchel, *Traité*, 26.

36. On this point, Kunow wrote: "The examination of family members … involves only the appraisal of their ability to work and serve in supervisory capacities. It is conducted in an extra room and should be carried out as gently as possible." In Kunow, *Musterung*, 69.

37. Anleitung für die militärärztliche Beurteilung der Kriegsbrauchbarkeit beim Kriegsmusterungsgeschäft, bei den Bezirkskommandos und bei der Truppe, 1916, Bundesarchiv—Militärarchiv Freiburg i.Br., Druckschriften Preussisches Heer, PHD 6/115, 19.

38. "Note pour le ministre" from the *Direction générale du Personnel et du matériel*, dated March 1, 1877, in Actes diverses sur le recrutement (between approx. 1870 and 1914), État major, SHAT 7 N 26. Kratz had delivered a similar report a few years earlier: Kratz, *Recrutirung*, 20–21.

39. In the same period, Switzerland also had similar technical difficulties: in the 1870s, the Swiss surgeon general reported that he had hoped that "the spring scale provided by the local administration would prove to be serviceable; unfortunately, given the transportation required and the [challenges of] hanging them in each location, this is not the case as often as one wishes. As a result, I have decided not to rely on them this year. Instead, I invite all regional doctors where possible to rent a good, properly calibrated scale—using either the Roman or the decimal system—and to use this to weigh [potential recruits]." Letter from the surgeon general to the division doctors, dated August 15, 1879, BA Bern, E 27 Tit 5855.

40. Roynette, *Bon pour le service*, 188.

41. Kunow, *Musterung*, 30.

42. Letter from the surgeon general to the division doctors, dated August 5, 1882, BA Bern, E 27 Tit 5855.

43. Heyberger shows this for the transition from the leveling board to the metering rule: Heyberger, *Révolution des corps*, 73ff.

44. For an important example, see the exchange between Otto Ammon and René Collignon: University of Freiburg, Archives, Ammon personal papers, C 75-59, especially the technical notes that both scientists exchanged between February and March 1892. See chapter 6 for more information on the particular anthropometric network between Ammon and Collignon.

45. Letter from the surgeon general to the division doctors, dated August 5, 1882, BA Bern, E 27 Tit 5855.

46. Antony and Loisson, "Examen du coeur à la Radioscopie au point de vue de l'aptitude au service militaire," in *Comptes Rendus du XIVe Congrès international de médecine, Madrid 23.–30.4. 1903, Section de médecine et hygiène militaires et navales* (Madrid: Imprenta Nacional, 1904), 175–187.

47. Statistics on contagious diseases of the eye among those liable for military service in Prussia, 1895–1897, BArch R 1501, Reichsministerium des Inneren—Militaria, Militärsanitätswesen, Band 112505.

48. Schwiening, *Beiträge*.

49. Bircher, *Der endemische Kropf.*

50. For example, in Switzerland: Erfassung der Ausmusterungsgründe für das Jahr 1906 BA Bern E 27 Tit 5847.

51. Letter from Minister of War Einem to the Department of the Interior, dated November 23, 1905, BArch R 1501, Reichsministerium des Inneren—Militaria, Militärsanitätswesen, Band 112506.

52. Kunow, *Musterung*, 29.

53. Ibid., 30. In the mid-century, vision problems were identified by reports compiled by local teachers and pastors. The examination thus was not limited only to those with medical expertise. *Instructionen*, § 2.

54. Albouze, "Notes sur les conseils de revision; modifications à y apporter," *Bulletin bi-mensuel de la Société de médecine militaire française* 7 (1913): 238–239.

55. Léon Joseph Du Cazal and Louis Catrin, *Médecine légale militaire* (Paris: Gauthier-Villars et fils, 1892), 27.

56. Du Cazal, *Petit guide.*

57. Borowski, *Aushebung,* 26.

58. Within the context of research on such simulation attempts during the conscription process, there is also ample evidence of how the scholars' exchange transcended borders—for example, in the following list of contemporary literature:"Beiträge zur Untersuchung und Beurtheilung der simulirten Krankheiten," *Der Militärarzt,* no. 15 (July 20, 1867); Mauricheau-Beaupré, *Ärztlich-Militärische Untersuchungen: Tabellarische Übersicht der wirklichen verheimlichten und verstellten Krankheiten und Gebrechen* (Weimar, 1882); Emile Boisseau, *Des maladies simulées et des moyens de les reconnaitre* (Paris: J.-B. Baillière et fils, 1870); M. Burchhardt, *Praktische Diagnostik der Simulationen von Gefühlslähmungen, von Schwerhörigkeit und von Schwachsichitigkeit* (Berlin: Otto Enslin, 1875); W. Derblich, *Die simulierten Krankheiten der Wehrpflichtigen* (Vienna: Urban und Schwarzenberg, 1878); H. Fröhlich, *Vortäuschung von Krankheiten* (Leipzig, 1895); Louis Froehlich, *Des procédés modernes pour reconnaitre la simulation de la cécité ou de la faiblesse visuelle* (Geneva, 1891); and von Hasselberg, *Tafeln zur Entlarvung der Simulation einseitiger Blindheit und Schwachsinnigkeit* (Wiesbaden, 1901).

59. On the topic of those symptoms of epilepsy that were addressed in the military context, see Lengwiler, *Zwischen Klinik,* 143ff.

60. The topic of cycles of some illnesses and their subsequent disappearance has been addressed at the conceptual level by Mark Micale—for the case of hysteria in France—and Edward Shorter: Mark S. Micale, "On the 'Disappearance' of Hysteria: A Study in the Clinical Deconstruction of a Diagnosis," *Isis* 84 (1993): 496–526; and Edward Shorter, "Paralysis: The Rise and Fall of a 'Hysterical' Symptom," *Journal of Social History* 19, no. 4 (1986): 549–582.

61. Andrew T. Scull, *Hysteria: The Biography* (Oxford: Oxford University Press, 2009), 115ff.

62. The relationship between the discourse over hysteria and gender constructions thus seems less linear than in Lamott's account: Franziska Lamott, *Die vermessene Frau: Hysterien um 1900* (Munich: Fink, 2001).

63. Lerner, *Hysterical Men,* 20–21.

64. "Beiträge zur Untersuchung."

65. *Manuel du recrutement des armées de terre et de mer contenant toute la legislation* (Paris: L. Baudoin, 1890), 243; and Billot, *Conférence.* The problem was more pronounced in France than in Germany, because the volunteers were not treated separately but subjected to an individualized test of fitness for service by the regimental doctor himself. Roynette, *Bon pour le service,* 181.

66. These one-year volunteers were subjected to a thorough examination in the barracks, which addressed not only their physical weaknesses but also their positive

abilities. In cases of weaker constitution, the suggestion was made that recruits be required to serve an additional six months and thus compensate for their deficiencies when compared to the regular recruits. Königlich Württembergische Prüfungskommission für Einjährig-Freiwillige an den K. Oberrekrutierungsrat in Stuttgart, 7. Mai 1914; Kriegsministerium Prüfungskommission Einjährig-Freiwillige 1905–1914, HStA S M 12 Bü 40. On these different approaches to conscription, see Schwiening and Nicolai, *Körperbeschaffenheit*, 1ff.

67. § 33 of *Anleitung für die militärärztliche Beurteilung der Kriegsbrauchbarkeit beim Kriegsmsuterungsgeschäft, bei den Bezirkskommandos und bei der Truppe. 1916*, Druckschriften Preussisches Heer, Bundesarchiv—Militärarchiv Freiburg i.br. PHD 6/115, 18.

68. Vincent, "Du choix du soldat ou étude sur la consitution des hommes de vingt ans, appliquée au recrutement de l'armée," in *Bulletin bimensuel* 32 (1876): 419.

69. Duponchel, *Traité*, 29.

70. Letter from the surgeon general to the division doctors, dated August 15, 1879, BA Bern, E 27 Tit 5855. On this topic, see also Marianne Rychner, "Männlichkeit, Nation und militärdiensttauglicher Körper in der Schweiz um 1875," in *Medizin, Gesellschaft und Geschichte* 18 (1999): 40–41.

71. § 41 of *Anleitung für die militärärztliche Beurteilung der Kriegsbrauchbarkeit beim Kriegsmusterungsgeschäft, bei den Bezirkskommandos und bei der Truppe. 1916*, Druckschriften Preussisches Heer, in Bundesarchiv—Militärarchiv Freiburg i.Br. PHD 6/115, 20–21.

72. "Dienstanweisungen zur Beurteilung der Militärdienstfähigkeit und zur Ausstellung von militärärztlichen Zeugnissen, 1909/2/9," Bundesarchiv—Militärachiv Freiburg i.Br., Druckschriften Preussisches Heer, PHD 6/115.

73. "Die Musterung," *Soldaten-Brevier*, 1907, Staatsarchiv Münster, Regierung Münster, VII-59, Blatt 3, cited from Bernd Ulrich, Jakob Vogel, and Benjamin Ziemann, *Untertan in Uniform: Militär und Militarismus im Kaiserreich 1871–1914: Quellen und Dokumente* (Frankfurt: Fischer, 2001), 58.

74. Borowski, *Die Aushebung*, 7.

75. For example, Kratz, *Recrutirung*, 21; Borowski, *Aushebung*, 24; and *Der Rekrut: Andenken an Musterung und Aushebung* (Rheinberg: Sattler & Koss, 1912), 28.

76. Ibid., 25.

77. Circular of the Swiss Department of the Military, September 25, 1875, BA Bern Militärdepartement, E 27 Tit 5862; on this point, see also Lustenberger, *Pädagogische Rekrutenprüfung.*

78. Philipp Reinhard, *Vaterlandskunde. Fragen gestellt an den Rekrutenprüfungen. Mit Bewilligung des eidg. Militärdepartements zusammengestellt und erweitert* (Bern: A. Francke, 1903), 4.

79. *Rekruten-Prüfung im Jahr 1876*, ed. Statistischen Bureau des eidgenössischen Departement des Inneren (Zurich: Orell Füssli, 1877).

80. See also Lustenberger, *Pädagogische Rekrutenprüfung*, 54ff.

81. Many authors highlighted this problem and warned about premature conclusions—for example: Johann Jakob Heuser, *Die Rekrutenprüfungen: Referat gehalten in der 56. ordentlichen Versammlung der Schulsynode am 23.9.1889 in Zürich* (Zurich: J. Schabelitz, 1889), 2; and *Bericht des Vorstandes der Schulsynode über die Erhebungen betr. die unbefriedigenden Resultate bei den Rekrutenprüfungen im Kanton Bern* (Bern: 1905).

82. August Müller, "Rekrutenprüfungen und Freiämter Schulwesen," in *Schlussbericht der Bezirksschule Muri 1907/1908*, ed. S. Schmid (Muri: A. Schibli-Keller, 1908); Eduard Niggli, *Die Ergebnisse der Rekrutenprüfungen im Aargau pro 1893 und ihre Ursachen: Referat vorgetragen an der aargauischen Kantonallehrerkonferenz vom 18.September 1893* (Baden, 1893); Anonymous, *Statistik über die Thurgauischen Rekrutenprüfungen vom Jahre 1908* (Frauenfeld, 1908); and Conference of Swiss directors of education, June 10, 1882, Presentation of the Education director from the canton of Geneva, in BA Bern Militärdepartement E 27 Tit 5862.

83. "By a vote of thirteen to six, the petition is approved: neither of the two tests should involve unilateral theoretical methods or overly specialized questions based on the school curriculum; instead the age of the candidate is to be considered and the focus should be on general knowledge essential to every Swiss citizen." Discussion at the conference of Swiss directors of education, June 10, 1882, in BA Bern Militärdepartement E 27 Tit 5862.

84. Correspondence between the Swiss Department of the Military and the surgeon general, February 3–12, 1896, in BA Bern E 27 Militärdepartement Tit 5862.

85. Compare chapter 2.

86. Excerpt from the minutes of the fifteenth meeting of the Swiss National Council, in BA Bern E 27 Militärdepartement Tit 5862.

87. Letter from the royal *Oberrekrutierungsrat* of Württemberg to the superior conscriptions commissions and the conscription commissions, dated April 22, 1908, in Kriegsministerium—Oberersatzkommission, HStA S M 11 Bü 2.

88. In this context, Martin Lengwiler points to the long tradition of psychological examinations within the German military as opposed to other European countries; Lengwiler, *Zwischen Klinik*, 277–278.

89. Borowski, *Aushebung*, 30.

90. Franz Stricker and Theodor Ziehen, *Über die Feststellung regelwidriger Geisteszustände bei Heerespflichtigen und Heereszugehörigen: Veröffentlichungen aus dem Gebiete des Militärsanitätswesens* (Berlin: A. Hirschwald, 1905), 14–15.

91. Stricker and Ziehen, *Feststellung*, 16; Ewald Stier, *Der Militärdienst der geistig Minderwertigen und die Hilfsschulen. Beiträge zur Kinderforschung und Heilerziehung* (Langensalza: Beyer, 1907), 12–13. For the case of Switzerland, see Lustenberger, *Pädagogische Rekrutenprüfung*, 70.

92. Stier, *Militärdienst*, 12.

93. Stricker and Ziehen, *Feststellung*, 8.

94. Instructions from the royal *Oberrekrutierungsrat* to the royal superior conscription commissions, royal conscription commissions, and the royal city administration of Stuttgart and the royal *Oberämter*, dated June 13, 1907, Kriegsministerium—Oberersatzkommission, HStA S M 11 Bü 2. The Prussian instructions for service issued in 1909 stipulated: "If there are indications that a candidate for conscription has ever belonged to a 'special school,' this shall not be considered proof of his unsuitability for military service without further [ado]; instead there should be inquiries from case to case as to whether these former "special pupils" are to be considered fit or not. "Dienstanweisungen zur Beurteilung der Militärdienstfähigkeit iud zur Ausstellung von militärärztlichen Zeugnissen, 2.9.1909," Druckschriften Preussisches Heer, in Bundesarchiv—Militärarchiv Freiburg i.Br. PHD 6/115. The requirement to report was perceived in other countries as a role model for efficient consideration of mental abnormalities; see Naville, *Contribution*, 36.

95. "Württemberg—Militärdienst geistig Minderwertiger," *Der Beobachter*, September 9, 1907.

96. Stier, *Militärdienst*, 21.

97. Schjerning, *Sanitätsstatistische Betrachtungen*, 26.

98. Report of the expert commission on the conscription examinations, dated June 17, 1901, BA Bern E 27 Tit 5869.

99. "Bericht über die Turnprüfung bei der Rekrutierung 1905," *Schweizerische Zeitschrift für Statistik* 42, no. 4 (1906).

100. Letter from Director Guillaume of the Swiss Statistical Bureau to the Department of the Interior, dated September 30, 1905, BA Bern E 86, Bd. 14-157.

101. Letter from the Swiss Department of the Interior to the Departmentof the military, dated October 2, 1905, BA Bern E 86, Bd. 14-157.

102. Report of the head of the Swiss Gymnastics Commission to the Department of the military, dated December 18, 1911, BA Bern, E 27 Tit 5879.

5 New Knowledge Systems

1. Alain Desrosières, *Politics of Large Numbers: The History of Statistic Reasoning* (Cambridge, MA: Harvard University Press, 2002).

2. Rabinbach describes the analogies which were made between unfitness for the army and industrial accidents, especially in France. Rabinbach, *The Human Motor*, 224–225. See also Martine Millot, "L'emergence de la notion d'aptitude dans la réglementation du travail après 1892," in *Les mains inutiles. Inaptitude au travail et emploi en Europe*, ed. Cathrine Omnès and Anne-Sophie Bruno (Paris: Belin, 2004), 32–41.

3. Dr. Wernher Gießen in *Archiv für klinische Chirurgie von Langenbeck*, cited from Fröhlich, "Musterungsstatistik," 93.

4. On this point, see Martin Lengwiler, "Kalkulierte Solidarität: Grenzen sozialstaatlicher Prognosen (1900–1970)," in *Zukunftswissen. Prognosen in Wirtschaft, Politik und Gesellschaft*, ed. Heinrich Hartmann and Jakob Vogel (Frankfurt: Campus, 2010), 37–38; Hartmann, "Normieren,"; and Hacking, *Taming*, 127ff.

5. Svenja Goltermann describes this process thus: "The body of the physically strong, muscular, disciplined, upright 'man'—in control of his body, nimble and thus well able to put up a fight—remained ... a sort of 'enduring symbol' which served as a constant reminder of the attributes of the 'masculine.' These are conveyed in the public sphere as well via the bodies, for these are the embodiment of the characteristics of the 'masculine.' As a kind of 'markers' that stuck to the body of a man prepared for battle, they were perceptible to the senses, [and] can even be interpreted as elements of a 'corporal rhetoric.'" Svenja Goltermann, *Körper der Nation: Habitusformierung und Politik des Turnens 1860–1890* (Göttingen: Vandenhoeck & Ruprecht, 1998), 302. On this point, see also Ute Planert, *Antifeminismus im Kaiserreich. Diskurs, soziale Formation und politische Mentalität* (Göttingen: Vandenhoeck & Ruprecht, 1998).

6. Felix Axster, *Koloniales Spektakel in 9 × 14. Bildpostkarten im Deutschen Kaiserreich* (Bielefeld: Transcript, 2014), 154ff.; Jens Jäger, "Bilder aus Afrika vor 1918: Zur visuellen Konstruktion Afrikas im europäischen Kolonialismus," in *Visual History: Ein Studienbuch*, ed. Gerhard Paul (Göttingen: Vandenhoeck & Ruprecht, 2006), 138ff. On the construction of race and gender through the visual technologies, see Anandi Ramamurthy, "Spectacles and Illusions: Photography and Commodity Cultures," in *Photography: A Critical Introduction*, 3rd. ed., ed. Liz Wells (London: Routledge, 2004), 214ff.

7. Eitner, *Militärärztliche Atteste und Gutachten. Zusammenstellung der für Militärärzte anwendbaren gesetzlichen Bestimmungen* (Berlin, 1873), 21; [xy] in original.

8. Georg Schwiening, *Die Dienstpflicht der Frauen: Ein Beitrag zur Lösung der "Arbeiterinnen"-Frage* (Kassel: Hühn, 1900); and Sarasin and Tanner, *Physiologie*. In the vein of intellectual history, see Rabinbach, *Human Motor*, 35ff.

9. Grosse, *Kolonialismus, Eugenik und bürgerliche Gesellschaft*, 229ff.

10. Lothar Bassenge, *Die Heranziehung und Erhaltung einer wehrfähigen Jugend: Vortrag gehalten am 9. Januar 1911* (Berlin: A. Hirschwald, 1911), 23.

11. Alsberg, *Militärtauglichkeit*, 2.

12. Borowski, *Aushebung*, 14ff; and Kunow, *Musterung*, 13.

13. Bindewald accordingly argued that women should not be employed due to the threat to public health in industrial regions; this was intended as a strategy for maintaining their fertility and minimizing the negative consequences for the strength of the military. Bindewald, *Wehrfähigkeit*, 50ff.

14. Staffan Müller-Wille and Hans-Jörg Rheinberger, *A Cultural History of Heredity* (Chicago: Chicago University Press, 2012).

15. Compare chapter 1.

16. Eugen Weber, "Gymnastics and Sports in Fin-de-Siècle France: Opium of the Classes?," *American Historical Review* 76, no. 1 (1971): 74–75; Pierre Arnaud and André Gounot, "Mobilisierung der Körper und republikanische Selbstinszenierung in Frankreich (1879–1889). Ansätze zu einer vergleichenden deutsch-französischen Sportgeschichte," in *Nation und Emotion: Deutschland und Frankreich im Vergleich 19. und 20. Jahrhundert*, ed. Etienne François, Hannes Siegrist, and Jakob Vogel (Göttingen: Vandenhoeck & Ruprecht, 1995), 301.

17. Weber, "Gymnastics," 77.

18. Maurice Larkin, "'La République en Danger'? The Pretenders, the Army and Déroulède, 1898–1899," *English Historical Review* 100, no. 394 (1985): 85–105.

19. Angelo Mosso, *Die körperliche Erziehung der Jugend* (Hamburg: Voss, 1894), 107–108.

20. Vogel, *Nationen*, 108ff; and Marcel Spivak, *Les Origines militaires de l'éducation physique française: 1774–1848* (Paris: Université Paul Valéry, 1975).

21. Gaston Moch, *L'armée d'une démocratie* (Paris: Editions de la Revue blanche, 1900), 406–407.

22. This was reflected, for example, in the ministry's introduction of a *certificat d'aptitude militaire* on September 17, 1900, into which both physical fitness and target practice were factored.

23. Dossier on the formulation of legislation on "préparation militaire" 1907–1910. "Premier bureau—effectifs," État major, SHAT 7 N 137.

24. This can be inferred from a circular of the French Ministry of Education dated April 15, 1909, and the answers of the prefects. Education militaire, AN F 1C I 201.

25. Mosso, *Die körperliche Erziehung*, 82ff.

26. Ibid., 106.

27. Frevert, *Nation in Barracks*, 200. The disciplining of youth was a central topic of the great classic of German militarism, Colmar von der Goltz's *Volk in Waffen*, published in 1883. See also Ulrich, Vogel, and Ziemann, *Untertan*, 90ff.

28. Stübig, *Bildung*, 145.

29. Hueppe, "Ueber die Körperübungen," 491.

30. Ibid., 510.

31. Colin Veitch, "Play up! Play up! And Win the War! Football, the Nation and the First World War 1914–15," *Journal of Contemporary History* 20, no. 3 (1985): 363–378; and Sonja Levsen, *Elite, Männlichkeit und Krieg: Tübinger und Cambridger Studenten 1900–1929* (Göttingen: Vandenhoeck & Ruprecht, 2006), 126ff. For a broad overview of the cleavages of athletic body culture, see Chrsitiane Eisenberg, *"English Sports" und Deutsche Bürger* (Paderborn: Schöningh, 1999); and Michael Hau, *Performance Anxiety: Sport and Work in Germany from the Empire to Nazism* (Toronto: University of Toronto Press, 2017), 18ff.

32. Thomas Schnitzler, "Fußball und Rassenhygiene: Der DFB-Gründungspräsident Ferdinand Hueppe," in *Zur Sozial- und Kulturgeschichte des Fußballs*, ed. Beatrix Bouvier (Trier: Studienzentrum Karl-Marx-Haus, 2006), 78–119.

33. Goltermann, *Körper*, 305ff.

34. Hueppe, "Ueber die Körperübungen," 499. On Hueppe, see Hau, *Performance Anxiety*, 15ff. Levsen also reaches the conclusion that, in the British context, the options for a transnational exchange on these questions of physical fitness were extensive despite the nationalist rhetoric. The discourse differentiated rather between two social proponent groups: the highly militarized English students spoke about national borders, but already reflected biological, racist thought patterns. Levsen, *Elite*, 155ff.

35. Letter of Chairman Emil von Schenkendorff to the Ministry of War of the Kingdom of Württemberg, dated May 24, 1899, HStA S M 1/4 Bü 801.

36. Ibid., appended program.

37. He published a report of his activities to date in 1904: Hermann Lorenz and Emil von Schenkendorff, *Wehrkraft durch Erziehung (Schriften des Zentralausschusses zur Förderung der Volks- und Jugendspiele in Deutschland)* (Leipzig: Voigtländer, 1904).

38. Correspondence between the ministry and the central committee, HStA S M 1/4 Bü 801. This correspondence continued until 1914.

39. Mayershofer, *Bevölkerung*, 301ff.

40. On this point, see also Bassenge, "Heranziehung," 30ff.

41. Memorandum on the results of the meeting of the "Ausschuss zur Förderung der Wehrkraft durch Erziehung" on March 12, 1911, HStA S M 1/4 Bü 801.

42. Ibid.

43. This was especially the case for certain aspects of the training, like dealing with weapons and target practice, in which areas Prussian Minister of War von Herringen had clearly put them in their place despite being sympathetic to their goals. Letter of the Prussian minister of war to Emil von Schenkendorff, January 22, 1911; included in Ulrich, Vogel, and Ziemann, *Untertan*, 92-93.

44. Report and guidelines sent to the ministry, May 29, 1914, HStA S M 1/4 Bü 801.

45. Tim Jeal, *Baden-Powell: Founder of the Boy Scouts* (New Haven, CT: Yale University Press, 2001).

46. Sonja Levsen, "Männliche Bierbäuche oder männliche Muskeln?," in *Männlichkeit und Gesundheit im historischen Wandel, ca. 1800–2000*, ed. Martin Dinges (Stuttgart: Steiner, 2007), 175–190.

47. Compare chapter 1.

48. Boudin, "Études," 30.

49. Ingenlath, *Mentale Aufrüstung*, 147–148.

50. *Resultate der Ärztlichen Rekrutenuntersuchung im Herbste 1885*, ed. Statistisches Bureau des eidgenössischen Departements des Inneren (Bern, 1886), viii.

51. Schwiening and Nicolai, *Körperbeschaffenheit*, 30.

52. Ibid.

53. Ibid.

54. Ibid.

55. For example, in France: "État major: Note pour la direction de l'infanterie," February 1895, SHAT 7 N 125.

56. Livi's study was based on the *foglii sanitarii*, conducted between 1880 and 1885, in which each individual soldier was measured at the point of being drafted and then periodically during his service in the military. After each soldier's discharge, the statistics were collected and analyzed by the central bureau in Rome. Livi, "Taille," 92–95.

57. Ibid., 94.

58. Such instruction was introduced in the German Empire in 1908 on a trial basis. According to the ministry's administration, it was modeled after programs in Italy and France, which had already introduced similar instruction. In addition to the positive effect on the soldiers' fitness, this instruction was intended to promote modern techniques and organization within the agricultural sector. Document collection on agricultural instruction in the army, Ministry of War, division for general matters of the army and personnel, HStA Stuttgart M 1/4 Bü 595.

59. Emile Lachaud, "Rapport fait à la chambre des députés. Annexe au procès-verbal de la séance du 11 juillet 1910," SHAT 7 N 137.

60. Fröhlich, "Musterungsstatistik."

61. Fröhlich, "Musterungsstatistik."

62. Gustave Lagneau, *Étude de statistique anthropologique sur la population parisienne* (Paris: A. Hennuyer, 1869); Lagneau, *Considérations médicales et anthropologiques sur la réorganization de l'armée en France, remarques relatives à quelques objections* (Paris: Masson, 1871); Lagneau, *Ethnogénie des populations du sud-ouest de la France, particulièrement du bassin de la Garonne et de ses affluents* (Paris: A. Hennuyer, 1873); Lagneau, *Anthropologie de la France, recherches ethnologiques sur les populations du bassin de la Saône et des autres affluents du cours moyen du Rhône* (Paris: A. Hennuyer, 1874); Lagneau, *Ethnogénie des populations du nord de la France* (Paris: A. Hennuyer, 1874); Lagneau, *Ethnogénie des populations du nord-ouest de la France* (Paris: A. Hennuyer, 1876); and Lagneau, *De la distinction ethnique des Celtes et des Gaëls et de leurs migrations au sud des Alpes* (Paris: A. Hennuyer, 1876); Lagneau summed up his research under the title "Du récrutement de l'armée sous le rapport anthropologique."

63. *Reichsland* was the official name for the annexed, formerly French Alsace-Lorraine.

64. Schwiening and Nicolai, *Körperbeschaffenheit.*

65. Seyffarth, "Beitrag zur Verwertbarkeit."

66. See chapter 1.

67. Note in the records of the Ministry of the Interior dated June 3, 1909. Conscription records, 1907–1913. Ministry of War, division for general matters of the army and personnel, HStA Stuttgart, M 1/4 Bü 610.

68. Memorandum of the Royal Conscription Council for Württemberg, dated March 6, 1906. Württemberg Ministry of War, Superior Conscription Commission. Marines 1889–1910, HStA Stuttgart M 11 Bü 12.

69. Lorimer, *Science, Race Relations and Resistance*, 208ff; Zweiniger-Bargielowska, *Managing the Body*, 62ff.

70. Dörte Lerp, *Imperiale Grenzräume: Bevölkerungspolitiken in Deutsch-Südwestafrika und den östlichen Provinzen Preußens 1884–1914* (Frankfurt: Campus, 2016); and Samuël Coghe, "Medical Demography in Interwar Angola: Measuring and Negotiating Health, Reproduction and Difference," in *Health and Difference: Rendering Human Variation in Colonial Engagements*, ed. Alexandra Widmer and Veronika Lipphardt (New York: Berghahn, 2016), 178–204.

71. Curtin, *Disease and Empire;* David P. Geggus, *Slavery, War, and Revolution: The British Occupation of Saint Domingue 1793–1798* (Oxford: Clarendon Press, 1982); and Geggus, "Yellow Fever in the 1790s: The British Army in Occupied Saint Domingue," *Medical History* 23 (1979): 38–58.

72. Karl Ittmann, "'Where Nature Dominates Man': Demographic Ideas and Policy in British Colonial Africa, 1890–1970," in *The Demographics of Empire: The Colonial Order and the Creation of Knowledge*, ed. Karl Ittmann, Dennis D. Cordell, and Gregory H. Maddox (Athens: Ohio University Press, 2010): 89–112; and Bouda Etemad, "Pour une approche démographique de l'expansion coloniale de l'Europe," *Annales de Démographie Historique* 1, no. 113 (January 2007): 17.

73. Etemad, "Pour une approche," 17.

74. Veronika Lipphardt and Kiran Klaus Patel, "Auf der Suche nach dem Europäer. Wissenschaftliche Konstruktionen des Homo Europaeus," *Themenportal Europäische Geschichte*, 2007, https://www.europa.clio-online.de/2007/Article=204.

75. "Knowledge of Africa began with the know-how necessary to survive in the climate." Johannes Fabian, *Out of Our Minds: Reason and Madness in the Exploration of Central Africa* (Berkeley: University of California Press, 2000), 58–59. See also Sandra Maß, "Welcome to the Jungle: Imperial Men, 'Inner Africa,' and Mental Disorder, 1870–1970," in *Helpless Imperialists: Imperial Failure, Fear and Radicalization*, ed. Maurus Reinkowski and Gregor Thum (Göttingen: Vandenhoeck and Ruprecht, 2012): 91–115; and Daniel J. Walther, *Sex and Control: Veneral Disease, Colonial Physicians, and Indigenous Agency in German Colonialism, 1884–1914* (New York: Berghahn, 2015).

76. Fabian, *Out of Our Minds*, 71; and Michael Pesek, *Koloniale Herrschaft in Deutsch-Ostafrika: Expeditionen, Militär und Verwaltung seit 1880* (Frankfurt: Campus, 2005), 140. Chief Pharmacist Alfred Dörppel, for example, reported of his deployment in German East Africa that it was the order of the day to adapt local remedies as a substitute for the lack of medical supplies and medication. Report of the chief pharmacist Alfred Dörppel, transcribed in 1953, BA Militärarchiv Freiburg, Kaiserliche Schutztruppen, RW 51/6.

77. Philip D. Curtin, "'The White Man's Grave': Image and Reality, 1780–1850," *Journal of British Studies* 1, no. 1 (1961): 94–110; Ittmann, "Where Nature Dominates Man"; and Gregory H. Maddox, "Disease and Environment in Africa: Imputed Dynamics and Unresolved Issues," in *The Demographics of Empire: The Colonial Order*

and the Creation of Knowledge, ed. Karl Ittmann, Dennis D. Cordell, and Gregory H. Maddox (Athens: Ohio University Press, 2010).

78. Eckart has shown, for example, how important the German doctors were in pushing for Germany to have its own colonial empire. Their enthusiasm was manifest in the attempts to develop a science of tropical hygiene. Eckart, *Medizin*, 25ff.; and Walther, *Sex and Control*, 91ff.

79. Dirk van Laak, *Über alles in der Welt: Deutscher Imperialismus im 19. und 20. Jahrhundert* (Munich: C. H. Beck, 2005), 81–82.

80. In a letter to Walter Woitum shortly before his graduation from secondary school, the Imperial Colonial Office outlined the standard procedure: "Imperial citizens who are obligated to perform military service and plan to do so in a German colony can be stationed in southwest Africa … or deployed in the [Chinese] colony of Kiauchau (under the authority of the Imperial Naval Office). The colonial troops in East Africa and Cameroon are drawn exclusively from the colored population. In Togo and the South Sea Islands, there are not stationed troops. … Shortly before their deployment, the volunteers are to appear in Berlin to the commando of the colonial troops for an examination to determine their ability to serve in the tropics. The candidates themselves are responsible for the related travel costs." Correspondence between high school student Walter Woitum (Karslruhe) and the Imperial Colonial Office, 1912, and the answer of the Imperial Colonial Office from September 30, 1912, BA-MA Freiburg Kaiserliche Schutztruppen RW 51/1.

81. Walther, *Sex and Control*, 75ff.

82. "Statistique médicale de l'armée des indes Néerlandaise orientales pour 1894." *Geneeskundig Tijdschrift voor Nederlandsch Indie*, no. 2 and no. 3 (1895).

83. H. Gros, "Les enseignements d'une statistique," *Archives de médecine navale* 78 (August 1902): 81–113, and 88 (September 1908): 161–195.

84. For the case of England, Ittman also concludes that there was hardly a systematic body of knowledge on demography before 1914. Instead, a diffuse angst spread throughout the British Empire that the colonial population could become too large. Karl Ittmann, "Where Nature Dominates Man," 61–62; and Deborah J. Neill, *Networks in Tropical Medicine: Internationalism, Colonialism, and the Rise of Medical Specialty* (Stanford, CA: Stanford University Press, 2012).

85. Hans Ziemann, *Wie erobert man Afrika für die weiße und farbige Rasse? Vortrag gehalten auf dem Internationalen Kongreß für Hygiene und Demographie zu Berlin 1907* (Leipzig: Barth, 1907).

86. Ziemann, *Wie erobert man Afrika*, 7.

87. Discussed in depth in chapter 1.

88. Steudel, "Die Beurteilung Der Tropendiensttauglichkeit bei Offizieren und Mannschaften," *Archiv für Schiffs- und Tropenhygiene* 12 (1908): 73–77.

89. G. Reynaud, "Jugement quant à l'aptitude des officiers et des soldats au service dans les pays tropiques," *Archiv für Schiffs- und Tropenhygiene* 12 (1908): 136.

90. Davies, "How to Judge of the Fitness of Officers and Men for Active Service in Tropical Countries," *Bericht*, vol. 3, 572.

91. This was parallel to Ziemann's call for an "international society for tropical medicine and hygiene," which was "to be comprised of the individual national curia"; Ziemann, *Wie erobert man Afrika*, 29.

92. Edward Charles Woodruff, *The Effects of Tropical Light on White Men* (New York: Rebman, 1905).

93. T. zur Verth, *Zur Hygiene europäischer Truppen bei tropischen Feldzügen* (Leipzig: Barth, 1909), 10.

94. The most extreme suggestion was that of a blood serum test, via which some military doctors expected to be able to accurately predict fitness for tropical climates. Reynaud, "Jugement"; Carl Bruck, "Die biologische Differenzierung von Affenarten und menschlichen Rassen durch spezifische Blutreaktionen," *Berliner klinische Wochenschrift* 26 (1907), 793–797; and Myriam Spörri, "'Reines Blut,' 'gemischtes Blut': Blutgruppen und Rassen zwischen 1900 und 1933," in *Transfusionen: Blut-Bilder und Bio-Politik in der Neuzeit*, ed. Anja Lauper (Zurich: Diaphanes, 2005), 211–225.

95. Juliano Moreira and Afriano Peixoto, "Les maladies mentales dans les pays tropicaux," in *XVe Congrès international de Médecine, Lisbonne 19–26 avril 1906, Section XVII Médecine coloniale et navale* (Lisbon, 1906), 190.

96. Friedrich Wulffert, *Die Akklimatisation der europäischen und insbesondere der germanischen Rasse in den Tropen und ihre hauptsächlichen Hindernisse* (Leipzig: Breitkopff & Härtel, 1900); the author nevertheless concludes "that the necessary conditions for the establishment of larger Germanic agricultural settlements in the hot countries will not be provided in the course of the entire twentieth century" (176). On this point, see also Grosse, *Kolonialismus*, 84–85.

97. Hugo Zöller, *Die deutschen Besitzungen an der westafrikanischen Küste*, vol. 2 (Berlin: Spemann, 1885).

98. Reinhold Pallmann, *Die Bewohnbarkeit der Tropen für Europäer: Eine kulturgeographische Studie aus den Quellen: Vortrag gehalten im Klub der Landwirthe zu Berlin on 21.12.1886* (Berlin: F. & P. Lehmann, 1887).

99. Pallmann, *Die Bewohnbarkeit*, 10ff.

100. Steudel, "Beurteilung," 74.

101. Zur Verth, *Hygiene*, 11.

102. However, he recommended moderate consumption of hashish and opium; Charles Richard Francis, "On Opium, Narcotics and Alcohol in the Tropics," in *VIIIe Congrès international d'Hygiène et de démographie, tenu à Budapest du 1er au 9 septembre 1894: Comptes-rendus et mémoires*, vol. 2 (Budapest, 1896), 722–729.

103. Ludwig Külz, *Zur Hygiene des Trinkens in den Tropen* (Flensburg: Verlag von Deutschlands Grossloge, 1905). This is the same argument made by Georges Deherme, one of the most influential social hygienists in France; Georges Deherme, "L'alcoolisme dans les colonies," *Annales antialcooliques* 3, no. 4 (April 1905).

104. Steudel, "Beurteilung," 75. "Alcoholic beverages in the hands of the soldiers during military campaigns in the tropics are tantamount to self-annihilation." Zur Verth, *Hygiene*, 42. "Drinking habits" were in fact listed in a number of publications on the concept of fitness for tropical climates as the primary obstacle to "acclimatization" in these climatic zones. This indicates a gradual transition from a purely biologistic definition of fitness for tropical climates toward one that considered cultural factors. Doctor H. Sunder, for example, concluded that "the fan … is as essential for the white race in the tropics as the stove is in a cold climate"; H. Sunder, *Kann die weiße Rasse sich in den Tropen akklimatisieren?* (Berlin: Süsserott, 1908). And Doctor F. Hey, in his guidebook for doctors working in the tropics, offered nutritional advice: "Eating spicy food and drinking alcohol while eating are … the bad habits of a deviant race of man." F. Hey, *Der Tropenarzt: Ausführlicher Ratgeber für Europäer in den Tropen sowie für Besitzer von Plantagen und Handelshäusern, Kolonial-Behörden und Missions-Verwaltungen*, 2nd ed. (Wismar: Hinstorff, 1912), 6.

105. The measures for tropical hygiene could lead to the creation of "artificial spheres of life" for representatives of the colonial powers, as Eric Jennings has shown with his recent study of French hydrotherapeutic pools in the colonies. Eric T. Jennings, *Curing the Colonizers: Hydrotherapy, Climatology, and French Colonial Spas* (Durham, NC: Duke University Press, 2006).

106. On this point, see the speech of the tropical doctor Schilling at the assembly of the colonial congress in 1910, titled "What Is the Significance of Recent Advances in Tropical Hygiene for Our Colonies?"

107. Quoted from a review by Reinhold Ruge: "Review of Steuber, Über die Verwendbarkeit europäischer Truppen in Kolonien vom gesundheitlichen Standpunkte," *Archiv für Schiffs- und Tropenhygiene* 11 (1907), 433.

108. This is reflected in slogans like: "Always [wear] sun protection—pith helmet! Never burden the white soldier with anything to carry except his weapon!" Ruge, "Zu Steuber," 432.

109. German scholars were especially fond of the claim that fitness for tropical climates was to be defined partly by the ability to swallow quinine tablets in the

prescribed size, a criterion according to which a fair number of the candidates for service in tropical climates were eliminated. Zur Verth, *Hygiene*, 14.

110. On the South African War, see Geoffrey R. Searle, *The Quest for National Efficiency: A Study in British Politics and Political Thought* (Oxford: Blackwell, 1971); and Levsen, *Elite*, 129–130.

111. Heather Streets-Salter, *Martial Races: The Military, Race, and Masculinity in British Imperial Culture, 1857–1914* (Manchester: Manchester University Press, 2004). On this point, see also Schubert's analysis of the function of biologistic categorization in the effectiveness of colonial power politics. Frank Schubert, "'Soldiers Can Get Anything Free': Idi Amin und das Erbe des Kolonialmilitärs in Afrika," *Historische Anthropologie: Kultur, Gesellschaft, Alltag* 14, no. 1 (2006): 93–104; Michels, *Schwarze deutsche Kolonialsoldaten*, 78ff; and Sandra Maß, *Weiße Helden, schwarze Krieger: Zur Geschichte kolonialer Männlichkeit in Deutschland 1918–1964* (Cologne: Böhlau, 2006).

112. Memorandum on the results of the meeting of the "Ausschuss zur Förderung der Wehrkraft durch Erziehung" on March 12, 1911; HStA S M 1/4 Bü 801.

113. Carole Reynaud Paligot, *La république raciale: Paradigme racial et idéologie républicaine (1860–1930)*, 2nd ed. (Paris: Presses universitaires de France, 2009), 227–228.

114. I draw here on Wolfgang Eckart's expression of a "special form of German colonial racism" in contrast to racism focused on the situation within Europe during this same era. Whether or not the differentiation between these two forms of racism is actually specific to Germany seems doubtful but requires further research. Eckart, *Medizin*, 63.

6 Beyond the Army

1. Paligot, *La république raciale*, 221.

2. See, for example, a report on the physical fitness for service of the varied ethnic groups represented in the French colony of La Réunion: Théron, "Le récrutement." In another context, the military strength of the colored population had been appraised in the United States during the Civil War as a "foreign element which had become domicilated [sic] among us by the act of our ancestors." Sanford B. Hund, "The Negro as a Soldier," *Anthropological Review* 7, no. 24 (1869): 40.

3. Immediate report of Imperial Chancellor Caprivi to the emperor concerning the failed deployment of Sudanese in Cameroon, dated August 24, 1894, Bundesarchiv Militärarchiv Freiburg i. Br., Kaiserliche Schutztruppen, MSg 101/147.

4. Ibid.

5. Grosse, *Kolonialismus, Eugenik und bürgerliche Gesellschaft*, 35ff.

6. On this point, see also Christian Koller, *Von Wilden*; Koller, "Feind-Bilder, Rassen- und Geschlechterstereotype in der Kolonialtruppendiskussion Deutschlands und Frankreichs, 1914–1923," in *Heimat-Front: Militär und Geschlechterverhältnisse im Zeitalter der Weltkriege*, ed. Karen Hagemann and Stefanie Schüler-Springorum (New York: Campus Verlag, 2002), 150–167; and Sandra Maß, *Weiße Helden*.

7. For an account of the recruiting practices in French Sénégal, see Joe Lunn, *L'odysée des combattants sénégalais, 1914–1918* (Paris: L'Harmattan, 2014), 37ff.; Marc Michel, *Les Africains et la Grande Guerre: L'appel à l'Afrique (1914–1918)* (Paris: Karthala, 2003); Christian Koller, "Farbige Truppen," in *Enzyklopädie Erster Weltkrieg*, ed. Gerhard Hirschfeld, Gerd Krumeich, and Irina Renz (Paderborn: Schöningh, 2003), 471–472.

8. For example, as in the Manifesto of the Ninety-Three, cited in Koller, *Von Wilden*, 53ff.; see also Koller, "Feind-Bilder," 151ff.

9. Wilhelm Waldeyer, *Die im Weltkrieg stehenden Völker in anthropologischer Betrachtung* (Berlin: Heymanns, 1915).

10. Andrew D. Evans, *Anthropology at War: World War I and the Science of Race in Germany* (Chicago: University of Chicago Press, 2010), 132ff. This has been shown for the prison camp in Wünsdorf: Britta Lange, "Die Welt im Ton: In deutschen Sonderlagern für Kolonialsoldaten entstanden ab 1915 einzigartige Aufnahmen," *iz3w*, no. 307 (August 2008): 22–25, http://www.freiburg-postkolonial.de/pdf/2008 -Lange-Welt-im-Ton.pdf.

11. Paligot, *La république raciale*, 224ff.

12. Adolphe Quetelet, *Anthropométrie ou mésure des différentes facultés de l'homme* (Brussels: C. Muquardt, 1870). For reasons that can no longer be determined, most publications cite this work as having appeared in 1871. Considering Quetelet's statements concerning the military fitness of modern men, this mistake is quite serious in the context of the Franco-Prussian War.

13. Rudolf Virchow, "Gesamtbericht über die Statistik der Farbe der Augen, der Haare und der Haut der Schulkinder in Deutschland," *Correspondenzblatt der Deutschen anthropologischen Gesellschaft* 16 (1885): 89–100; and Virchow, "Gesamtbericht über die von der deutschen anthropologischen Gesellschaft veranlassten Erhebungen über die Farbe der Augen, der Haare und der Haut der Schulkinder in Deutschland," *Archiv für Anthropologie* 16 (1886): 275–475. On Virchow's project, see Christian Geulen, "Blonde bevorzugt: Virchow und Boas: Eine Fallstudie zur Verschränkung von 'Rasse' und 'Kultur' im ideologischen Feld der Ethnizität 1900," *Archiv für Sozialgeschichte* 40 (2000): 147–170; and Andrew Zimmerman, "Anti-Semitism as a Skill: Rudolf Vichow's *Schulstatistik* and the Racial Composition of Germany," *Central European History* 32 (1999): 409–429.

14. For example, the anthropologist in Basel, Julius Kollmann, who began conducting a study in 1877 that was commissioned by the Swiss Society of Anthropology and requested by its German counterparts. Julius Kollmann, *Die statistischen Erhebungen über die Farbe der Auge, Haare und der Haut in den Schulen der Schweiz* (Basel: Georg, 1881). This project was continued later in other European countries: in Bulgaria, the pediatrician and anthropologist Stephan Wateff even combined the results of examinations of school children and potential conscripts. Stephan Wateff, "Anthropologische Beobachtungen an den Schülern und Soldaten in Bulgarien," *Correspondenzblatt der Deutschen anthropologischen Gesellschaft* 32 (1901): 29–30. On this point, see also Christian Promitzer, "Vermessene Körper: 'Rassenkundliche' Grenzziehungen im südöstlichen Europa," in *Europa und die Grenzen im Kopf*, ed. Karl Kaser and Lojze Wieser (Klagenfurt: Wieser, 2003), 375–376.

15. Goschler, *Virchow*, 339; see also statements made in Bischoff, *Brauchbarkeit*, 17. Compare also chapter 1 of this book.

16. This method was outlined, for example, by Granjux and Simon at the International Congress of Hygiene and Demography in 1907: "In the statistics compiled by most armies, the physical value of the various conscription groups is typically expressed in terms of the number of those judged unfit by the conscription examinations." Granjux and Simon, "De la statistique," 1204.

17. Jakob Tanner, "Die 'Alkoholfrage' in der Schweiz im 19. und 20. Jahrhundert," in *Zur Sozialgeschichte des Alkohols in der Neuzeit Europas*, ed. W. Hermann Fahrenkrug (Lausanne: ISPA Press, 1986), 150.

18. Rabinbach, *Human Motor*, 153ff.; and Mary Poovey, *Making a Social Body: British Cultural Formation, 1830–1864* (Chicago: University of Chicago Press, 1995).

19. James K. Shuttleworth, *The Moral and Physical Condition of the Working Classes Employed in the Cotton Manufacture in Manchester, Enlarged and Containing an Introductory Letter to the Reverend T. Chalmers* (London: Ridgway, 1832); and Léon Faucher, *Etudes sur l'Angleterre* (Paris: Guillaumin, 1845 [and subsequent years]). Around the turn of the century, this fear had become so widespread within the United Kingdom that the government commissioned several ambitious statistical studies on this topic. *Report of the Inter-Departmental Committee on Physical Deterioration, Vl 1*, starting in 1904 and updated versions published every year. See also Rabinbach, *Human Motor*, 154.

20. Begun quite early by Paul Rabinow, *French Modern: Norms and Forms of the Social Environment* (Chicago: University of Chicago Press, 1995), 30ff. More generally, see Robert Aisenberg, *Contagion: Disease, Government and the "Social Question" in Nineteenth-Century France* (Stanford, CA: Stanford University Press, 1999), 15ff. More than palpable in Josef Goldstein, *Bevölkerungsprobleme und Berufsgliederung in Frankreich* (Berlin: J. Guttentag, 1900), 36; Gustave Le Bon, *Psychologie des Foules* (Paris: Alcan, 1895); Georg Simmel, "Die Großstädte und das Geistesleben," in *Aufsätze und*

Abhandlungen 1901–1908 (Frankfurt: Suhrkamp, 1995), 121ff.; Bertillon, *La dépopulation*; and Enklaar, *La constitution des conscripts dans les différentes classes sociales* (Utrecht, 1912). Cautious about reaching premature conclusions was Fischer, *Militärtauglichkeit*, 5–6.

21. Ulrich Herbert, "Traditionen des Rassismus," in *Arbeit, Volkstum, Weltanschauung: Über Fremde und Deutsche im 20. Jahrhundert*, ed. Ulrich Herbert (Frankfurt: Fischer, 1995), 20.

22. *Report of the Inter-Departmental Committee.*

23. Heinrich Harkner, "Die Entartungsfrage in England," *Jahrbuch für Gesetzgebung, Verwaltung und Volkswirtschaft im Deutschen Reich: Schmollers Jahrbuch* 31, no. 2 (1907): 357–378.

24. Schwiening, *Beiträge.*

25. Rabinow, *French Modern*, 129ff.; and Müller-Wille and Rheinberger, *Cultural History.*

26. Müller-Wille and Rheinberger, *Cultural History*, 103.

27. Ibid., 82ff.

28. Weindling refers here to a "professional middle class." Weindling, *Health*, 145–146.

29. See the chapter titled "Gesetzmässigkieten der Vererbung: Mendeln," in Max von Gruber and Ernst Rüdin, eds., *Fortpflanzung, Vererbung, Rassenhygiene: Katalog der Gruppe Rassenhygiene der Internationalen Hygiene-Ausstellung 1911 in Dresden* (Munich: Lehmann, 1911), 41–58.

30. For example, in the widely circulated anonymous pamphlet: *Ein Vermächtnis Motke's*. On this point, see also Hartmann, "Normieren."

31. Hansen, *Die drei Bevölkerungsstufen*, 39.

32. See the chapter titled "Kapitel Degeneration," in Max von Gruber and Ernst Rüdin, eds., *Fortpflanzung, Vererbung, Rassenhygiene*, 91–108, esp. pp. 96–101.

33. This background story has been outlined in Heinrich Hartmann, "Une affaire de marge: L'anthropométrie au conseil de révision, France-Allemagne 1880–1900," *Mouvement Social* 256 (2016): 81–99. See also Thomas Etzemüller, *Auf der Suche nach der nordischen Rasse: Die deutsche Rassenanthropologie in der modernen Welt* (Bielefeld: Transcript, 2015), 65ff.

34. See the correspondence between Ammon and the commission at Archives of the University of Freiburg, Ammon papers C 75 file 13.

35. Ammon started the project via an extensive exchange on the methods to apply with Rudolph Virchow in 1886 and 1887. At first very respectful, the correspon-

dence soon took a different course and ended in a dispute. University of Freiburg, Ammon papers C 75 file 61. In his later correspondence, Ammon stated that "the craniometer of Virchow is so terrible, that by the metallic elasticity, we will have deviations of several millimeters. But Virchow is such an authority that we will not be able to convince him." Letter to René Collignon, May 28, 1891, University of Freiburg, Ammon papers C 75 file 59.

36. Otto Ammon, *Die Natürliche Auslese beim Menschen: Auf Grund der Anthropologischen Untersuchungen der Wehrpflichtigen in Baden und anderer Materialien dargstellt* (Jena: Fischer, 1893), 92.

37. Jon Savage, *Teenage: Die Erfindung der Jugend (1870–1945)* (Frankfurt: Campus, 2008), 101. For Italy, see Alfredo Niceforo, *Antropologia delle classi povere* (Milan: Vallardi, 1908), 46ff.

38. C. H. Alden, "The Identification of the Individual: With Special Reference to the System in Use in the Office of the Surgeon General, U.S. Army," *American Anthropologist* 9, no. 9 (September 1896): 295–310.

39. Robert Michels, "Das Prolatariat in der Wissenschaft und die ökonomisch-anthropologische Synthese," foreword to Niceforo, *Anthropologie*, 13.

40. This is most explicitly and prominently outlined in Alfred Plötz, "Die Begriffe Rasse und Gesellschaft und einige damit zusammenhängende Probleme," in *Verhandlungen des Ersten Deutschen Soziologentages, 19.–22.10.1910 in Frankfurt am Main* (Tübingen: Mohr, 1911), 133ff. On this point, and Max Weber's response, see Max Weber, "Entgegnung auf Alfred Plötz," in *Verhandlungen des Ersten Deutschen Soziologentages, 19.–22.10.1910 in Frankfurt/M* (Tübingen: Mohr, 1911), 151–157.

41. Alsberg, *Erbliche Entartung*; and Herbert, "Traditionen," 15.

42. Zheng Kang, "La Société de Statistique de Paris au XIXe siècle: Un lieu de savoir social," *Les Cahiers du Centre de Recherches Historiques* 9 (April 15, 1992), 11, doi:10.4000/ccrh.2808.

43. Hans-Konrad Schmutz, "Vermessene Nation. Eine Skizze der imagologischen Anthropologie nach 1860," in *Anthropologie nach Haeckel*, ed. Dirk Preuß, Uwe Hoßfeld, and Olaf Breidbach (Stuttgart: Steiner, 2006), 184–194; and Andrew Zimmerman, *Anthropology and Antihumanism in Imperial Germany* (Chicago: University of Chicago Press, 2001), 88–89. Ammon himself was in close contact with William Rippley and Vacher de Lapouge, who both visited him before the end of the century. His original research also drew methodologically on the field of prehistory and early history, until he believed he had found a broader body of sources with the records of the conscription examinations: Hilkea Lichtsinn, *Otto Ammon und die Sozialanthropologie* (Frankfurt: P. Lang, 1987), 11.

44. Letter to René Collignon, March 11, 1892, University of Freiburg, Ammon papers C 75 file 59.

45. See chapter 4 for the parallel reflections.

46. See the argument of Etzemüller, *Auf der Suche*, 65ff.

47. Müller-Wille and Rheinberger, *Cultural History*, 65ff.

48. Peter Walkenhorst, *Nation—Volk—Rasse: Radikaler Nationalismus im Deutschen Kaiserreich, 1890–1914* (Göttingen: Vandenhoeck & Ruprecht, 2007).

49. Schmutz, *Vermessene Nation*, 190ff.; and Simona Boscani Leoni, "Einleitung," in *Wissenschaft—Berge—Ideologien: Johann Jakob Scheuchzer (1672–1733) und die frühneuzeitliche Naturforschung/Scienza—montagna—ideologie: Johann Jakob Scheuchzer (1672–1733) e la ricerca naturalistica in epoca moderna*, ed. Simona Boscani Leoni (Basel: Schwabe, 2010), 9–22.

50. For the Swiss case, this is convincingly shown by Pascal Germann, *Laboratorien der Vererbung: Rassenforschung und Humangenetik in der Schweiz, 1900–1970* (Göttingen: Wallstein, 2016).

51. Georges Vacher de Lapouge, *L'aryen: Son rôle social: Cours libre de science politique* (Paris: Fontemoing, 1899); and William Ripley, *Races of Europe: A Selected Bibliography of the Anthropology and Ethnology of Europe* (New York: Appleton, 1899).

52. Weindling, *Health*, 125ff.

53. Schmutz, *Vermessene Nation*. On the practices of research settings in closed, alpine-laboratory-like conditions as one of the important anthropometric approaches of the time, see Germann, *Laboratorien der Vererbung*, 71ff.

54. Within the German-speaking sphere especially, such maps of ethnicity were often drawn along linguistic borders in the late nineteenth century. On the numerous complications and rejections, see Labbé, "Grenzen."

55. Claude Blanckaert, "La crise de l'anthropométrie: Des arts anthropotechniques aux dérives militants," in *Les politiques de l'anthropologie: Discours et pratiques en France (1860–1940)*, ed. Claude Blanckaert (Paris: L'Harmattan, 2009), 220–245.

56. See Hartmann, "Affaire de marge."

57. He published his first anthropometric works on the anthropology of Lorraine. René Collignon, *La race Lorraine étudiée sur des ossements trouvés à Nancy* (Nancy: Berger-Levrault, 1881); and René Collignon, *Anthropologie de la Lorraine* (Nancy: Berger-Levrault, 1886).

58. Letter to Ammon, Feburary 9 and 18, and March 9, 1892, University of Freiburg, Ammon papers C 75 file 59.

59. René Collignon, *L'Anthropologie au conseil de revision: Méthode à suivre, son application à l'étude des populations des Côtes-du-Nord* (Paris: Hennuyer, 1891).

60. Hartmann, "Affaire de marge," 94ff.

61. Later to be published as William Z. Ripley, *The Races of Europe: A Sociological Study* (New York: D. Appleton, 1899). On this, see Jon Røyne Kyllingstad, *Measuring the Masterrace: Physical Anthropology in Norway, 1890–1945* (Cambridge: Open Book Publishers, 2014), 58–59.

62. Ammon to Ripley, May 30, 1896, University of Freiburg, Ammon papers C 75 file 60.

63. Ammon to Ripley, July 4, 1896, University of Freiburg, Ammon papers C 75 file 60. We know such rather shaky ways of anthropological evidence from other contexts. Schmutz tells a similar story about how the phenotypes of the Swiss Canton of Graubünden were fixed: Schmutz, "Vermessene Nation," 189–190.

64. Also, Ammon and Collignon advocated for international coordination on these questions: René Collignon, "Projet d'entente internationale au sujet des recherches anthropométriques dans les conseils de révision," *Bulletins de la Société d'anthropologie de Paris* 3 (1892): 186–188. See also Kyllingstad, *Measuring the Masterrace*, 45ff.

65. Hugo Meißner, "Rekrutierungsstatistik," *Archiv für Rassen- und Gesellschaftsbiologie* 6 (1909): 59–72; and Brentano, "Unbrauchbarkeit."

66. Cited from Kaup, *Ernährung*, 6.

67. In reference to this first generation around Virchow and its rather limited nationalist determination, Weindling speaks of a "liberal anthropology": Weindling, *Health*, 50–51. On this point, see also Goschler, *Virchow*, 333ff.

68. This argument was made repeatedly by the president of the Anthopological Society, Gustav Schwalbe—for example, in Gustav A. Schwalbe, "Eröffnung der XXXVIII. allgemeinen Versammlung der deutschen Anthropologischen Gesellschaft in Strassburg vom 4. bis 8. August 1907. Aufgaben der Sozialanthropologie," *Korrespondenz-Blatt der deutschen Gesellschaft für Anthropologie, Ethnologie und Urgeschichte*, no. 9/12 (September/December 1907): 66; and most clearly in Albrecht Wirth, *Volk und Rasse* (Halle: Max Niemeyer, 1914).

69. Chris Manias, "The *Race prusienne* Controversy: Scientific Internationalism and the Nation," *Isis* 100 (2009): 733–757. On a more general note, this argument has been repeatedly made in the case of France and Germany around 1900—for example, Harry W. Paul, *The Sorcerer's Apprentice: The French Scientists: The French Scientist's Image of German Science, 1840–1919* (Gainesville: University of Florida Press, 1972); Maurice Crosland, "Science and the Franco-Prussian War," *Social Studies of Science* 6 (1976): 185–214; Kai Thorsten Kanz, *Nationalismus und internationale Zusammenarbeit in den Naturwissenschaften: Die deutsch-französischen Wissenschaftsbeziehungen zwischen Revolution und Restauration, 1789–1832* (Stuttgart: Steiner, 1997); and Ralph Jessen and Jakob Vogel, "Die Naturwissenschaften und die Nation: Perspektiven einer Wechselbeziehung in der europäischen Geschichte," in *Wissenschaft und*

Nation in der Europäischen Geschichte, ed. Ralph Jessen and Jakob Vogel (Frankfurt: Campus, 2002), 7–37.

70. Heyberger, *Révolution des corps*, 56ff.; Wolfgang Freund, *Volk, Reich und West-grenze: Deutschtumswissenschaften und Politik in der Pfalz im Saarland und im annekti-erten Lothringen 1925–1945* (Saarbrücken: Saarländische Druckerei und Verlag, 2006), 214ff.

71. Christian Bonah, "Sciences et prestige national; trajectoires de médecins mor-phologistes," in *La science sous influence: L'université de Strasbourg, enjeu des conflits franco-allemands, 1872–1945*, ed. Elisabeth Crawford and Josiane Olff-Nathan (Stras-bourg: La Nuée bleue, 2005), 129–130; and Bonah, "Espace national et porteurs de culture: Le double jeu géopolitique des sciences exactes lors de la création de l'université d'Empire de Strasbourg, 1872–1884," in *Les espaces de l'Allemagne au XIXe siècle: Frontières, centers et question nationale*, ed. Catherine Maurer (Strasbourg: Presses universitaires de Strasbourg, 2010), 210ff.

72. Gustav Adolf Brandt, *Die Körpergröße der Wehrpflichtigen des Reichslandes Elsass-Lothringen: Nach amtlichen Quellen* (Strasbourg: Trübner, 1898).

73. Ibid., and Collignon, *Anthropologie de la France: Dordogne, Charente, Corrèze, Creuse, Haute-Vienne* (Paris, 1894).

74. Georges Hervé, "La taille en Alsace," *Revue mensuelle de l'Ecole d'anthropologie de Paris* (1901): 161–177.

75. Even though this could not be reproduced for all countries. Heinrich Bircher's disappointment about this, for example, was palpable: "If the difference in height between north and south allows for the proof of ethnic heredity, we can only hope in vain to achieve such a demarcation for Switzerland because the mixing of the races is too significant." Bircher, *Rekrutirung und Ausmusterung*, 20.

76. John Beddoe, "President's Address," *Journal of the Anthropological Institute of Great Britain and Ireland* 19 (1890): 483.

77. Benjamin A. Gould, *Investigations in the Military and Anthropological Statistics of American Soldiers* (New York: Riverside Press, 1869).

78. S. Guida, "Il foglio di sanità nel libretto personale del soldato e la matricola sani-taria," *Giornale di medicina militare* 27 (1879).

79. Ridolfo Livi, "Essai d'anthropométrie militaire," *Bulletin de l'Institut International de Statistique* 7 (1894): 273–285.

80. W. H. Duckworth, "Ridolfo Livi (1856–1920) [Obituary]," *Man* 20 (1920): 139–143.

81. Livi, "Taille"; Livi, "Statistique anthropométrique militaire," *Bulletin de l'institut international de statistique* 15 (1906): 46–49.

82. Schmid-Monard, "Über den Werth."

83. "Bevölkerung und deren Aufnahme," BArch Reichskanzlei Gr. 44—Statistik, R 43/2070. Keywords are underlined in the original.

84. Arbo concluded that Norwegians, like the rest of the Scandinavian neighbors, were descended from the Neanderthals and a migratory race from the Mediterranean: Carl Oscar Eugen Arbo, "Sur l'indice céphalique en Norwège, sa répartition topographique et ses rapports avec la taille," in *Comptes-Rendus du XII congrès international de médecine, Moscou 7–14 août 1897, Séction 1—Anatomie, Anthropologie—Histologie* (Moscow, 1899), 22–25. On the topic of, at that time, Swedish Norway and Sweden itself, see also the later studies: Carl Oscar Eugen Arbo, *Sveriges anthropologi med sammenlignende bemaerkninger til Norges* (Christiania: Dybwad, 1903); and Carl Fürst and Gustav Retzius, *Anthropometria suecica: Beiträge zur Anthropologie der Schweden* (Stockholm: Aftonbladets Druckerei, 1902). On the functional character of skull measurement for Norwegian nationalism, see Kyllingstad, *Measuring the Masterrace*, 35ff.

85. Hans-Ulrich Wehler, *Deutsche Gesellschaftsgeschichte*, vol. 3, *Von der "deutschen Doppelrevolution" bis zum Beginn des Ersten Weltkrieges 1849–1914*, 3rd. ed. (Munich: C. H. Beck, 1995), 660ff.

86. On Rudolf Martin's role as intermediary between anthropometric methods and cultural ethnology, see Germann, *Laboratorien der Vererbung*; and Christoph Keller, *Der Schädelvermesser: Otto Schlaginhaufen—Anthropologe und Rassenhygieniker: Eine biographische Reportage* (Zurich: Limmat, 1995), 20ff.

87. Letter to His Excellency Dr. Count of Posadowsky-Wehner, Royal Prussian Minister of State, Undersecretary of State, June 1904; BArch Reichskanzlei Gr. 44—Statistik, R 43/2070.

88. During this period, the anthropological society vehemently pursued the goal of compiling a racial map of the European continent; although this was to be based on ethnographic and prehistorical data, it was hoped that statistics gathered in contemporary surveys might provide a form of secondary evidence. Lissauer, "Bericht der vorbereitenden Commission zur Herstellung von Typenkarten," *Correspondenzblatt der Deutschen anthropologischen Gesellschaft*, no. 11 (1903): 123–125.

89. Gustav Schwalbe, "Bericht über die Thätigkeit der Commission für eine physisch-anthropologische Untersuchung des deutschen Reiches," *Correspondenzblatt der Deutschen anthropologischen Gesellschaft*, no. 9 (1904): 75–79.

90. Ibid., 77.

91. This was the procedure for the newly introduced examinations in Denmark, for example, where estimates for the general population were made based on the measurements collected from those who had already been drafted. Mackeprang, "Die

Körperhöhe der Stadtbevölkerung," *Correspondenz-Blatt der deutschen Gesellschaft für Anthropologie, Ethnologie und Urgeschichte* 6 (June 1910): 41–42.

92. *Heerordnung, Militärische Ergänzungsbestimmungen zur Deutschen Wehrordnung vom 22.11.188: Neuabdruck unter Berücksichtigung der bis April 1904 eingetretenen Änderungen* (Berlin: Mittler 1904), § 10, 13–14.

93. Wilhelm Waldeyer, "Eröffnungsrede der XLI. allgemeinen Versammlung der Deutschen Anthropologischen Gesellschaft in Cöln am Rh. Über Zukunftsaufgaben für die anthropologische Forschung und für die anthropologischen Vereine," *Correspondenz-Blatt der deutschen Gesellschaft für Anthropologie, Ethnologie und Urgeschichte*, no. 9/12 (September/December 1910): 69–70.

94. Armand Quatrefages, *La rasse prusienne* (Paris: Hachette, 1871); Manias, "The Race Prusienne Controversy"; and Schmutz, "Vermessene Nation."

95. Evans, *Anthropology at War*; Christian Geulen, "The Common Grounds of Conflict: Racial Visions of World Order," in *Competing Visions of World Order: Global Order and Movements, 1880s–1930s*, ed. Sebastian Conrad and Dominik Sachsenmaier (New York: Palgrave, 2007), 69–96.

96. Wilhelm Waldeyer, *Die im Weltkrieg stehenden Völker in anthropologischer Betrachtung* (Berlin: Heymanns, 1915); and Evans, *Anthropology at War*, 115ff.

97. Evans, *Anthropology at War*, 123ff.

98. For more information on people such as Rudolf Martin, see Germann, *Laboratorien der Vererbung*, 77ff.

99. Evans, *Anthropology at War*, 77ff.

100. Schwiening and Nicolai, *Körperbeschaffenheit*, 157.

101. Goschler, *Virchow*, 343ff.; Weindling, *Health*, 57ff.; and Paligot, *La République racial*, 91–92.

102. Zimmerman, *Anthropology*, 136ff.

103. Interesting in this context is Grosse's argument that, in the years before the war broke out, eugenicists were often unable to take a stance regarding militarized nationalism because it was not clear how war would affect the eugenic development of the national collective. Grosse, *Kolonialismus*, 210ff.

104. Fabio Frassetto, "A Uniform Blank of Measurements to be Used in Recruiting: A Plea for the Standardization of Anthropological Methods," *American Anthropologist*, n.s., 21, no. 2 (1919): 179. *European* here referred to the nation states of Western Europe and the Austro-Hungarian Empire. Frassetto's essay, however, also highlights the failure not only of the coordination in the context of the military but also more generally that of the field of anthropology to introduce standardized methods of measurement. For example, there was no agreement on the metric system as a frame

of reference, which complicated international comparisons and resulted in astonishing imprecision: Frassetto, "Uniform," 175–176.

105. Jakob Tanner, "Eugenik und Rassenhygiene in Wissenschaft und Politik seit dem ausgehenden 19. Jahrhundert: Ein historischer Überblick," in *Zwischen Erziehung und Vernichtung: Zigeunerpolitik und Zigeunerforschung im Europa des 20. Jahrhunderts*, ed. Michael Zimmermann (Stuttgart: Steiner, 2007), 112; and Stefan Kühl, *Die Internationale der Rassisten: Aufstieg und Niedergang der Internationalen Bewegung für Eugenik und Rassenhygiene im 20. Jahrhundert* (Frankfurt: Campus, 1997).

106. Michl, *Im Dienste*.

Conclusion

1. Jakob Vogel, "Lernen vom Feind: Das Militär als Träger des deutsch-französischen Kulturtransfers im 19. Jahrhundert," in *Vom Gegner lernen: Feindschaften und Kulturtransfers im Europa des 19. und 20. Jahrhunderts*, ed. Martin Aust and Daniel Schönpflug (Frankfurt: Campus, 2007), 95–113.

2. Grosse, *Kolonialismus*, 220ff.

3. Wilhelm Schmidt, *Rasse und Volk: Eine Untersuchung zur Bestimmung ihrer Grenzen und zur Erfassung ihrer Beziehungen* (Munich: J. Kösel & F. Pustet, 1927), 4ff.

4. Christoph Keller, *Der Schädelvermesser: Otto Schlaginhaufen, Anthropologe und Rassenhygieniker: Eine biographische Reportage* (Zurich: Limmat, 1995), 110ff.

5. For example, Friedrich Burgdörfer, *Volks- und Wehrkraft, Krieg und Rasse* (Berlin: Metzner, 1936).

Bibliography

Abelsdorff, Walter. *Die Wehrfähigkeit zweier Generationen mit Rücksicht auf Herkunft und Beruf.* Berlin: G. Reimer, 1905.

Aisenberg, Andrew Robert. *Contagion: Disease, Government, and the "Social Question" in Nineteenth-Century France.* Stanford, CA: Stanford University Press, 1999.

Albouze. "Notes sur les conseils de revision; modifications à y apporter." *Bulletin bi-mensuel de la Société de médecine militaire française* 7 (1913): 238–247.

Alden, C. H. "The Identification of the Individual: With Special Reference to the System in Use in the Office of the Surgeon General, U.S. Army." *American Anthropologist* 9, no. 9 (September 1896): 295–310.

Aldenhoff-Hübinger, Rita. "'Les nations anciennes, écrasées ...' Agrarprotektionismus in Deutschland und Frankreich, 1880–1914." *Geschichte und Gesellschaft* 26 (2000): 439–470.

Alsberg, Moritz. *Erbliche Entartung bedingt durch Soziale Einflüsse.* Kassel: Th. G. Fisher, 1903.

Alsberg, Moritz. *Militäruntauglichkeit und Großstadt-Einfluß: Hygienisch-volkswirtschaftliche Betrachtungen und Vorschläge.* Leipzig: Teubner, 1909.

Ammon, Otto. *Die Natürliche Auslese beim Menschen: Auf Grund der Anthropologischen Untersuchungen der Wehrpflichtigen in Baden und anderer Materialien dargstellt.* Jena: Fischer, 1893.

Ammon, Otto. *Die Bedeutung des Bauernstandes für den Staat und die Gesellschaft.* Berlin: Trowitsch, 1894.

Annuario estadistico de Espana correspondiendo á 1839 y 1860. Madrid: Imprenta Nacional, 1860.

Antony and Loisson. "Examen du coeur à la Radioscopie au point de vue de l'aptitude au service militaire." In *Comptes rendus du XIVe congrès international de médecine, Madrid 23.–30.4. 1903, Section de médecine et hygiène militaires et navales,* 175–187. Madrid: Imprenta Nacional, 1904.

Arbo, Carl Oscar Eugen. "Sur l'indice céphalique en Norwège, sa répartition topographique et ses rapports avec la taille." In *Comptes-Rendus du XII congrès international de médecine, Moscou 7–14 août 1897, Séction 1—Anatomie, Anthropologie—Histologie,* 22–25. Moscow, 1899.

Arbo, Carl Oscar Eugen. *Sveriges anthropologi med sammenlignende bemaerkninger til Norges.* Christiania: Dybwad, 1903.

Army Medical Department Report for the Year 1878. London, 1880.

Arnaud, Pierre, and André Gounot. "Mobilisierung der Körper und republikanische Selbstinszenierung in Frankreich (1879–1889). Ansätze zu einer vergleichenden deutsch-französischen Sportgeschichte." In *Nation und Emotion: Deutschland und Frankreich im Vergleich 19. und 20. Jahrhundert,* edited by Etienne François, Hannes Siegrist, and Jakob Vogel, 300–320. Göttingen: Vandenhoeck & Ruprecht, 1995.

Aron, Jean-Paul, Paul Dumont, and Emmanuel Le Roy Ladurie. *Anthropologie du conscrit français: D'après les comptes numériques et sommaires du recrutement de l'armée (1819–1826).* Paris: Mouton de Gruyter, 1972.

Ash, Mitchell G. "Wissenschaft und Politik als Ressourcen füreinander." In *Wissenschaften und Wissenschaftspolitik: Bestandsaufnahmen zu Formationen, Brüchen und Kontinuitäten im Deutschland des 20. Jahrhunderts,* edited by Rüdiger Bruch and Brigitte Kaderas, 32–51. Stuttgart: Steiner, 2002.

Atti dell'XI Congresso Medico Internazionale, Roma, 29 Marzo–5 Aprile 1894, vol. 4. Rome: 1895.

Axster, Felix. *Koloniales Spektakel in 9 × 14. Bildpostkarten im Deutschen Kaiserreich.* Bielefeld: Transcript, 2014.

Baldwin, Peter. *Contagion and the State in Europe, 1830–1930.* Cambridge: Cambridge University Press, 1999.

Ballod, Carl. *Die Lebensfähigkeit der städtischen und ländlichen Bevölkerung.* Leipzig: Duncker & Humblot, 1897.

Ballod, Carl. "Zur 'agrarischen' Beweisführung." *Schweizerische Blätter für Wirtschafts—und Socialpolitik,* no. 4 (1903): 217–222.

Barlösius, Eva. "Bilder des demografischen Wandels." In *Zukunftswissen: Prognosen in Wirtschaft, Politik und Gesellschaft seit 1900,* edited by Heinrich Hartmann and Jakob Vogel, 231–248. Frankfurt: Campus, 2010.

Barthélemy, Adrien. *L'examen de la vision devant les conseils de revision et de réforme dans la marine et dans l'armée et devant les commissions des chemins de fer.* Paris: J.-B. Baillière et fils, 1889.

Bashford, Alison. "Nation, Empire, Globe: The Spaces of Population Debate in the Interwar Years." *Comparative Studies in Society and History* 49, no. 1 (2007): 170–201.

Bassenge, Lothar. *Die Heranziehung und Erhaltung einer wehrfähigen Jugend: Vortrag gehalten am 9. Januar 1911.* Berlin: A. Hirschwald, 1911.

Becker, Frank. "'Bewaffnetes Volk' oder 'Volk in Waffen'? Militärpolitik und Militarismus in Deutschland und Frankreich 1870–1914." In *Der Bürger als Soldat: Die Militarisierung europaischer Gesellschaften im langen 19. Jahrhundert: Ein internationaler Vergleich,* edited by Christian Jansen, 158–174. Essen: Klartext, 2004.

Becker, Frank. "Synthetischer Militarismus: Die Einigungskriege und der Stellenwert des Militärischen in der deutschen Gesellschaft." In *Das Militär und der Aufbruch in die Moderne 1860 bis 1890: Armeen, Marinen und der Wandel von Politik, Gesellschaft und Wirtschaft in Europa, den USA sowie Japan,* edited by Michael Epkenhans and P. Gerhard Groß, 125–141. Munich: Oldenbourg, 2003.

Becker, Peter, and Richard Wetzell, eds. *The History of Criminology in International Perspective.* Cambridge: Cambridege University Press, 2006.

Beck, Stefan, and Jörg Niewöhner. "Somatographic Investigations across Levels of Complexity." *Biosocieties* 1, no. 2 (June 2006): 219–227.

Beddoe, John. "President's Address." *Journal of the Anthropological Institute of Great Britain and Ireland* 19 (1890): 481–493.

Benecke, Werner. "Die Allgemeine Wehrpflicht in Russland: Zwischen militärischem Anspruch und zivilen Interessen." *Journal of Modern European History* 5, no. 2 (2007): 244–263.

Benecke, Werner. *Militär, Reform und Gesellschaft im Zarenreich: Die Wehrpflicht in Russland 1874–1914.* Paderborn: Schöningh Paderborn, 2006.

Benoiston de Châteauneuf, Louis. "Essai sur la mortalité dans l'infanterie française." *Annales d'hygiène publique et de médecine légale* 10 (1833).

Bericht über den XIV. Internationalen Kongress für Hygiene und Demographie, Berlin, 23.–29. September 1907. Berlin: A. Hirschwald, 1908.

Bericht des Vorstandes der Schulsynode über die Erhebungen betr. die unbefriedigenden Resultate bei den Rekrutenprüfungen im Kanton Bern. Bern: 1905.

Bernstein, S. *Körperlänge, Brustumfang und Körpergewicht zur Beurteilung der physischen Widerstandskraft der Soldaten.* Vienna, 1865.

Bertillon, Jacques. "La colonisation de l'Europe par les Allemands." *La réforme économique: Revue des question sociales, politiques, fiscales, scientifiques, industrielles, agricoles et commerciales* 1 (1875): 154–169.

Bertillon, Jacques. *La dépopulation de la France: Ses conséquences, ses causes: Mesures à prendre pour la combattre*. Paris: Alcan, 1911.

Beyrau, Dietrich. "Aus der Subalternität in die Sphären der Macht: Die Juden im Zarenreich und in Sowjetrussland (1860–1930)." In *Moderne Zeiten? Krieg, Revolution und Gewalt im 20. Jahrhundert*, edited by Jörg Barberowski, 60–93. Göttingen: Vandenhoeck & Ruprecht, 2006.

Beyrau, Dietrich. *Militär und Gesellschaft im vorrevolutionären Russland*. Cologne: Böhlau, 1984.

Billot, Camille. *Conférence: Rôle du médecin dans le regiment*. Paris, 1891.

Bindewald, Georg. *Die Wehrfähigkeit der ländlichen und städtischen Bevölkerung*. Halle: Pierer, 1901.

Bircher, Heinrich. *Der endemische Kropf und seine Beziehung zur Taubstummheit und zum Cretinismus*. Basel: Schwabe, 1883.

Bircher, Heinrich. *Die Armeeorganisation und Militärkreiseinteilung der schweizerischen Eidgenossenschaft auf Grundlage der Tauglichkeitsziffern*. Aarau: Sauerländer, 1886.

Bircher, Heinrich. *Die Rekrutierung und Ausmusterung der schweizerischen Armee*. Aarau: Sauerländer, 1886.

Bischoff, Hans. *Festschrift zur 50jährigen Stiftungsfeier der Berliner Militärärztlichen Gesellschaft am 20.2.1914*. Berlin: Mittler, 1914.

Bischoff, Thomas L. W. *Über die Brauchbarkeit der in verschiedenen europäischen Staaten veröffentlichten Resultate des Recrutirungs-Geschäftes zur Beurtheilung des Entwicklungs- und Gesundheitszustandes ihrer Bevölkerung*. München: Verlag der königlichen Akademie, 1867.

Blanckaert, Claude. "La crise de l'anthropométrie: Des arts anthropotechniques aux dérives militants." In *Les politiques de l'anthropologie: Discours et pratiques en France (1860–1940)*, edited by Claude Blanckaert, 220–245. Paris: L'Harmattan, 2009.

Boisseau, Emile. *Des maladies simulées et des moyens de les reconnaitre*. Paris: J.-B. Baillière et fils, 1870.

Bonah, Christian. "Espace national et porteurs de culture: Le double jeu géopolitique des sciences exactes lors de la création de l'université d'Empire de Strasbourg, 1872–1884." In *Les espaces de l'Allemagne au 19e siècle: Frontières, centres et question nationale*, edited by Catherine Maurer, 195–220. Strasbourg: Presses universitaires de Strasbourg, 2010.

Bonah, Christian. "Sciences et prestige national; trajectoires de médecins morphologistes." In *La science sous influence: L'université de Strasbourg, enjeu des conflits franco-allemands 1872–1945*, edited by Elisabeth Crawford and Josiane Olff-Nathan, 121–134. Strasbourg: La Nuée bleue, 2005.

Borowski. *Die Aushebung: Ein Ratgeber für die Ober-Ersatz und Ersatzkommissionen.* Berlin: Liebmann, 1890.

Boscani Leoni, Simona. "Einleitung." In *Wissenschaft—Berge—Ideologien. Johann Jakob Scheuchzer (1672–1733) und die frühneuzeitliche Naturforschung/Scienza—montagna—ideologie: Johann Jakob Scheuchzer (1672–1733) e la ricerca naturalistica in epoca moderna,* edited by Simona Boscani Leoni, 9–22. Basel: Schwabe, 2010.

Bostridge, Mark. *Florence Nightingale: The Woman and Her Legend.* Facsimile edition. London: Viking, 2008.

Boudin, Jean-Christian. "Études sur le récrutement de l'armée." *Annales d'Hygiène Publique et de médecine légale* 41 (1849).

Boudin, Jean-Christian. *Hygiène militaire comparée, et statistique médicale des armées de terre et de mer.* Paris: J.-B. Baillière et fils, 1848.

Bracke, Nele. "For State and Society: The Production of Official Statistics in 19th-Century Belgium." In *Jenseits von Humboldt: Wissenschaft im Staat 1850–1990,* edited by Axel C. Hüntelmann and Michael C. Schneider, 257–267. Frankfurt: Peter Lang, 2010.

Brandt, Gustav Adolf. *Die Körpergröße der Wehrpflichtigen des Reichslandes Elsass-Lothringen: Nach amtlichen Quellen.* Strasbourg: Trübner, 1898.

Brentano, Lujo. "Die Agrarreform in Preußen." *Die Nation,* no. 24 (March 13, 1897): 359–362, no. 25 (March 20, 1897): 374–379, no. 26 (March 27, 1897): 392–396, and no. 27 (April 3, 1897): 407–410.

Brentano, Lujo. "Die Grundlage der Deutschen Wehrkraft noch einmal." *Die Nation* 8 (November 27, 1897): 111–113.

Brentano, Lujo. "Die heutige Grundlage der deutschen Wehrkraft." *Die Nation* 5 (October 30, 1897): 67–71.

Brentano, Lujo. "Die Krisis der deutschen Wirtschaftswissenschaften." *Die Nation,* no. 48 (August 28, 1897): 727–730, and no. 49 (September 4, 1897): 738–742.

Brentano, Lujo. "Ein agrarisches Zugeständnis." *Die Nation,* no. 7 (November 20, 1897): 97.

Brentano, Lujo. "Wollen oder Erkennen? Ein ernstes Wort an Herrn Prof. Dr. Max Sering." *Die Nation,* no. 43 (July 24, 1897): 649–653.

Brentano, Lujo, and Robert René Kuczynski. *Die heutige Grundlage der deutschen Wehrkraft.* Stuttgart: Cotta, 1900.

Bronfen, Elisabeth. *Specters of War: Hollywood's Engagement with Military Conflict.* New Brunswick, NJ: Rutgers University Press, 2012.

Bruck, Carl. "Die biologische Differenzierung von Affenarten und menschlichen Rassen durch spezifische Blutreaktionen." *Berliner klinische Wochenschrift* 26 (1907): 793–797.

Burchhardt, M. *Praktische Diagnostik der Simulationen von Gefühlslähmungen, von Schwerhörigkeit und von Schwachsichitigkeit.* Berlin: Otto Enslin, 1875.

Burgdörfer, Friedrich. *Volks- und Wehrkraft, Krieg und Rasse.* Berlin: Metzner, 1936.

Busch, H. *Grösse, Gewicht und Brustumfang von Soldaten: Studien über ihre Entwicklung ihren Einfluss auf die militairische Tauglichkeit.* Berlin: A. Hirschwald, 1878.

Callon, Michael, ed. *La Science et ses réseaux: Genèse et circulation des faits scientifiques.* Paris: Editions La Découverte, 1989.

Caradec, François. *Alphonse Allais.* Paris: Belfond, 1994.

Chanet, Jean-François. *Vers l'armée nouvelle: République conservatrice et réforme militaire, 1871–1879.* Rennes: Presses universitaires de Rennes, 2006.

Chassagne. *Les cahiers de 1889 de la médecine militaire française: Officiers du corps de santé miliaire de l'armée active, réserve et armée territoriale.* Paris: H. Charles-Lavauzelle, 1889.

Chenu, Jean-Charles. *Rapport aux Conseil de Santé des armées sur les résultats du service médico-chirurgial aux Ambulances du Crimée et aux hôpitaux militaires français de Turquie pendant la campagne d'Orient en 1854–1855–1856.* Paris: Masson et fils, 1865.

Chenu, Jean-Charles. *Recrutement de l'armée et population de la France.* Paris: Masson et fils, 1867.

Cheysson, Emile. "Les méthodes de la statistique: Conférence faite le 30 Novembre 1889 à la réunion des Officiers. In *Œuvres choisies*, 155–184. Paris: A. Rousseau, 1911.

Claaßen, Walter. "Die abnehmende Kriegstüchtigkeit im Deutschen Reiche in Stadt und Land." *Archiv für Rassen—und Gesellschaftsbiologie*, no. 1 (1909).

Coghe, Samuël. "Medical Demography in Interwar Angola: Measuring and Negotiating Health, Reproduction and Difference." In *Health and Difference: Rendering Human Variation in Colonial Engagements*, edited by Alexandra Widmer and Veronika Lipphardt, 178–204. New York: Berghahn, 2016.

Collignon, René. *Anthropologie de la France: Dordogne, Charente, Corrèze, Creuse, Haute-Vienne.* Paris, 1894.

Collignon, René. *Anthropologie de la Lorraine.* Nancy: Berger-Levrault, 1886.

Collignon, René. *L'Anthropologie au conseil de revision: Méthode à suivre, son application à l'étude des populations des Côtes-du-Nord.* Paris: Hennuyer, 1891.

Collignon, René. *La race Lorraine étudiée sur des ossements trouvés à Nancy.* Nancy: Berger-Levrault, 1881.

Collignon, René. "Projet d'entente internationale au sujet des recherches anthropométriques dans les conseils de révision." *Bulletins de la Société d'anthropologie de Paris* 3 (1892): 186–188.

Colombo, Jean Pierre. *Heinrich Bircher (1850–1923): Chirurg, Demograph und Militärarzt.* Stuttgart: B. Schwabe, 1961.

Conrad, Sebastian, and Jürgen Osterhammel. "Einleitung." In *Das Kaiserreich transnational: Deutschland in der Welt 1871–1914*, edited by Sebastian Conrad and Jürgen Osterhammel, 7–27. Göttingen: Vandenhoeck & Ruprecht, 2004.

Crépin, Annie. *Défendre la France: Les Français, la guerre et le service militaire, de la guerre de Sept Ans à Verdun.* Rennes: Presses universitaires de Rennes, 2005.

Crépin, Annie. *La conscription en débat ou Le triple apprentissage de la nation, de la citoyenneté, de la République: 1798–1889.* Arras: Artois presses université, 1998.

Crosland, Maurice. "Science and the Franco-Prussian War." *Social Studies of Science* 6 (1976): 185–214.

Curtin, Philip D. *Disease and Empire: The Health of European Troops in the Conquest of Africa.* Cambridge: Cambridge University Press, 1998.

Curtin, Philip D. "'The White Man's Grave': Image and Reality, 1780–1850." *Journal of British Studies* 1, no. 1 (1961): 94–110.

Dade. *Die Notwendigkeit der Erhaltung und Vermehrung des Deutschen Bauern—und Landarbeiterstandes für die Volks—und Wehrkraft.* Leipzig: Deichert, 1914.

Davies. "How to Judge of the Fitness of Officers and Men for Active Service in Tropical Countries,." In *Bericht über den XIV: Internationalen Kongress für Hygiene und Demographie, Berlin, 23.–29. September 1907.* Vol. 3, 572. Berlin: A. Hirschwald, 1908.

Davison, Graeme. "The City as Natural System: Theories of Urban History." In *The Pursuit of Urban History*, edited by Derek Fraser and Anthony Sutcliffe, 349–370. London: E. Arnold, 1983.

de Bondy, François Marie Taillepied. *Recrutement de l'armée. Observations pratiques sur les inégalités du mode actuel de répartition des contingents entre les départements et les cantons, et proposition d'un nouveau mode.* Auxerre: E. Perriquet, 1841.

Deherme, Georges. "L'alcoolisme dans les colonies." *Annales antialcooliques* 3, no. 4 (1905).

De Luca Barrusse, Virginie. *Les familles nombreuses: Une question démographique, un enjeu politique: France, 1880–1940.* Rennes: Presses universitaires de Rennes, 2008.

Derblich, W. *Die simulierten Krankheiten der Wehrpflichtigen.* Vienna: Urban und Schwarzenberg, 1878.

Dermoor, Jean, Jean Massart, and Emile Vandervelde. *L'évolution régressive en biologie et en sociologie.* Paris: Alcan, 1897.

Der Rekrut: Andenken an Musterung und Aushebung. Rheinberg: Sattler & Koss, 1912.

Desrosières, Alain. *Politics of Large Numbers: The History of Statistic Reasoning.* Cambridge, MA: Harvard University Press, 2002.

Dienel, Christiane. *Kinderzahl und Staatsräson: Empfängnisverhütung und Bevölker- ungspolitik in Deutschland und Frankreich bis 1918.* Münster: Westfälisches Dampf- boot, 1995.

Dienstanweisung zur Beurteilung der Militärdienstfähigkeit und zur Ausstellung von militärärztlichen Zeugnissen. Berlin: Mittler, 1909.

Dix, Arthur. "Ueber Volksvermehrung und Wehrkraft in Deutschland." *Preußische Jahrbücher* 91 (January 1898): 51–68.

Dragomir, Eneia. "Programmierte Instruktion—gesteuertes Verhalten? Die Ausein- andersetzung um die Ausbildung der Schweizer Armee und die Anthropologie des Soldaten nach 1945." In *Pulverdampf und Kreidestaub: Beiträge zum Verhältnis zwischen Militär und Schule im 19. und 20. Jahrhundert,* edited by Lukas Boser, Patrick Bühler, Michèle Hofmann, and Philippe Müller, 365–387. Bern: Bibliothek am Guisanplatz, 2016.

Du Cazal, Léon Joseph. *Petit guide adminsitratif du Médecin militaire.* Paris: Berger Levrault, 1882.

Du Cazal, Léon Joseph, and Louis Catrin. *Médecine légale militaire.* Paris: Gauthier- Villars et fils, 1892.

Duckworth, W. H. "Ridolfo Livi (1856–1920) [Obituary]." *Man* 20 (1920): 139–143.

Dumas, Alphonse. *Le conseil de révision: Ce qu'il est, ce qu'il devrait être.* Montpellier: C. Boehm, 1891.

Dumas, Alphonse. *Les étudiants en médecine: La loi de "deux ans."* Montpellier: Delord- Boehm et Martial, 1904.

Duponchel, Emile. *Du diagnostic de la faiblesse de constitution au point de vue du recrutement militaire.* Paris: O. Doin, 1887.

Duponchel, Emile. *Traité de médecine légale militaire.* Paris: O. Doin, 1890.

Duvergier, J.-B., ed. *Collection complète des lois, décrets, ordonnances et règlements, Nou- velle série,* vol. 13. Paris: A. Guyot et Scribe, 1913.

Eckart, Wolfgang U. *Medizin und Kolonialimperialismus: Deutschland 1884–1945.* Paderborn: Schöningh, 1997.

Ein Vermächtnis Moltke's: Stärkung der sinkenden Wehrkraft. Berlin: Eisenschmidt, 1892.

Eisenberg, Christiane. *"English Sports" und Deutsche Bürger.* Paderborn: Schöningh, 1999.

Eitner. *Militärärztliche Atteste und Gutachten. Zusammenstellung der für Militärärzte anwendbaren gesetzlichen Bestimmungen.* Berlin, 1873.

Eley, Geoff. "Anti-Semitism, Agrarian Mobilization, and the Conservative Party: Radicalism and Containment in the Founding of the Agrarian League, 1890–93." In *Between Reform, Reaction, and Resistance: Studies in the History of German Conservatism from 1789 to 1945,* edited by Larry Eugene Jones and James N. Retallack, 187–228. Providence: Berg, 1993.

Elliott, Ezekiel B. *On the Military Statistics of the United States of America.* Berlin: Congrès international de statistique, 1863.

Engel, Ernst, ed. *Compte-rendu général des travaux du "Congrès international de statistique" dans ses sénaces tenues à Bruxelles 1853, Paris 1855, Vienne 1857, et Londres 1860.* Berlin: Imprimerie Royale, 1863.

Engel, Ernst, ed. *Der Internationale Statistische Congreß in Berlin: Ein Bericht an die Vorbereitungs-Commission der V. Sitzungsperiode des Congreßes über die Gegenstände der Tagesordnung derselben.* Berlin: R. Decker, 1863.

Enklaar. *La constitution des conscrits dans les différentes classes sociales.* Utrecht, 1912.

Etemad, Bouda. "Pour Une Approche Démographique de L'expansion Coloniale de l'Europe." *Annales de Démographie Historique* 1, no. 113 (January 2007): 13–32.

Etzemüller, Thomas. *Auf der Suche nach der nordischen Rasse: Die deutsche Rassenanthropologie in der modernen Welt.* Bielefeld: Transcript, 2015.

Evans, Andrew D. *Anthropology at War: World War I and the Science of Race in Germany.* Chicago: The University of Chicago Press, 2010.

Ewald, François. *Der Vorsorgestaat.* Frankfurt: Suhrkamp, 1993.

Fabian, Johannes. *Out of Our Minds: Reason and Madness in the Exploration of Central Africa.* Berkeley: University of California Press, 2000.

Faucher, Léon. *Etudes sur l'Angleterre.* Paris: Guillaumin, 1845 [and subsequent years].

Felsch, Philipp. *Laborlandschaften: Physiologische Alpenreisen im 19. Jahrhundert.* Göttingen: Wallstein, 2007.

Ferdinand, Ursula. *Das Malthusische Erbe: Entwicklungsstränge der Bevölkerungstheorie im 19. Jahrhundert und ihr Einfluß auf die radikale Frauenbewegung in Deutschland.* Münster: LIT, 1999.

Ferdinand, Ursula. "Die Debatte 'Agrar- versus Industriestaat' und die Bevölkerungsfrage." In *Das Konstrukt "Bevölkerung" vor, im und nach dem Dritten Reich",* edited by Rainer Mackensen and Jürgen Reulecke, 111–149. Wiesbaden: VS Verlag für Sozialwissenschaften, 2005.

Ferdinand, Ursula. "Geburtenrückgangstheorien und 'Geburtenrückgangs-Gespenster' 1900–1930." In *Herausforderung Bevölkerung: Zu Entwicklungen des modernen Denkens über die Bevölkerung vor, im und nach dem "Dritten Reich",* edited by Josef Ehmer, Ursula Ferdinand, and Jürgen Reulecke, 77–98. Wiesbaden: VS Verlag für Sozialwissenschaften, 2007.

Fischer, Alfons. *Militärtauglichkeit und Industriestaat.* Leipzig: Dietrich, 1912.

Fisher, Kate, and Sarah Toulalan, eds. *The Routledge History of Sex and the Body: 1500 to the Present.* London: Routledge, 2013.

Förster, Stig. "Militär und staatsbürgerliche Partizipation: Die allgemeine Wehrpflicht im Deutschen Kaiserreich 1871–1914." In *Die Wehrpflicht Entstehung, Erscheinungsformen und politisch-militärische Wirkung,* edited by Roland G. Foerster, 55–70. Munich: R. Oldenbourg, 1994.

Fox, Lane. "Note on the Chest Measurement of Recruits." *Journal of the Anthropological Institute of Great Britain and Ireland* 5 (1876): 101–106.

Francis, Charles Richard. "On Opium, Narcotics and Alcohol in the Tropics." In *VIIIe Congrès international d'Hygiène et de démographie, tenu à Budapest du 1er au 9 septembre 1894: Comptes-rendus et mémoires,* vol. 2, 722–729. Budapest, 1896.

Frassetto, Fabio. "A Uniform Blank of Measurements to be Used in Recruiting. A Plea for the Standardization of Anthropological Methods." *American Anthropologist, n.s.,* 21, no. 2 (1919): 175–181.

Fredj, Claire. "Médecins en campagne, médecine des lointains: Le service de santé des armées en campagne dans les expéditions lointaines du Second Empire (Crimée, Chine-Cochinchine, Mexique)." PhD thesis, École des Hautes Études en Sciences Sociales, 2006.

French, David. *Military Identities: The Regimental System, the British Army, and the British People, c.1870–2000.* Oxford: Oxford University Press, 2005.

Freund, Wolfgang. *Volk, Reich und Westgrenze: Deutschtumswissenschaften und Politik in der Pfalz, im Saarland und im annektierten Lothringen 1925–1945.* Saarbrücken: Saarländische Druckerei und Verlag, 2006.

Frevert, Ute. "Das Jakobinische Modell: Allgemeine Wehrpflicht und Nationsbildung in Preußen-Deutschland." In *Militär und Gesellschaft im 19. und 20. Jahrhundert*, edited by Ute Frevert, 17–46. Stuttgart: Klett-Cotta, 1997.

Frevert, Ute. *A Nation in Barracks: Modern Germany, Military Conscription and Civil Society*. Oxford: Berg Publishers, 2004.

Frocard, Paul Marie. *Aptitude militaire des contingents français*. Paris: F. Fournier, 1911.

Froehlich, Louis. *Des procédés modernes pour reconnaitre la simulation de la cécité ou de la faiblesse visuelle*. Geneva: 1891.

Fröhlich, H. *Vortäuschung von Krankheiten*. Leipzig, 1895.

Fuhrer, Hans Rudolf. "Das Schweizer System: Friedenssicherung und Selbstverteidigung im 19. und 20. Jahrhundert." In *Die Wehrpflicht: Entstehung, Erscheinungsformen und politisch-militärische Wirkung*, edited by Roland G. Foerster, 193–206. Munich: Oldenbourg, 1994.

Fuhrer, Hans Rudolf. "Wehrpflicht in der Schweiz—ein historischer Überblick." In *Wehrpflicht und Miliz—Ende einer Epoche? Der europäische Streitkräftewandel und die Schweizer Miliz*, edited by Karl W. Haltiner and Andreas Kühner, 67–78. Baden-Baden: Nomos, 1999.

Funck, Marcus. "Militär, Krieg und Gesellschaft: Soldaten und militärische Eliten in der Sozialgeschichte." In *Was ist Militärgeschichte?*, edited by Thomas Kühne and Benjamin Ziemann, 157–174. Paderborn: Schöningh, 2000.

Fürst, Carl, and Gustav Retzius. *Anthropometria suecica: Beiträge zur Anthropologie der Schweden*. Stockholm: Aftonbladets Druckerei, 1902.

Geggus, David P. *Slavery, War, and Revolution: The British Occupation of Saint Domingue 1793–1798*. Oxford: Clarendon Press, 1982.

Geggus, David P. "Yellow Fever in the 1790s: The British Army in Occupied Saint Domingue." *Medical History* 23 (1979): 38–58.

Gehring, Petra. "Biologische Politik um 1900: Reform, Therapie, Experiment?" In *Kulturgeschichte des Menschenversuchs im 20. Jahrhundert*, edited by Birgit Griesecke, 48–77. Frankfurt: Suhrkamp, 2009.

Germann, Pascal. *Laboratorien der Vererbung: Rassenforschung und Humangenetik in der Schweiz, 1900–1970*. Göttingen: Wallstein, 2016.

Geulen, Christian. "Blonde bevorzugt: Virchow und Boas: Eine Fallstudie zur Verschränkung von 'Rasse' und 'Kultur' im ideologischen Feld der Ethnizität 1900." *Archiv für Sozialgeschichte* 40 (2000): 147–170.

Geulen, Christian. "The Common Grounds of Conflict: Racial Visions of World Order." In *Competing Visions of World Order: Global Order and Movements,*

1880s–1930s, edited by Sebastian Conrad and Dominik Sachsenmaier, 69–96. New York: Palgrave, 2007.

Geyer, Martin H., and Johannes Paulmann. "Einleitung." In *The Mechanics of Internationalism: Culture, Society, and Politics from the 1840s to the First World War*, edited by Martin H. Geyer and Johannes Paulmann, 1–26. Oxford: Oxford University Press, 2001.

Gibson, Mary. *Born to Crime: Cesare Lombroso and the Origins of Biological Criminology*. London: Praeger, 2002.

Glenn, Penny H. "Wissenschaft in einer polyzentrischen Nation: Der Fall der deutschen Ethnologie." In *Wissenschaft und Nation in der europäischen Geschichte*, edited by Ralph Jessen and Jakob Vogel, 80–96. Frankfurt: Campus, 2002.

Goldscheid, Rudolf. *Entwicklungswerttheorie, Entwicklungsökonomie, Menschenökonomie: Eine Programmschrift*. Leipzig: Klinkhartdt, 1908.

Goldstein, Josef. *Bevölkerungsprobleme und Berufsgliederung in Frankreich*. Berlin: J. Guttentag, 1900.

Goldstein, Josef. "Zur 'agrarischen' Beweisführung." *Schweizerische Blätter für Wirtschafts— und Socialpolitik*, no. 1 (1900): 372–375.

Goldstein, Josef. "Zur 'agrarischen' Beweisführung." *Schweizerische Blätter für Wirtschafts— und Socialpolitik*, no. 4 (1903): 382–384.

Goltermann, Svenja. *Körper der Nation: Habitusformierung und die Politik des Turnens 1860–1890*. Göttingen: Vandenhoeck & Ruprecht, 1998.

Goschler, Constantin. *Rudolf Virchow: Mediziner, Anthropologe, Politiker*. Cologne: Böhlau, 2002.

Gordon, Rae Beth. *Dances with Darwin, 1875–1910: Vernacular Modernity in France*. Surrey: Ashgate, 2009.

Gould, Benjamin A. *Investigations in the Military and Anthropological Statistics of American Soldiers*. New York: Riverside Press, 1869.

Granjux, Alphonse, and Simon. "De la statistique du recrutement." In *Bericht über den XIV: Internationalen Kongress für Hygiene und Demographie, Berlin 23.-29.9.1907*, vol. 3/2, 1203–1207. Berlin: A. Hirschwald, 1908.

Gros, H. "Les enseignements d'une statistiques." *Archives de médecine navale* 78 (August 1902): 81–113, and 88 (September 1908): 161–195.

Grosse, Pascal. *Kolonialismus, Eugenik und bürgerliche Gesellschaft in Deutschland 1850–1918*. Frankfurt: Campus, 2000.

Gruber, Max von. *Ursachen und Bekämpfung des Geburtenrückgangs im Deutschen Reich: Bericht erstattet an die 38. Versammlung des Deutschen Vereins für öffentliche Gesundheitspflege am 19 September 1913 in Aachen.* Munich: J. F. Lehmann, 1914.

Gruber, Max von, and Ernst Rudin, eds. *Fortpflanzung, Vererbung, Rassenhygiene: Katalog der Gruppe Rassenhygiene der Internationalen Hygiene-Ausstellung 1911 in Dresden.* Munich: Lehmann, 1911.

Guggenbühl, Johann Jakob."Hülfsruf aus den Alpen, zur Bekämpfung des schrecklichen Cretinismus." In *Maltens Bibliothek der neuesten Weltkunde*, vol. 1. Aarau: Sauerländer, 1840.

Guida, S. "Il foglio di sanità nel libretto personale del soldato e la matricola sanitaria." *Giornale di Medicina Militare* 27 (1879).

Hacking, Ian. "Prussian Numbers 1860–1882." In *The Probabilistic Revolution*, vol. 1, edited by Lorraine J. Daston et al., 377–394. Cambridge, MA: MIT Press, 1987.

Hacking, Ian. *The Social Construction of What?* Cambridge, MA: Harvard University Press, 1999.

Hacking, Ian. *The Taming of Chance.* Cambridge: Cambridge University Press, 1990.

Hämmerle, Christa. "Ein gescheitertes Experiment? Die allgemeine Wehrpflicht in der multiethnischen Armee der Habsburgermonarchie." *Journal of Modern European History* 5 (2007): 222–243.

Hansen, Georg. *Die drei Bevölkerungsstufen: Ein Versuch, die Ursachen für das Blühen und das Altern der Bevölkerungen nachzuweisen.* Munich: Lindauer, 1889.

Happel, Jörn. *Nomadische Lebenswelten und zarische Politik: Der Aufstand in Zentralasien 1916.* Stuttgart: Franz Steiner Verlag, 2010.

Hargenvilliers, Antoine-Audet. *Recherches et considérations sur la formation et le recrutement de l'Armée en France.* Paris: Didot, 1817.

Harkner, Heinrich. "Die Entartungsfrage in England." *Schmollers Jahrbuch* 31, no. 2 (1907): 357–378.

Hartmann, Heinrich. "Die Produktion der Wehrbevölkerung: Musterungskommissionen als Begegnungsort von Demographie und medizinischen Expertenwissen, 1890–1914." In *Jenseits von Humboldt: Wissenschaft im Staat 1850–1990*, edited by Axel C. Hüntelmann and Michael C. Schneider, 149–164. Frankfurt: Peter Lang, 2010.

Hartmann, Heinrich. "Normieren und Errechnen: Zur Korrelation von Bevölkerungsprognosen und Musterung vor 1914." In *Zukunftswissen: Prognosen in Wirtschaft, Politik und Gesellschaft seit 1900*, edited by Heinrich Hartmann and Jakob Vogel, 137–152. Frankfurt: Campus, 2010.

Hartmann, Heinrich. "Soldaten in den Tropen, Soldaten aus den Tropen: Neudefinitionen der Wehrkraft im kolonialen Kontext zwischen 1884 und 1914." In *Koloniale Politik und Praktiken Deutschlands und Frankreichs 1880–1962/Politiques et pratiques coloniales dans les empires allemands et français, 1880–1962*, edited by Alain Chatriot and Dieter Gosewinkel, 223–246. Stuttgart: Steiner, 2010.

Hartmann, Heinrich. "Une affaire de marge: L'anthropométrie au conseil de révision, France-Allemagne 1880–1900." *Mouvement Social* 256 (2016): 81–99.

Hasse, Hermann. *Die Statistik als Hilfsmittel der Sozialwissenschaften: Mit besonderer Berücksichtigung des Schaubildes*. Leipzig: Dietrich, 1911.

Hau, Michael. *The Cult of Health and Beauty in Germany: A Social History 1890–1930*. Chicago: University of Chicago Press, 2003.

Hau, Michael. *Performance Anxiety: Sport and Work in Germany from the Empire to Nazism*. Toronto: University of Toronto Press, 2017.

Hecht, Jacqueline. "L'idée de dénombrement jusqu'à la révolution." In *Pour une histoire de la statistique*, vol. 1, edited by Institut national de la statistique et des études économiques, 21–81. Paris: INSEE, 1977.

Heer, Oswald. *Beitrag zur Kenntnis der Rekrutierungsverhältnisse der landwirtschaftlichen und industriellen Bevölkerung der Schweiz*. Schaffhausen, 1897.

Heerordnung. Militärische Ergänzungsbestimmungen zur Deutschen Wehrordnung vom 22.11.188: Neuabdruck unter Berücksichtigung der bis April 1904 eingetretenen Änderungen. Berlin: Mittler, 1904.

Hennock, E. Peter. *The Origin of the Welfare State in England and Germany, 1850–1914: Social Policies Compared*. Cambridge: Cambridge University Press, 2007.

Herbert, Ulrich. "Traditionen des Rassismus." In *Arbeit, Volkstum, Weltanschauung: Über Fremde und Deutsche im 20. Jahrhundert*, edited by Ulrich Herbert, 7–29. Frankfurt: Fischer, 1995.

Herman, Arthur. *The Idea of Decline in Western History*. New York: Free Press, 1997.

Herren, Madeleine. "'Die Erweiterung des Wissens beruht vorzugsweise auf dem Kontakt mit der Aussenwelt': Wissenschaftliche Netzwerke aus Historischer Perspektive." *Zeitschrift für Geschichtswissenschaft* 49 (2001): 197–207.

Hertel. *Über die Methoden der Untersuchung der Brustorgane beim Ersatzgeschäft*. Lecture to the Berlin Society of Medical Military Personnel, December 21, 1872.

Hervé, Georges. "La taille en Alsace." *Revue mensuelle de l'Ecole d'anthropologie de Paris* 11 (1901): 161–177.

Heuser, Johann Jakob. *Die Rekrutenprüfungen: Referat gehalten in der 56. ordentlichen Versammlung der Schulsynode am 23.9.1889 in Zürich*. Zurich: J. Schabelitz, 1889.

Hey, F. *Der Tropenarzt: Ausführlicher Ratgeber für Europäer in den Tropen sowie für Besitzer von Plantagen und Handelshäusern, Kolonial-Behörden und Missions-Verwaltungen.* Wismar: Hinstorff, 1912.

Heyberger, Laurent. *L'histoire anthropométrique.* Bern: Peter Lang, 2011.

Heyberger, Laurent. *La révolution des corps: Décroissance et croissance staturale des habitants des villes et des campagnes en France, 1780–1940.* Strasbourg: Presses Universitaires de Strasbourg, 2005.

Hippler, Thomas. *Citizens, Soldiers and National Armies: Military Service in France and Germany, 1789–1830.* London: Routledge, 2008.

Histoire de la médecine aux Armées. Vol. 2, *De la Révolution française au conflit mondial de 1914.* Edited by Comité d'Histoire du Service de Santé. Paris: C. Lavauzelle, 1984.

Hoffmann, Karl. "Wieviel Rekruten stellt die Landwirtschaft." *Die Grenzboten: Zeitschrift für Politik, Literatur und Kunst* 57 (January 27, 1898): 201–210.

Horn, David G. *The Criminal Body: Lombroso and the Anatomy of Deviance.* London: Routledge, 2003.

Horn, David G. *Social Bodies: Science, Reproduction and Italian Modernity.* Princeton, NJ: Princeton University Press, 2001.

Hueppe, Ferdinand. "Ueber die Körperübungen in Schule und Volk und ihren Werth für die militaerischen Uebungen." In *Festschrift zur 100 jährigen Stiftungsfeier des medizinisch-chirurgischen Friedrich-Wilhelms-Instituts, 2. Dezember 1895.* Berlin: Mittler, 1895.

Hull, Isabel V. *Absolute Destruction: Military Culture and the Practices of War in Imperial Germany.* Ithaca, NY: Cornell University Press, 2004.

Hund, Sanford B. "The Negro as a Soldier." *Anthropological Review* 7, no. 24 (1869): 40–54.

Hüntelmann, Axel C. *Hygiene im Namen des Staates: Das Reichsgesundheitsamt, 1876–1933.* Göttingen: Wallstein Verlag, 2008.

Hurley, Kelly. *The Gothic Body: Sexuality, Materialism, and Degeneration at the Fin de Siècle.* Cambridge: Cambridge University Press, 1996.

Hürlimann, Josef. *Ueber die Ergebnisse der Sanitarischen Rekruten-Musterung in der Schweiz während der Jahre 1875 bis 1879: Eine populäre militärärztliche Skizze (erstes Referat an die Festversammlung der schweizerischen gemeinnützigen Gesellschaft, 21.09.1880 in Zug).* Zurich: J. Herzog, 1880.

Ingenlath, Markus. *Mentale Aufrüstung: Militarisierungstendenzen in Frankreich und Deutschland vor dem Ersten Weltkrieg.* Frankfurt: Campus, 1998.

Instruction relative aux opérations du conseil de revision pour la formation des classes. Paris: R. Chapelot, 1890 [and subsequent years].

Instructionen für die, zu den Rekruten-Aushebungen commandirten Militäraerzte. Berlin, n.d. [1858].

Ittmann, Karl. "'Where Nature Dominates Man': Demographic Ideas and Policy in British Colonial Africa, 1890–1970." In *The Demographics of Empire: The Colonial Order and the Creation of Knowledge,* edited by Karl Ittmann, Dennis D. Cordell, and Gregory H. Maddox, 59–88. Athens: Ohio University Press, 2010.

Jäger, Jens. "Bilder aus Afrika vor 1918: Zur visuellen Konstruktion Afrikas im europäischen Kolonialismus." In *Visual History: Ein Studienbuch,* edited by Gerhard Paul, 134–148. Göttingen: Vandenhoeck & Ruprecht, 2006.

Jaun, Rudolf. *Preussen vor Augen: Das schweizerische Offizierskorps im militärischen und gesellschaftlichen Wandel des Fin de siècle.* Zurich: Chronos, 1999.

Jeal, Tim. *Baden-Powell: Founder of the Boy Scouts.* New Haven, CT: Yale University Press, 2001.

Jeismann, Michael. *Das Vaterland der Feinde: Studien zum nationalen Feindbegriff und Selbstverständnis in Deutschland und Frankreich, 1792–1918.* Stuttgart: Klett-Cotta, 1992.

Jennings, Eric T.. *Curing the Colonizers: Hydrotherapy, Climatology, and French Colonial Spas.* Durham, NC: Duke University Press, 2006.

Jessen, Ralph, and Jakob Vogel. "Die Naturwissenschaften und die Nation: Perspektiven einer Wechselbeziehung in der europäischen Geschichte." In *Wissenschaft und Nation in der Europäischen Geschichte,* edited by Ralph Jessen and Jakob Vogel, 7–37. Frankfurt: Campus, 2002.

Joppich, Robin. "Otto von Schjerning (4.10.1853–28.06.1921): Wissenschaftler, Generalstabsarzt der preußischen Armee und Chef des deutschen Feldsanitätswesens im Ersten Weltkrieg." PhD thesis, Heidelberg University, 1997.

Kang, Zheng. "La Société de Statistique de Paris au XIXe siècle: Un lieu de savoir social." *Les Cahiers du Centre de Recherches Historiques* 9 (April 15, 1992). doi:10.4000/ccrh.2808.

Kanz, Kai Thorsten. *Nationalismus und internationale Zusammenarbeit in den Naturwissenschaften: Die deutsch-französischen Wissenschaftsbeziehungen zwischen Revolution und Restauration, 1789–1832.* Stuttgart: Steiner, 1997.

Kaschuba, Wolfgang. "Die Nation als Körper: Zur symbolischen Konstruktion 'nationaler' Alltagswelt." In *Nation und Emotion: Deutschland und Frankreich im Vergleich 19. und 20. Jahrhundert,* edited by Etienne François, Hannes Siegrist, and Jakob Vogel, 291–299. Göttingen: Vandenhoeck & Ruprecht, 1995.

Kaup, Ignaz. *Ernährung und Lebenskraft der ländlichen Bevölkerung.* Berlin: Heymann, 1910.

Keller, Christoph. *Der Schädelvermesser: Otto Schlaginhaufen, Anthropologe und Rassenhygieniker: Eine biographische Reportage.* Zurich: Limmat, 1995.

Kienitz, Sabine. *Beschädigte Helden: Kriegsinvalidität und Körperbilder, 1914–1923.* Paderborn: Schöningh, 2008.

Kiesewetter, Hubert. *Industrielle Revolution in Deutschland: 1815–1914.* Frankfurt: Suhrkamp, 1989.

Koller, Christian. "Farbige Truppen." In *Enzyklopädie Erster Weltkrieg,* edited by Gerhard Hirschfeld, Gerd Krumeich, and Irina Renz, 471–472. Paderborn: Schöningh, 2003.

Koller, Christian. "Feind-Bilder, Rassen- und Geschlechterstereotype in der Kolonialtruppendiskussion Deutschlands und Frankreichs, 1914–1923." In *Heimat-Front: Militär und Geschlechterverhältnisse im Zeitalter der Weltkriege,* edited by Karen Hagemann and Stefanie Schüler-Springorum, 150–167. New York: Campus Verlag, 2002.

Koller, Christian. *"Von Wilden aller Rassen niedergemetzelt": Die Diskussion um die Verwendung von Kolonialtruppen in Europa zwischen Rassismus, Kolonial- und Militärpolitik (1914–1930).* Stuttgart: Steiner, 2001.

Kollmann, Julius. *Die statistischen Erhebungen über die Farbe der Auge, Haare und der Haut in den Schulen der Schweiz.* Basel: Georg, 1881.

Komlos, John. "Stature and Nutrition in the Habsburg Monarchy: The Standard of Living and Economic Development." *American Historical Review* 90 (1985): 1149–1161.

Kratz, F. *Recrutirung und Invalidisierung: Eine militärärztliche Studie.* Erlangen, 1872.

Krüger, Dieter. *Nationalökonomen im wilhelminischen Deutschland.* Göttingen: Vandenhoeck & Ruprecht, 1983.

Krumeich, Gerd. "Zur Entwicklung der 'nation armée' in Frankreich bis zum Ersten Weltkrieg." In *Die Wehrpflicht Entstehung, Erscheinungsformen und politisch-militärische Wirkung,* edited by Roland G. Foerster, 133–145. Munich: R. Oldenbourg, 1994.

Kuczynski, Robert René. *Der Zug nach der Stadt, Statistische Studien über die Bevölkerungsbewegungen im Deutschen Reich.* Stuttgart: Cotta, 1897.

Kuczynski, Robert René. *Ist die Landwirtschaft die wichtigste Grundlage der deutschen Wehrkraft?* Berlin: Simion, 1905.

Kuczynski, Robert René. "Ueber Voksvermehrungen und Wehrkraft in Deutschland: Eine Entgegnung." *Preußische Jahrbücher* 92 (1898): 138–153.

Kühl, Stefan. *Die Internationale der Rassisten: Aufstieg und Niedergang der internationalen Bewegung für Eugenik und Rassenhygiene im 20. Jahrhundert.* Frankfurt: Campus, 1997.

Külz, Ludwig. *Zur Hygiene des Trinkens in den Tropen.* Flensburg: Verlag von Deutschlands Grossloge, 1905.

Kunow, O. *Musterung, Aushebung und Prüfungsgeschäft: Für Sanitätsoffiziere und die bei diesen Geschäften mitwirkenden Offiziere und Zivilbeamten.* Berlin: Mittler, 1907.

Kyllingstad, Jon Røyne. *Measuring the Masterrace: Physical Anthropology in Norway, 1890–1945.* Cambridge: Open Book Publishers, 2014.

Labbé, Morgane. "Die Grenzen der Deutschen Nation: Raum der Karte, Statistik, Erzählung." In *Die Grenze als Raum, Erfahrung und Konstruktion: Deutschland, Frankreich und Polen,* edited by Etienne François, Jörg Seifarth, and Bernhard Struck, 293–319. Frankfurt: Campus, 2007.

Labbé, Morgane. "Le Séminaire de statistiques du Bureau Prussien de statistique (1862–1900): Former des administrateurs à la statistique." *Journal Électronique d'Histoire Des Probabilités et de la Statistique* 2, no. 2 (2006). https://eudml.org/doc/117567.

Lachaud, Edouard. *Pour la race: Notre Soldat, sa caserne.* Paris: H. Charles-Lavauzelle, 1909.

Lagneau, Gustave. *Anthropologie de la France, recherches ethnologiques sur les populations du bassin de la Saône et des autres affluents du cours moyen du Rhône.* Paris: A. Hennuyer, 1874.

Lagneau, Gustave. *Considérations médicales et anthropologiques sur la réorganisation de l'armée en France: Mémoire lu à l'académie de médecine le 18 juillet 1871.* Paris: Masson, 1871.

Lagneau, Gustave. *De la distinction ethnique des Celtes et des Gaëls et de leurs migrations au sud des Alpes.* Paris: A. Hennuyer, 1876.

Lagneau, Gustave. *Ethnogénie des populations du nord de la France.* Paris: A. Hennuyer, 1874.

Lagneau, Gustave. *Ethnogénie des populations du nord-ouest de la France.* Paris: A. Hennuyer, 1876.

Lagneau, Gustave. *Ethnogénie des populations du sud-ouest de la France, particulièrement du bassin de la Garonne et de ses affluents.* Paris: A. Hennuyer, 1873.

Lagneau, Gustave. *Étude de statistique anthropologique sur la population parisienne.* Paris: J.-B. Baillière et fils, 1869.

Lamott, Franziska. *Die vermessene Frau: Hysterien um 1900.* Munich: Fink, 2001.

Lange, Britta. "Die Welt im Ton: In deutschen Sonderlagern für Kolonialsoldaten entstanden ab 1915 einzigartige Aufnahmen." *iz3w*, no. 307 (August 2008): 22–25.

La Patrie est en danger. Paris: Alliance nationale pour l'accroissement de la population française, 1913.

Larkin, Maurice. "'La République en Danger'? The Pretenders, the Army and Déroulède, 1898–1899." *English Historical Review* 100, no. 394 (1985): 85–105.

Lasalle, C. *Code-manuel des obligations: Manuel général du recrutement et des reserves.* Paris: Berger-Levrault, 1893.

Latour, Bruno, and Steve Woolgar. *Laboratory Life: The Social Construction of Scientific Facts.* Beverly Hills: Sage Publications, 1979.

Laur, Ernst. *Die Wehrkraft des Schweizer Volkes und der Bauernstand.* Zürich: Rascher, 1915.

Le Bon, Gustave. *Psychologie des Foules.* Paris: Alcan, 1895.

Leendertz, Ariane. *Ordnung schaffen: Deutsche Raumplanung im 20. Jahrhundert.* Göttingen: Wallstein, 2008.

Lengwiler, Martin. "Kalkulierte Solidarität: Grenzen sozialstaatlicher Prognosen (1900–1970)." In *Zukunftswissen: Prognosen in Wirtschaft, Politik und Gesellschaft seit 1900*, edited by Heinrich Hartmann and Jakob Vogel, 33–54. Frankfurt: Campus, 2010.

Lengwiler, Martin. *Zwischen Klinik und Kaserne: Die Geschichte der Militärpsychiatrie in Deutschland und der Schweiz 1870–1914.* Zurich: Chronos, 2000.

Leonhard, Jörn. *Bellizismus und Nation: Kriegsdeutung und Nationsbestimmung in Europa und den Vereinigten Staaten 1750–1914.* Munich: R. Oldenbourg, 2008.

Leonhard, Jörn, and Ulrike von Hirschhausen. *Empires und Nationalstaaten im 19. Jahrhundert.* 2nd ed. Göttingen: Vandenhoeck & Ruprecht, 2011.

Lerner, Paul Frederick. *Hysterical Men: War, Psychiatry, and the Politics of Trauma in Germany, 1890–1930.* Ithaca, NY: Cornell University Press, 2003.

Lerp, Dörte. *Imperiale Grenzräume: Bevölkerungspolitiken in Deutsch-Südwestafrika und den östlichen Provinzen Preußens 1884–1914.* Frankfurt: Campus, 2016.

Levsen, Sonja. *Elite, Männlichkeit und Krieg: Tübinger und Cambridger Studenten 1900–1929.* Göttingen: Vandenhoeck & Ruprecht, 2006.

Levsen, Sonja. "Männliche Bierbäuche oder männliche Muskeln? Studenten, Männlichkeit und Gesundheit zwischen 1900 und 1930." In *Männlichkeit und Gesundheit im historischen Wandel, ca. 1800–ca. 2000*, edited by Martin Dinges, 175–190. Stuttgart: Steiner, 2007.

Lichtsinn, Hilkea. *Otto Ammon und die Sozialanthropologie.* Frankfurt: P. Lang, 1987.

Lindenlaub, Dieter. *Richtungskämpfe im Verein für Sozialpolitik: Wissenschaft und Sozialpolitik im Kaiserreich vornehmlich vom Beginn des "Neuen Kurses" bis zum Ausbruch des 1. Weltkrieges (1890–1914).* Wiesbaden: F. Steiner, 1967.

Lipp, Anne. "Diskurs und Praxis. Militärgeschichte als Kulturgeschichte." In *Was ist Militärgeschichte?*, edited by Thomas Kühne and Benjamin Ziemann, 211–228. Paderborn: Schöningh, 2000.

Lipphardt, Veronika, and Kiran Klaus Patel. "Auf der Suche nach dem Europäer: wissenschaftliche Konstruktionen des Homo Europaeus." *Themenportal Europäische Geschichte*, 2007. https://www.europa.clio-online.de/2007/Article=204.

Lissauer. "Bericht der vorbereitenden Commission zur Herstellung von Typenkarten." *Correspondenz-Blatt der Deutschen anthropologischen Gesellschaft*, no. 11 (1903): 123–125.

Livi, Ridolfo. "Essai d'anthropométrie militaire." *Bulletin de l'Institut International de Statistique* 7 (1894): 273–285.

Livi, Ridolfo. "Statistique anthropométrique militaire." *Bulletin de l'institut international de statistique* 15 (1906): 46–49.

Livi, Ridolfo. "Taille et périmètre thoracique des militaires en rapport avec les professions." In *Comptes rendus du XII congrès international de médecine. Moskau 7.–14. août 1897, Séction X: Médecine militaire*, 92–95. Moscow, 1899.

Lorenz, Hermann, and Emil von Schenkendorff. *Wehrkraft durch Erziehung (Schriften des Zentralausschusses zur Förderung der Volks- und Jugendspiele in Deutschland).* Leipzig: Voigtländer, 1904.

Lorimer, Douglas. *Science, Race Relations and Resistance: Britain, 1870–1914.* Manchester: Manchester University Press, 2013.

Lunn, Joe. *L'odysée des combattants sénégalais, 1914–1918.* Paris: L'Harmattan, 2014.

Lustenberger, Werner. *Pädagogische Rekrutenprüfungen: Ein Beitrag zur Schweizer Schulgeschichte.* Chur: Rüegger, 1996.

Maß, Sandra. *Weiße Helden, schwarze Krieger: Zur Geschichte kolonialer Männlichkeit in Deutschland 1918–1964.* Cologne: Böhlau, 2006.

Maß, Sandra. "Welcome to the Jungle: Imperial Men, 'Inner Africa,' and Mental Disorder, 1870–1970." In *Helpless Imperialists: Imperial Failure, Fear and Radicalization*, edited by Maurus Reinkowski and Gregor Thum, 91–115. Göttingen: Vandenhoeck and Ruprecht, 2012.

Mackeprang. "Die Körperhöhe der Stadtbevölkerung." Correspondenz-Blatt der deutschen Gesellschaft für Anthropologie, *Ethnologie und Urgeschichte* 6 (June 1910): 41–42.

Maddox, Gregory H. "Disease and Environment in Africa: Imputed Dynamics and Unresolved Issues." In *The Demographics of Empire: The Colonial Order and the Creation of Knowledge*, edited by Karl Ittmann, Dennis D. Cordell, and Gregory H. Maddox, 198–216. Athens: Ohio University Press, 2010.

Maitrote de La Motte-Capron, Albert. *Nos fronitères de l'est et du nord: Le service de deux ans et sa répercussion sur leur défense*. Paris: H. Charles-Lavauzelle, 1913.

Manias, Chris. "The *Race prusienne* Controversy: Scientific Internationalism and the Nation." *Isis* 100 (2009): 733–757.

Manuel du recrutement des armées de terre et de mer contenant toute la legislation. Paris: L. Baudoin, 1890.

Manuel du recrutement ou recueil des ordonnances, instructions approuvées par le Roi, circulaires et décisions ministérielles, auxquelles l'exécution de la loi du 10 mars 1818 a donné lieu. Edited by the Ministry of War of France. Paris: Imprimerie nationale, 1820.

Marcinkowski, Adam, and Andrzej Rzepniewski. "Die Wehrdienst- und Wehrpflichtformen in Polen zwischen der Verfassung von 1791 und der Gegenwart." In *Die Wehrpflicht: Entstehung, Erscheinungsformen und politisch-militärische Wirkung*, edited by Roland G. Foerster, 147–170. Munich: R. Oldenbourg, 1994.

Mauricheau-Beaupré. *Ärztlich-Militärische Untersuchungen: Tabellarische Übersicht der wirklichen verheimlichten und verstellten Krankheiten und Gebrechen*. Weimar: 1882.

Mayershofer, Ingrid. *Bevölkerung und Militär in Bamberg 1860–1923: Eine bayerische Stadt und der preussisch-deutsche Militarismus*. Paderborn: Schöningh, 2010.

Mayr, Georg. "Statistik und Gesellschaftslehre." In *VIIIe congrès international d'hygiène et de démographie tenu à Budapest du 1er au 9 septembre, Comptes rendu et mémoires*, 290–301. Budapest, 1895.

Meienberg, Niklaus. *Die Welt als Wille und Wahn: Elemente zur Naturgeschichte eines Clans*. Zurich: Limmat Verlag, 1987.

Meißner, Hugo. "Rekrutierungsstatistik." *Archiv für Rassen- und Gesellschaftsbiologie* 6 (1909): 59–72.

Menne, Jonas. *"Lombroso redivivus?" Biowissenschaften, Kriminologie und Kriminalpolitik von 1876 bis in die Gegenwart*. Tübingen: Mohr, 2017.

Messimy, Adolphe. *Le statut des indigènes algériens*. Paris: H. Charles-Lavauzelle, 1913.

Meyenne, Armand Joseph. *Eléments de statistiques médicales militaires*. Brussels: 1859.

Micale, Mark S. "On the 'Disappearance' of Hysteria: A Study in the Clinical Deconstruction of a Diagnosis." *Isis* 84 (1993): 496–526.

Michel, Harald. *Der Bevölkerungsgedanke Zeitalter des Merkantilismus*. Berlin: Institut für Angewandte Demographie, 1994.

Michel, Marc. *Les Africains et la Grande Guerre: L'appel à l'Afrique (1914–1918)*. Paris: Karthala, 2003.

Michels, Robert. "Das Prolatariat in der Wissenschaft und die ökonomisch-anthropologische Synthese." Foreword to *Anthropologie der Nichtbesitzenden Klassen: Studien und Untersuchungen*, Alfredo Niceforo, 3–30. Leipzig: Maas & van Suchtelen, 1910.

Michels, Stefanie. *Schwarze deutsche Kolonialsoldaten: Mehrdeutige Repräsentationsräume und früher Kosmopolitismus in Afrika*. Bielefeld: Transcript, 2009.

Michl, Susanne. *Im Dienste des "Volkskörpers": Deutsche und französische Ärzte im Ersten Weltkrieg*. Göttingen: Vandenhoeck & Ruprecht, 2007.

Millot, Martine. "L'emergence de la notion d'aptitude dans la réglementation du travail après 1892." In *Les mains inutiles: Inaptitude au travail et emploi en Europe*, edited by Catherine Omnès and Anne-Sophie Bruno, 32–41. Paris: Belin, 2004.

Moch, Gaston. *L'armée d'une démocratie*. Paris: Editions de la Revue blanche, 1900.

Mombert, Paul. "Die Anschauungen des 17. und 18. Jahrhunderts über die Abnahme der Bevölkerung." *Jahrbücher für Nationalökonomie und Statistik* 135, no. 4 (1931): 481–503.

Morache, Georges. *Considérations sur le recrutement de l'armée et sur l'aptitude militaires dans la presse française*. Paris: J. Dumaine, 1873.

Moreira, Juliano, and Afriano Peixoto. "Les maladies mentales dans les pays tropicaux." In *XVe Congrès international de Médecine, Lisbonne 19–26 avril 1906, Section XVII Médecine coloniale et navale*, 175–192. Lisbon: 1906.

Morel, Bénédict Augustin. *Traité des dégénérances*. Paris: J.-B. Baillière et fils, 1857.

Mosso, Angelo. *Die Ermüdung*. Leipzig: Hirzel, 1892.

Mosso, Angelo. *Die körperliche Erziehung der Jugend*. Hamburg: Voss, 1894.

Mosso, Angelo. *L'Educazione Fisica della Gioventù*. Milan: Fratelli Treves, 1893.

Mosso, Angelo. *Una Ascensione d'inverno al Monte Rosa*. Milan: Fratelli Treves, 1885.

Müller, August. "Rekrutenprüfungen und Freiämter Schulwesen." In *Schlussbericht der Bezirksschule Muri 1907/1908*, edited by S. Schmid. Muri: A. Schibli-Keller, 1908.

Müller-Wille, Staffan, and Hans-Jörg Rheinberger. *A Cultural History of Heredity*. Chicago: Chicago University Press, 2012.

Naville, François. *Contribution à l'étude de l'aliénation mentale dans l'armée suisse et dans les armées étrangères: Etude clinique, statistique, et de prophylaxie*. Geneva: Librairie Kündig, 1910.

Neill, Deborah J. *Networks in Tropical Medicine: Internationalism, Colonialism, and the Rise of Medical Specialty*. Stanford, CA: Stanford University Press, 2012.

Nelson, Robert L. "The Archive for Inner Colonization, the German East, and World War." In *Germans, Poland, and Colonial Expansion to the East: 1850 through the Present*, edited by Robert L. Nelson, 65–94. New York: Palgrave Macmillan, 2009.

Niceforo, Alfredo. *Anthropologie der Nichtbesitzenden Klassen: Studien und Untersuchungen*. Leipzig: Maas & van Suchtelen, 1910.

Niceforo, Alfredo. *Antropologia delle classi povere*. Milan: Vallardi, 1908.

Niggli, Eduard. *Die Ergebnisse der Rekrutenprüfungen im Aargau pro 1893 und ihre Ursachen: Referat vorgetragen an der aargauischen Kantonallehrerkonferenz vom 18.September 1893*. Baden, 1893.

Nightingale, Florence. "Notes on Nursing." In *Florence Nightingale: The Nightingale School, Collected Works of Florence Nightingale*, vol. 12, edited by Lynn McDonald, 575–712. Waterloo, Ontario: Wilfrid Laurier University Press, 2009.

Nikolow, Sybilla. "Die Nation als statistisches Kollektiv: Bevölkerungskonstruktionen im Kaiserreich und in der Weimarer Republik." In *Wissenschaft und Nation in der europäischen Geschichte*, edited by Ralph Jessen and Jakob Vogel, 235–259. Frankfurt: Campus, 2002.

Nikolow, Sybilla, and Christina Wessely. "Öffentlichkeit als epistemologische und politische Ressource für die Genese umstrittener Wissenschaftskonzepte." In *Wissenschaft und Öffentlichkeit als Ressource füreinander: Studien zur Wissenschaftsgeschichte im 20. Jahrhundert*, edited by Sybilla Nikolow and Arne Schirrmacher, 273–285. Frankfurt: Campus, 2007.

Nivet, Vincent. *Etudes sur le goitre épidémique*. Paris: J.-B. Baillière et fils, 1873.

Nowosadtko, Jutta. *Krieg, Gewalt und Ordnung: Einführung in die Militärgeschichte: Historische Einführungen*. Tübingen: Edition Diskord, 2002.

Nye, Robert. "Degeneration, Neurasthenia and the Culture of Sport in Belle Epoque France." *Journal of Contemporary History* 17 (1982): 51–68.

Otto, Eduard. *Zur Geschichte der Theorie der allgemeinen Wehrpflicht in Deutschland*. Hamburg: J. F. Richter, 1900.

Overath, Petra. "Bevölkerungsforschung transnational: Eine Skizze zu Interaktionen zwischen Wissenschaft und Politik am Beispiel der International Union for the Scientific Study of Population." In *Die vergangene Zukunft Europas: Bevölkerungsforschung und -prognosen im 20. und 21. Jahrhundert*, edited by Petra Overath, 57–83. Cologne: Böhlau, 2011.

Overath, Petra. "Transfer als Verengung? Zur internationalen Diskussion über den Geburtenrückgang in Frankreich in Texten von Fernand Boverat, Roderich von Ungern-Sternberg sowie Joseph John Spengler in den späten 30er Jahren des 20. Jahrhunderts." In *Les figures de l'État en Allemagne et en France/Figurationen des Staates in Deutschland und Frankreich (1870–1945)*, edited by Alain Chatriot and Dieter Gosewinkel, 185–214. Munich: Oldenbourg Verlag, 2006.

Paligot, Reynaud Carole. *La république raciale: Paradigme racial et idéologie républicaine (1860–1930)*. Paris: Presses universitaires de France, 2009.

Pallmann, Reinhold. *Die Bewohnbarkeit der Tropen für Europäer: Eine kulturgeographische Studie aus den Quellen: Vortrag gehalten im Klub der Landwirthe zu Berlin am 21.12.1886.* Berlin: F. & P. Lehmann, 1887.

Paul, Harry W. *The Sorcerer's Apprentice: The French Scientist's Image of German Science, 1840–1919.* Gainesville: University of Florida Press, 1972.

Pesek, Michael. *Koloniale Herrschaft in Deutsch-Ostafrika: Expeditionen, Militär und Verwaltung seit 1880.* Frankfurt: Campus, 2005.

Pick, Daniel. *Faces of Degeneration: A European Disorder, c. 1848–1918.* Cambridge: Cambridge University Press, 1989.

Planert, Ute. *Antifeminismus im Kaiserreich: Diskurs, soziale Formation und politische Mentalität.* Göttingen: Vandenhoeck & Ruprecht, 1998.

Planert, Ute. "Der Dreifache Körper des Volkes: Sexualität, Biopolitik und die Wissenschaften vom Leben." *Geschichte und Gesellschaft* 26, no. 4 (2000): 539–576.

Plötz, Alfred. "Die Begriffe Rasse und Gesellschft und einige damit zusammenhängende Probleme." In *Verhandlungen des Ersten Deutschen Soziologentages, 19.-22.10.1910 in Frankfurt am Main*, 111–136. Tübingen: Mohr, 1911.

Poovey, Mary. *Making a Social Body: British Cultural Formation, 1830–1864.* Chicago: University of Chicago Press, 1995.

Porter, Theodore M. *Karl Pearson: The Scientific Life in a Statistical Age.* Princeton, NJ: Princeton University Press, 2004.

Porter, Theodore M. *The Rise of Statistical Thinking, 1820–1900.* Princeton, NJ: Princeton University Press, 1986.

Porter, Theodore M. *Trust in Numbers: The Pursuit of Objectivity in Science and Public Life.* Princeton, NJ: Princeton University Press, 1995.

Promitzer, Christian. "Vermessene Körper: 'Rassenkundliche' Grenzziehungen im südöstlichen Europa." In *Europa und die Grenzen im Kopf*, edited by Karl Kaser and Lojze Wieser, 365–394. Klagenfurt: Wieser, 2003.

Pröve, Ralf. *Militär, Staat und Gesellschaft im 19. Jahrhundert*. Munich: R. Oldenbourg, 2006.

Quatrefages, Armand. *La rasse prusienne*. Paris: Hachette, 1871.

Quetelet, Adolphe. *Anthropométrie ou mésures des différentes facultés de l'homme*. Brussels: C. Muquardt, 1870.

Quetelet, Adolphe. *Sur l'homme et le développement de ses facultés*. Paris: Bachelier, 1835.

Quinkert, Babette, Philipp Rauh, and Ulrike Winkler, eds. *Krieg und Psychiatrie 1914–1950*. Göttingen: Wallstein, 2010.

Rabinbach, Anson. *The Human Motor: Energy, Fatigue, and the Origins of Modernity*. New York: Basic Books, 1990.

Rabinow, Paul. *French Modern: Norms and Forms of the Social Environment*. Chicago: University of Chicago Press, 1995.

Ramamurthy, Anandi. "Spectacles and Illusions: Photography and Commodity Cultures." In *Photography: A Critical Introduction*, 3rd ed., edited by Liz Wells, 193–244. London: Routledge, 2004.

Rappaport, Helen. *No Place for Ladies: The Untold Story of Women in the Crimean War*. London: Aurum, 2007.

Rebel, Hermann. "Massensterben und die Frage nach der Biologie in der Geschichte: Eine Antwort an John Komlos." *Österreichische Zeitschrift für Geschichtswissenschaft* 5 (1994): 279–286.

Reed, Matt T. "From Aliéné to Dégénéré: Moral Agency and Psychiatric Imagination in Nineteenth-Century France." In *Confronting Modernity in Fin-de-Siècle France: Bodies, Minds and Gender*, edited by Christopher E. Forth and Elinor Accampo, 67–89. Hampshire: Palgrave Macmillan, 2010.

Rehe, Rolf. "Wilhelm August Roth (1833–1892)." *Sächsische Biografie*, edited by Institut für Sächsische Geschichte und Volkskunde e.V, 2007. http://saebi.isgv.de/biografie-druck/Wilhelm_August_Roth_(1833-1892).

Reidegeld, Eckart. *Staatliche Sozialpolitik in Deutschland*.Vol. 1, *Von den Ursprüngen bis zum Untergang des Kaiserreiches 1918*, 2nd ed. Wiesbaden: VS Verlag für Sozialwissenschaften, 2006.

Reinhard, Philipp. *Vaterlandskunde. Fragen gestellt an den Rekrutenprüfungen. Mit Bewilligung des eidg. Militärdepartements zusammengestellt und erweitert*. Bern: A. Francke, 1903.

Rekruten-Prüfung im Jahr 1876. Edited by Statistisches Bureau des eidgenössischen Departement des Inneren. Zurich: Orell Füssli, 1877.

Report of the Inter-Departmental Committee on Physical Deterioration, Band 1: Report and Appendix. Edited by Houses of Parliament by Command of His Majesty. London: H. M. Stationery Office, 1904.

Resultate der Ärztlichen Recrutenuntersuchung im Herbste 1885. Edited by Statistisches Bureau des eidgenössischen Departements des Inneren. Bern, 1886.

Reynaud, G. "Jugement quant à l'aptitude des officiers et des soldats au service dans les pays tropiques: Vortrag gehalten auf dem XIV. Internationalen Kongreß für Hygiene und Demographie zu Berlin." *Archiv für Schiffs- und Tropen-Hygiene* 12 (1908): 136.

Rheinberger, Hans-Jörg. "Objekt und Repräsentation." In *Mit dem Auge denken: Strategien der Sichtbarmachung in wissenschaftlichen und virtuellen Welten,* edited by Bettina Heintz and Jörg Huber, 55–61. Zurich: Springer, 2001.

Riegler, Johannes. *Das medicinische Berlin.* Berlin: Staude, 1873.

Rigal, Pierre-Mathieu. *De l'aptitude et de ses modifications sous l'influence des exercises militaires et des marches en pays de montagne: Etude sur le récrutement et l'examen des hommes du 12e bataillon de chasseurs.* Paris: Berger-Levrault, 1882.

Rilke, Rainer Maria. *Diaries of a Young Poet.* Translated by Edward Snow and Michael Winkler. New York: W. W. Norton & Company, 1998.

Rilke, Rainer Maria. *Sämtliche Werke.* Vol. 4. *Frühe Erzählungen und Dramen.* Frankfurt: Insel-Verlag, 1961.

Ripley, William Z. *The Races of Europe: A Sociological Study.* New York: Appleton, 1899.

Robert. "Rapport médical d'inspection générale de 1899 sur le 4e régiment de tirailleurs tonkinois." *Archives de médecine navale* 73 (1900): 321–366.

Ronsin, Francis. *La grève des ventres: Propagande néo-malthusienne et baisse de la natalité française, XIXe–XXe siècles.* Paris: Aubier Montaigne, 1980.

Rosental, Paul-André. "Pour une histoire politique des populations." *Annales* 61 (2006): 7–29.

Roth, Wilhelm August. *Jahresbericht über die Leistungen und Fortschritte auf dem Gebiete des Militär-Sanitätswesens, Nr. 7.* Berlin: Mittler, 1881.

Roynette, Odile. *"Bons pour le service": L'expérience de la caserne en France à la fin du XIXe siècle.* Paris: Belin, 2000.

Roynette, Odile. "La statistique médicale de l'armée française au XIXe siècle: Un instrument de savoir et de pouvoir démographiques?" In *Bevölkerungsfragen: Prozesse des Wissenstransfers in Deutschland und Frankreich (1870–1939)*, edited by Petra Overath and Patrick Krassnitzer, 67–78. Cologne: Böhlau, 2007.

Ruge, Reinhold. "Review of Steuber, Über die Verwendbarkeit europäischer Truppen in Kolonien vom gesundheitlichen Standpunkte." *Archiv für Schiffs-und Tropen-Hygiene* 11 (1907): 432–434.

Rychner, Marianne. "Frau Doktorin besichtigt die Männerwelt–ein Experiment aus dem Jahr 1883 zur Konstruktion von Männlichkeit im Militär." In *Soziale Konstruktion: Militär und Geschlechterverhältnis*, edited by Christine Eifler and Ruth Seifert, 94–109. Münster: Dampfboot, 1999.

Rychner, Marianne. "Männlichkeit, Nation und militärdiensttauglicher Körper in der Schweiz um 1875." *Medizin, Gesellschaft und Geschichte* 18 (1999): 37–56.

Rychner, Marianne. "'Mit entblösstem Oberkörper'—Blicke auf den Mann im Untersuchungszimmer: Männlichkeit, Nation und Militärdiensttauglichkeit in der Schweiz um 1875." Unpublished licentiate thesis, 1996.

Rychner, Marianne, and Kathrin Däniker. "'Unter Männern': Geschlechtliche Zuschreibungen in der Schweizerarmee zwischen 1870 und 1914." In *Weiblich, männlich: Geschlechterverhältnisse in der Schweiz: Rechtsprechung, Diskurs, Praktiken = Féminin, masculin: Rapports sociaux de sexes en Suisse: Législation, discours, pratiques*, edited by Rudolf Jaun and Brigitte Studer, 159–170. Zurich: Chronos, 1995.

"Sanitätsbericht über die Königlich Preußische Armee." Berlin, 1882 [and subsequent years].

Sarasin, Philipp, and Jakob Tanner. "Physiologie und industrielle Gesellschaft." In *Physiologie und industrielle Gesellschaft: Studien zur Verwissenschaftlichung des Körpers im 19. und 20. Jahrhundert*, edited by Philipp Sarasin and Jakob Tanner, 12–43. Frankfurt: Suhrkamp, 1998.

Savage, Jon. *Teenage: Die Erfindung der Jugend (1875–1945)*. Frankfurt: Campus, 2008.

Schiff, Arthur. "Über die Morbiditätsstatistik der Krankenkassen." In *Bericht über den XIV. Internationalen Kongress für Hygiene und Demographie, Berlin 23.–29. September 1907*, vol. 4, 800–809. Berlin, 1908.

Schirrmacher, Arne. "Nach der Popularisierung: Zur Relation von Wissenschaft und Öffentlichkeit im 20. Jahrhundert." *Geschichte und Gesellschaft* 34, no. 1 (2008): 73–95.

Schjerning, Otto von. "Ansprache Seiner Exzellenz des Generalstabsarztes des Armee Professors Dr. Schjerning bei Eröffnung des XIV. internationalen Kongresses für Hygiene und Demographie am 23. September 1907." In *Bericht über den XIV. Internationalen Kongress für Hygiene und Demographie, Berlin 23.–29. September 1907*, vol. 1, 817–819. Berlin, 1908.

Schjerning, Otto von. *Sanitätsstatistische Betrachtungen über Volk und Heer.* Berlin: Hirschwald, 1910.

Schmid-Monnard. "Über den Werth von Körpermaassen zur Beurtheilung des Körperzustandes von Kindern." *Korrespondenz-Blatt der deutschen Gesellschaft für Anthropologie, Ethnologie und Urgeschichte,* no. 11–12 (November–December 1900): 130–133.

Schmidt, Daniel. *Statistik und Staatlichkeit.* Wiesbaden: VS Verlag für Sozialwissenschaften, 2005.

Schmidt, Hermann. *Die Kaiser Wilhelms-Akademie für das militärärztliche Bildungswesen. Von 1895 bis 1910. Festschrift zur Einweihung des Neubaues der Akademie.* Berlin: Mittler, 1910.

Schmidt, Wilhelm. *Rasse und Volk: Eine Untersuchung zur Bestimmung ihrer Grenzen und zur Erfassung ihrer Beziehungen.* Munich: J. Kösel & F. Pustet, 1927.

Schmidt-Richberg, Wiegand. "Die Regierungszeit Wilhelms II." In *Handbuch zur deutschen Militärgeschichte, 1648-1939.* Vol. 5, *Von der Entlassung Bismarcks bis zum Ende des Ersten Weltkriegs (1890–1918),* edited by Hans Meier-Welcker and Wolfgang von Grothe, 9–155. Frankfurt: Bernard und Graefe Verlag, 1968.

Schmutz, Hans-Konrad. "Vermessene Nation. Eine Skizze der imagologischen Anthropologie nach 1860." In *Anthropologie nach Haeckel,* edited by Dirk Preuß, Uwe Hoßfeld, and Olaf Breidbach, 184–194. Stuttgart: Steiner, 2006.

Schnitzler, Thomas. "Fußball und Rassenhygiene: Der DFB-Gründungspräsident Ferdinand Hueppe." In *Zur Sozial- und Kulturgeschichte des Fussballs,* edited by Beatrix Bouvier, 78–119. Trier: Studienzentrum Karl-Marx-Haus, 2006.

Schubert, Frank. "'Soldiers Can Get Anything Free': Idi Amin und das Erbe des Kolonialmilitärs in Afrika." *Historische Anthropologie: Kultur, Gesellschaft, Alltag* 14, no. 1 (2006): 93–104.

Schwalbe, Gustav A. "Bericht über die Thätigkeit der Commission für eine physisch-anthropologische Untersuchung des deutschen Reiches." *Correspondenzblatt der Deutschen anthropologischen Gesellschaft,* no. 9 (1904): 75–79.

Schwalbe, Gustav A. "Eröffnung der XXXVIII. allgemeinen Versammlung der deutschen Anthropologischen Gesellschaft in Strassburg vom 4. bis 8. August 1907. Aufgaben der Sozialanthropologie." *Korrespondenz-Blatt der deutschen Gesellschaft für Anthropologie, Ethnologie und Urgeschichte,* no. 9/12 (September/December 1907): 65–69.

Schweber, Libby. *Disciplining Statistics: Demography and Vital Statistics in France and England, 1830–1885.* Durham, NC: Duke University Press, 2006.

Schwiening, Georg. *Die Dienstpflicht der Frauen: Ein Beitrag zur Lösung der "Arbeiterinnen"-Frage.* Kassel: Hühn, 1900.

Schwiening, Heinrich. *Beiträge zur Kenntnis der Verbreitung der venerischen Krankheiten in den europäischen Heeren sowie in der militärpflichtigen Jugend Deutschlands*. Berlin: A. Hirschwald, 1907.

Schwiening, Heinrich, and Wilhelm Nicolai. *Über die Körperbeschaffenheit der zum einjährig-freiwilligen Dienst berechtigten Wehrpflichtigen Deutschlands: Auf Grundlage amtlichen Materials*. Berlin: A. Hirschwald, 1909.

Scull, Andrew T. *Hysteria: The Biography*. Oxford: Oxford University Press, 2009.

Searle, Geoffrey R. *The Quest for National Efficiency: A Study in British Politics and Political Thought, 1899–1914*. Oxford: Blackwell, 1971.

Seeberg, Reinhold. *Der Geburtenrückgang in Deutschland*. Leipzig: Deichert, 1913.

Seitz, Anne. *Wimmeln und Wabern: Ansteckung und Gesellschaft im französischen Roman des Naturalismus und Fin-de-siècle*. Bielefeld: Aisthesis, 2015.

Selig, Jean-Michel. *Malnutrition et développement écnomique dans l'Alsace du XIXe siècle*. Strasbourg: Presses Universitaires de Strasbourg, 1996.

Sering, Max. "Rede vor dem Deutschen Landwirtschaftsrat." *Archiv des Deutschen Landwirthschaftsraths* 20 (1892).

Seyffarth. "Beitrag zur Verwertbarkeit des Pignetschen Verfahrens." *Militärärztliche Zeitschrift*, no. 21 (1908): 835–841.

Sheard, Sally, and Helen J. Power, eds. *Body and City: Histories of Urban Public Health*. Aldershot, England: Ashgate, 2000.

Shorter, Edward. "Paralysis: The Rise and Fall of a 'Hysterical' Symptom." *Journal of Social History* 19, no. 4 (1986): 549–582.

Shuttleworth, James K. *The Moral and Physical Condition of the Working Classes Employed in the Cotton Manufacture in Manchester, Enlarged and Containing an Introductory Letter to the Reverend T. Chalmers*. London: Ridgway, 1832.

Simmel, Georg. "Die Großstädte und das Geistesleben." In *Aufsätze und Abhandlungen 1901–1908*, edited by Georg Simmel, 116–131. Frankfurt: Suhrkamp, 1995.

Smith, Helmut Walser. "An Preußens Rändern, oder: Die Welt die dem Nationalismus verloren ging." In *Das Kaiserreich transnational: Deutschland in der Welt 1871–1914*, edited by Sebastian Conrad and Jürgen Osterhammel, 149–169. Göttingen: Vandenhoeck & Ruprecht, 2004.

Soloway, Richard A. *Demography and Degeneration: Eugenics and the Declining Birthrate in Twentieth-Century Britain*. Chapel Hill: University of North Carolina Press, 1990.

Soudjian, Guy. *Anthropologie du conscrit parisien sous le second Empire*. Paris: Lavauzelle, 1978.

Spivak, Marcel. *Les Origines militaires de l'éducation physique française: 1774–1848*. Paris: Université Paul Valéry, 1975.

Spörri, Myriam. "'Reines' und 'gemischtes Blut: Blutgruppen und 'Rassen' zwischen 1900 und 1933." In *Transfusionen: Blut-Bilder und Bio-Politik in der Neuzeit*, edited by Anja Lauper, 211–225. Zurich: Diaphanes, 2005.

Starkenburg, Heinz. "Volkswirthschaftliche Fabeln in wissenschaftlicher Beleuchtung." *Neuland: Monatsschrift* (February 1898): 289–305.

Statistical Report, on the Sickness and Mortality in the Army of the United States. Washington, DC: Bowman, 1840.

"Statistique médicale de l'armée des indes Néerlandaise orientales pour 1894." *Geneeskundig Tijdschrift voor Nederlandsch Indie*, no. 2 and 3 (1895).

"Statistique médicale de l'armée pendant l'année 1862." Paris, 1864.

"Statistische Sanitätsbericht über die Kaiserlich Deutsche Marine." Edited by Medizinalabteilung des Reichsmarineamtes. Berlin, 1874–1899.

Steudel. "Die Beurteilung der Tropendiensttauglichkeit bei Offizieren und Mannschaften." *Archiv für Schiffs—und Tropen-Hygiene* 12 (1908): 73–77.

Stier, Ewald. *Der Militärdienst der geistig Minderwertigen und die Hilfsschulen: Beiträge zur Kinderforschung und Heilerziehung*. Langensalza: Beyer, 1907.

Strachan, Hew. "Militär, Empire und Civil Society: Großbritannien im 19. Jahrhundert." In *Militär und Gesellschaft im 19. Und 20. Jahrhundert*, edited by Ute Frevert, 78–94. Stuttgart: Klett-Cotta, 1997.

Streets-Salter, Heather. *Martial Races: The Military, Race and Masculinity in British Imperial Culture, 1857–1914*. Manchester: Manchester University Press, 2004.

Stricker, Franz, and Theodor Ziehen. *Über die Feststellung regelwidriger Geisteszustände bei Heerespflichtigen und Heereszugehörigen: Veröffentlichungen aus dem Gebiete des Militärsanitätswesens*. Berlin: A. Hirschwald, 1905.

Stübig, Heinz. *Bildung, Militär und Gesellschaft in Deutschland: Studien zur Entwicklung im 19. Jahrhundert*. Cologne: Böhlau, 1994.

Sunder, H. *Kann die weiße Rasse sich in den Tropen akklimatisieren?* Berlin: Süsserott, 1908.

Süssmilch, Johann Peter. *Die göttliche Ordnung in den Veränderungen des menschlichen Geschlechts, aus der Geburt: Dem Tod und der Fortpflanzung desselben*. 2nd ed. Berlin: Verlag des Buchladen der Realschule, 1761.

Tanner, Jakob. "Eugenik und Rassenhygiene in Wissenschaft und Politik seit dem ausgehenden 19. Jahrhundert: Ein historischer Überblick." In *Zwischen Erziehung und Vernichtung: Zigeunerpolitik und Zigeunerforschung im Europa des 20. Jahrhunderts*, edited by Michael Zimmermann, 109–121. Stuttgart: Steiner, 2007.

Tanner, Jakob. "Die 'Alkoholfrage' in der Schweiz im 19. und 20. Jahrhundert." In *Zur Sozialgeschichte des Alkohols in der Neuzeit Europas*, edited by W. Hermann Fahrenkrug, 147–168. Lausanne: ISPA Press, 1986.

Théron, Fernand. "Le récrutement à la Réunion." *Archives de la médecine navale et colonial* 68 (July 1897): 5–18.

Toldt, Carl. *Studien über die Anatomie der menschlichen Brustgegend mit Bezug auf die Messung derselben und auf die Verwerthung des Brust-Umfanges zur Beurtheilung der Kriegsdiensttauglichkeit.* Stuttgart: Enke, 1875.

Ulrich, Bernd, Jakob Vogel, and Benjamin Ziemann. *Untertan in Uniform: Militär und Militarismus im Kaiserreich 1871–1914: Quellen und Dokumente.* Frankfurt: Fischer, 2001.

Vacher de Lapouge, Georges. *L'aryen: Son rôle social: Cours libre de science politique.* Paris: Fontemoing, 1899.

van Laak, Dirk. *Über alles in der Welt: Deutscher Imperialismus im 19. und 20. Jahrhundert.* Munich: C. H. Beck, 2005.

Vascik, George. "Agrarian Conservatism in Wilhelmine Germany: Diederich Hahn and the Agrarian League." In *Between Reform, Reaction, and Resistance: Studies in the History of German Conservatism from 1789 to 1945*, edited by Larry Eugene Jones and James N. Retallack, 229–260. Providence: Berg, 1993.

Vatin, François. "Arbeit und Ermüdung: Entstehung und Scheitern der Psychophysiologie der Arbeit." In *Physiologie und Industrielle Gesellschaft: Studien zur Verwissenschaftlichung des Körpers im 19. und 20. Jahrhundert*, edited by Philipp Sarasin and Jakob Tanner, 347–368. Frankfurt: Suhrkamp, 1998.

Veitch, Colin. "'Play up! Play up! And Win the War!' Football, the Nation and the First World War 1914–15." *Journal of Contemporary History* 20, no. 3 (1985): 363–378.

"Verhandlungen der XXX: Plenarversammlung des Deutschen Landwirthschaftsraths, 1902." *Archiv des Deutschen Landwirthschaftsraths* 30 (1902).

"Verhandlungen der XXXII: Plenarversammlung des Deutschen Landwirtschaftsraths." *Archiv des Deutschen Landwirthschaftsraths* 32 (1904): 259–301.

Villaret, Alfred. "Militär-Sanitätswesen." In *Verhandlungen des X. Internationalen Medicinischen Congresses, Berlin 4.–9. August 1890*, vol. 1, 324–332. Berlin, 1891.

Vincent. "Du choix du soldat ou étude sur la consitution des hommes de vingt ans, appliquée au recrutement de l'armée." *Bulletin bimensuel* 32 (1876): 419.

Virchow, Rudolf. "Gesamtbericht über die Statistik der Farbe der Augen, der Haare und der Haut der Schulkinder in Deutschland." *Correspondenzblatt der Deutschen anthropologischen Gesellschaft* 16 (1885): 89–100.

Virchow, Rudolf. "Gesamtbericht über die von der deutschen anthropologischen Gesellschaft veranlassten Erhebungen über die Farbe der Augen, der Haare und der Haut der Schulkinder in Deutschland." *Archiv für Anthropologie* 16 (1886): 275–475.

Vitu, Auguste Charles Joseph. *Histoire civile de l'armée ou conditions du service militaire en France depuis les temps les plus reculés jusqu'à la formation de l'armée permanente.* Paris: Didier, 1868.

Vogel, Jakob. "Der Undank der Nation: Die Veteranen der Einigungskriege und die Debatte um ihren 'Ehrensold' im Kaiserreich." *Militaergeschichtliche Zeitschrift* 60, no. 2 (2001): 343–366.

Vogel, Jakob. "Lernen vom Feind: Das Militär als Träger des deutsch-französischen Kulturtransfers im 19. Jahrhundert." In *Vom Gegner lernen: Feindschaften und Kulturtransfers im Europa des 19. und 20. Jahrhunderts*, edited by Martin Aust and Daniel Schönpflug, 95–113. Frankfurt: Campus, 2007.

Vogel, Jakob. *Nationen im Gleichschritt: Der Kult der "Nation in Waffen" in Deutschland und Frankreich, 1871–1914.* Göttingen: Vandenhoeck & Ruprecht, 1997.

Vogel, Jakob. "Von Der Wissenschafts—zur Wissensgeschichte: Für eine Historisierung der 'Wissensgesellschaft.'" *Geschichte und Gesellschaft* 30, no. 4 (2004): 639–660.

von Blume, Wilhelm. *Die Wehrkraft Deutschlands im Vergleich mit der der anderen europäischen Großmächte.* Berlin: Mittler, 1913.

von Hasselberg. *Tafeln zur Entlarvung der Simulation einseitiger Blindheit und Schwachsinnigkeit.* Wiesbaden: 1901.

von Justi, Johann Heinrich Gottlieb. *Staatswirtschaft oder systematische Abhandlung aller ökonomischen u. Cameralwissenschaften.* Vol. 1. 2nd ed. Leipzig, 1758.

von Myrdacz, Paul. "Ergebnisse der internatioanlen Militärsanitätsstatistik." In *Compte rendu du XVI congrès international de médecine, Budapest août-septembre 1909. Séction XX: Services sanitaires militaire et maritime*, 298–328. Budapest: 1910.

von Schmidt. *Vergleiche zwischen der Deutschen und französischen Armee: Vortrag gehalten im Deutschen Wehrverein, Ortsgruppe Stuttgart am 29.3.1912 und ergänzt nach dem Stand Ende 1912.* Stuttgart: Grüninger, 1913.

von Streitberg, Gisela. *Die Bevölkerungsfrage in weiblicher Beurteilung*, vols. 1–6. Leipzig: Dietrich, 1908–1909.

Waldeyer, Wilhelm. "Eröffnungsrede der XLI. allgemeinen Versammlung der Deutschen Anthropologischen Gesellschaft in Cöln am Rh. Über Zukunftsaufgaben für die anthropologische Forschung und für die anthropologischen Vereine." *Correspondenz-Blatt der deutschen Gesellschaft für Anthropologie, Ethnologie und Urgeschichte*, no. 9/12 (September/December 1910): 69–70.

Waldeyer, Wilhelm. *Die im Weltkrieg stehenden Völker in anthropologischer Betrachtung*. Berlin: Heymanns, 1915.

Walkenhorst, Peter. *Nation—Volk—Rasse: Radikaler Nationalismus im Deutschen Kaiserreich, 1890–1914*. Göttingen: Vandenhoeck & Ruprecht, 2007.

Walther, Daniel J. *Sex and Control: Veneral Disease, Colonial Physicians, and Indigenous Agency in German Colonialism, 1884–1914*. New York: Berghahn, 2015.

Wateff, Stephan. "Anthropologische Beobachtungen an den Schülern und Soldaten in Bulgarien." *Correspondenzblatt der Deutschen anthropologischen Gesellschaft* 32 (1901): 29–30.

Weber, Eugen. "Gymnastics and Sports in Fin-de-Siècle France: Opium of the Classes?" *American Historical Review* 76, no. 1 (1971): 70–98.

Weber, Eugen. *Peasants into Frenchmen: The Modernization of Rural France, 1870–1914*. Stanford, CA: Stanford University Press, 1976.

Weber, Max. "Entgegnung auf Alfred Plötz." In *Verhandlungen des Ersten Deutschen Soziologentages, 19.–22.10.1910 in Frankfurt/M*, 151–157. Tübingen: Mohr, 1911.

Wehler, Hans-Ulrich. "Der Aufbruch in die Moderne 1860 bis 1890: Armee, Marine und Politik in Europa, den USA und Japan." In *Das Militär und der Aufbruch in die Moderne 1860 bis 1890: Armeen, Marinen und der Wandel von Politik, Gesellschaft und Wirtschaft in Europa, den USA sowie Japan*, edited Michael Epkenhans and Gerhard P. Groß, xxi–xxix. Munich: Oldenbourg Verlag, 2003.

Wehler, Hans-Ulrich. *Deutsche Gesellschaftsgeschichte*. Vol. 1, *Vom Feudalismus des Alten Reiches bis zur Defensiven Modernisierung der Reformära 1700–1815*. 3rd ed. Munich: C. H. Beck, 1996.

Wehler, Hans-Ulrich. *Deutsche Gesellschaftsgeschichte*. Vol. 3, *Von der "deutschen Doppelrevolution" bis zum Beginn des Ersten Weltkrieges 1849–1914*. Munich: C. H. Beck, 1995.

Weindling, Paul. *Health, Race, and German Politics between National Unification and Nazism, 1870–1945*. Cambridge: Cambridge University Press, 1989.

Wirth, Albrecht. *Volk und Rasse*. Halle: Max Niemeyer, 1914.

Wolf, Julius. *Geburtenrückgang: Die Rationalisierung des Sexuallebens in unserer Zeit*. Jena: Fischer, 1912.

Woodruff, Edward. *The Effects of Tropical Light on White Men*. New York: Rebman, 1905.

"Worth a Thousand Words." *Economist*, December 22, 2007, 70–72.

Wulffert, Friedrich. *Die Akklimatisation der europäischen und insbesondere der germanischen Rasse in den Tropen und ihre hauptsächlichen Hindernisse*. Leipzig: Breitkopff & Härtel, 1900.

Zemanek, Adolf. *Werth und Bedeutung der Militär-Sanitäts-Statistik*. Vienna, 1884.

Zemanek, Adolf. "Discussion." In *Comptes rendus du XII congrès international de médecine, Moscou 7.–14. août 1897, Séction X: Médecine militaire*, 95. Moscow, 1899.

Ziemann, Hans. *Wie erobert man Afrika für die weiße und farbige Rasse? Vortrag gehalten auf dem Internationalen Kongreß für Hygiene und Demographie zu Berlin 1907*. Leipzig: Barth, 1907.

Zimmerman, Andrew. *Anthropology and Antihumanism in Imperial Germany*. Chicago: University of Chicago Press, 2001.

Zimmerman, Andrew. "Anti-Semitism as a Skill: Rudolf Vichow's *Schulstatistik* and the Racial Composition of Germany." *Central European History* 32 (1999): 409–429.

Zöller, Hugo. *Die deutschen Besitzungen an der westafrikanischen Küste, vol. 2*. Berlin: Spemann, 1885.

Zur Verth, T. *Zur Hygiene europäischer Truppen bei tropischen Feldzügen*. Leipzig: Barth, 1909.

Zweiniger-Bargielowska, Ina. *Managing the Body: Beauty, Health and Fitness in Britain, 1880–1939*. Oxford: Oxford University Press, 2010.

Newspapers and Periodicals

Alldeutsche Blätter

Allgemeine Zeitung

Allgemeine militärärztliche Zeitschrift

Archives de médecine navale

Berliner Tageblatt

Bulletin bi-mensuel—Société de médecine militaire française

Correspondenzblatt für Schweizer Aerzte

Der Beobachter

Der Militärarzt. Internationales Organ für das gesammte Sanitätswesen der Armeen

Frankfurter Zeitung und Handelsblatt

Le Démocrate

Mittheilungen des statistischen Bureaus in Berlin

Münchener Neueste Nachrichten

Neue Preußische Zeitung (Kreuzzeitung)

Neueste Mittheilungen

Norddeutsche Allgemeine Zeitung

Schweizerische Zeitschrift für Statistik

Tägliche Rundschau

Volkszeitung. Organ für Jedermann aus dem Volke

Zeitschrift des Königlich preussischen statistischen Bureaus

Archives

Archives of the University of Freiburg
  Otto Ammon Papers (C75)
Bibliothèque Nationale de France—Historical Collections
  Receuil de pièces "Tirage au sort du service militaire"
Bundesarchiv Berlin (BArch)
  Reichsgesundheitsamt R 86
  Reichsministerium des Innneren R 1501
  Reichsministerium des Inneren—Militaria (div.)
  Reichskanzlei R 43
Bundesarchiv Bern (BA Bern)
  Ausstellung und Kongresse E 14
  Eidgenössisches Militärdepartement E 27
  Departement des Inneren—Statistisches Bureau E 86
Bundesarchiv—Militärarchiv Freiburg i.Br.
  Kaiserliche Schutztruppen MSg 101
  Druckschriften Preußisches Heer
Deutsches Historisches Museum Berlin
  Postkartensammlung (DHM PK)

Hauptstaatsarchiv Stuttgart (HStA)
    Oberersatzkommission S M 11
    Prüfungskommission Einjährig Freiwillige S M 12
    Kriegsministerium S M 1/4
Landesarchiv Berlin (LaB)
Medizinhistorisches Archiv Zürich
    Sammlung Heinrich und Eugen Bircher
Service Historique de l'Armée de Terre/Vincennes (SHAT)
Sozialarchiv Zürich
Zentral und Landesbibliothek Berlin Kuczynski (KUC)

Index